About the Author

Marc Frank joined the U.S. peace and justice movement in the late 1960s at age 16. He helped organize Massachusetts high school students against the Vietnam war, worked to humanize the state's juvenile justice system and to organize street gangs to fight for a better life instead of each other. Marc Frank moved to New Jersey in 1970 and graduated from Rutgers University in 1972 with a BA in political science and urban studies. Between 1972 and 1984 he worked in New Jersey as a community and labor organizer and elected union official. In 1984 Marc Frank moved to Cuba where he lived and worked as a journalist for seven years. The U.S. community and trade union activist turned journalist has written over 1,000 articles on Cuba, Latin America and inter-American relations. Marc Frank has toured the United States from coast to coast lecturing on Cuba, been a guest on numerous talk shows, and has been extensively quoted in the U.S. press. CUBA LOOKS TOWARD THE YEAR 2000 is Marc Frank's first book.

CUBA
Looks
TO THE YEAR
2000

For Dhara, Beth, Gabriela, Carima and Julian in hopes they will follow the example of the late Sandy Pollack.

A Special thanks to my friend and editor Gail Reed for her help with the final draft of the manuscript.

CUBA
Looks
TO THE YEAR
2000

MARC FRANK

INTERNATIONAL PUBLISHERS, New York

© 1993 International Publishers Co., New York
1st printing, 1993

Manufactured in the United States of America

Library of Congress Cataloging-in-Publication Data

Frank, Marc.
    Cuba looks to the year 2000 / Marc Frank.
        p.   cm.
    Includes bibliographical references and index.
    ISBN 0-7178-0704-5 : $9.95
        1. Cuba--Economic conditions--1959- 2. Cuba--Politics and
government--1959- 3. Cuba--Forecasting. 4. Communism--Cuba-
-History.   I. Title.
HC152.5.F7   1992
330.97291'001'12--dc20   92-39652
                                                          CIP

CONTENTS

Acknowledgements

This book would never have made it into print without the support, cooperation and advice of scores of people. My wife, Mary Murray, discussed the manuscript with me many times; Ida Estrella Cuellar not only made sure I understood her country but managed to find countless ways to make life easier in Havana. My sister Michele and friend Adelaide Bean urged me on. My father Tom, his wife Kate, my brothers Paul and Guy, and sister Anara lent support as only family can. My Grandfather, the late Waldo Frank, inspired me. My friend, Georgina Chabau, cut red tape as needed. The staffs at Jose Marti publishers and Radio Havana Cuba were always ready to help with my research. Graciella Tabio stepped in at the last moment, combing the photo archives of Cuba's National Information Service (AIN), Prensa Latina (PL) and Granma for many of the photos that appear in this book. Carmen González, Loreli Parodi, Maria Sequera Rodríguez and her family, Ramón Díaz, Jorge Ruiz, Plácido Sánchez and many others let me into their hearts and homes, enriched mine, and provided the diverse reference points from which the manuscript took shape.

Preface: The Magic Mirror

Coming to grips with as complex and controversial a country as Cuba is quite a challenge. That is especially so if one visits the island for just a few days, weeks or months. Cuba, like all nations, is composed of many, constantly changing realities and no book, video, article or photo can be expected to capture them all. The 10.5 million souls living on the island are a diverse and dynamic lot. No two Cubans think, act, look, or are exactly alike.

During my seven years in Cuba I became almost as fascinated by visitors' reactions to the island as I was by the drama of its daily life. Cuba, perhaps because it is so diverse and controversial, appeared to be a some sort of magic mirror. People passing through, friend and foe alike, saw reflected in their mind's eye that part of Cuban reality that coincided with their own point of view. Unfortunately, this magic mirror phenomena was compounded by many trained observers— mainstream journalists who came and went during my stay. Too often they had written their stories about a grey, oppressive and even desperate Cuba before setting foot on the island. I discovered that many journalists spent a week in Cuba doing little else than confirming their preconceptions. More often than not their stories went like this.

Cuba is stagnant, unchanging, caught in a time warp best illustrated by the vintage U.S. cars still found on the streets. Amidst decaying buildings, long lines, and shortages, government officials mechanically rattle off the Party line. On the street, opposition, while still insignificant, is growing. An unidentified (for his or her own security) source, is quoted confirming the hidden horrors of everyday life. The reporter concludes that despite the above, because Fidel Castro has hypnotized and bludgeoned his people into submission, there is no indication change (i.e., the establishment of a U.S. style political, social and economic system) will come soon.

Journalists have a special responsibility to go beyond their own beliefs, first impressions and the politics of their government and editors. Our job is to enlighten our readers. It is sad but true that when it comes to Cuba, many journalists have fallen short on the job. For example— Havana has a population of some 2.2 million people. Most hotels are in the City's 50 square block Vedado section. At most five percent, or 110,000 Havana residents, make their living black marketing, changing currency and in general hustling foreigners. These Cubans naturally congregate in Vedado around the hotels. A foreign journalist steps out into the Havana night and confronts a gauntlet of strangers offering to change money, sell black market goods, show him around town and yes, go to bed. The experience, along with a few quotes from Havana's petty criminal element, becomes yet another article depicting the scene as typical of Cuban reality. You, the reader, have no clue that another two million hard working, law abiding Havana residents exist. Nor are you given a glimpse of their daily lives, their thoughts, hopes and dreams. It's rare indeed to read an article in the Western press that includes an interview with a well known cultural figure, scientist, doctor, soldier, teacher, nurse, engineer, farmer, factory or office worker.

I do not claim to have escaped the subjectivity that distorts every observer's perceptions. Like most people, I believe in a nation's right to independence and that, more than anything, is what the Cuba controversy is all about. I also dislike bullies, and it's a fact that the United States, the wealthiest and most powerful country in history, has been knocking tiny Cuba around for a long, long time. But as a journalist, I recognize the danger of my own subjectivity, and the magic mirror phenomenon. And I have worked hard to overcome my own subjectivity, to break through that magic mirror and capture for you, the reader, what goes on in the hearts and minds of Cuba's not so silent majority, those two million Havana residents and their eight million countrymen and women that we know so little about.

I lived and worked in Cuba from 1984 through 1988 before beginning work on the manuscript. I remained in Cuba through March, 1991, as I developed the book. Finally, I returned to Cuba in June, 1992, before submitting my final draft to the publisher. I've combined four basic sources to capture what I believe to be the dominant and most important aspects of life on the island. First, my experience as someone who lived in Cuba for seven years. Second, over 100 interviews with Cubans ranging from the highest officials to the man and woman on the street. Third, quotes from Fidel Castro's most important speeches during the 1986—1992 period. Fourth, statistics gleaned from international and Cuban studies and reports. Unless otherwise indicated the interviews took place between 1989 and 1991 and are not footnoted. Though I was present for most of Fidel Castro's speeches I provide English language references, when available, in the notes.

This account of Cuba consists of an introduction, two parts and a conclusion. The four sections, taken together, capture the Cuba I came to know and provide a context for understanding where the island is headed as the world tumbles, turns and gropes its way toward the year 2000. The introduction analyzes some of the differences between

European socialism and Cuban socialism, clarifying why the latter remains and the former does not. Part One takes an inside look at Cuba's rectification movement between 1986 and 1990 and the dramatic changes it brought while the world's attention was fixed on events in the Soviet Union and Eastern Europe. Part Two examines how Cuba is coping with the fall of European socialism, the "New World Order" and stepped up U.S. pressure. The conclusion delves into Cuba's plans for the future, in particular to transform the superstructure and economy.

CUBA
Looks
TO THE YEAR
2000

INTRODUCTION: SOCIALIST EUROPE AND CUBA—IS THERE A DIFFERENCE?

Fidel Castro

"Mr. President, Mr. President," shouted the NBC TV correspondent over the clamor of his 250 colleagues jostling to be recognized by Fidel Castro. "There are many Cubans living in Florida who say you won't be in power within a year, and they're ready to come here and take over when you leave. What would you say to them?"

It was April 3, 1990, and Cuba's President was holding a nationally televised press conference at Havana's International Convention Center. The Soviet Union was in crisis, and East European socialism in disarray; Panama was occupied by U.S. troops and Nicaragua's Sandinistas were out. The U.S. had just begun transmitting TV Martí into Cuba, a first ever attempt by one nation to impose a TV station on another. Havana was considering retaliating with AM radio broadcasts into the United States, and Washington threatened to bomb the island's radio transmitters if it dared.

"Well," joked Fidel Castro, who appeared in excellent humor, "neither of us can say. Only God knows whether I'll be here in a year . . . But the truth is that they have been saying that for three decades now . . . They pay too much attention to me. What's really unbelievable is how little attention they pay to the Cuban people, how much they underestimate our people . . ."[1]

Just two months earlier I had toured 20 states in the USA to talk about Cuba. I had five years in Cuba and over 1,000 articles under my belt as the Havana-based *People's Daily World* Latin American correspondent. But they were not just any five years. They were the Gorbachev years during which the bulwark of the world socialist movement, the Soviet Union and Eastern Europe, came unglued. Years during which the international alliance against colonialism and neocolonialism blew apart from within. Years during which the United States and its allies emerged practically unchallenged on the world scene.

As European socialism crumbled, I could find no sign that a similar process would take place in Cuba. I wondered if perhaps I was missing something. I hit the streets like never before. I cultivated my contacts, searched out the discontented and attended the never ending stream of grass roots meetings that are a constant in Cuba's daily life. Yet, I found no signs that Cuban socialism would follow European socialism into the dustbin of history. In fact, events in socialist Europe and increasing U.S. pressure on the island seemed to be rallying the Cubans around their flag, government and socialism like never before. Despite increasing economic hardships socialist Cuba appeared united and determined to defend its independence and unique system of social justice.

Why hasn't Cuban socialism crumbled? The quality of Cuba's leadership, and in particular Fidel Castro's, is certainly part of the answer. No world leader alive today generates as much interest and controversy as Fidel Castro. For over three decades, a furious U.S. government backed by a complacent media has painted an image of the Cuban President as an iron fisted tyrant. Yet, a glowing Mother Teresa, after meeting with Castro in July of 1986, lauded Cuba's social and economic advances and then told the press: "the most beautiful gift God has given me is my meeting with President Fidel Castro." The millionaire President of the Cuban-American National Foundation and unofficial U.S. candidate for Cuban President, Jorge Mas Canosa, charges Fidel Castro with genocide. Yet, the United Nations Children's Fund, the Latin American Pediatrics Association and Pan-American Health Organization have showered the Cuban President with praise and awards for the island's social gains, which they say have saved countless lives.

My first vivid memory of Fidel Castro dates back to June 27, 1984. He was standing side-by-side with then U.S. presidential candidate Rev. Jesse Jackson in the pulpit of one of Havana's many churches. The occasion marked the end of the Cuban Methodists' annual Martin Luther King Jr., Theological Seminar, attended by representatives from the United States and Cuban religious communities. Castro and Jackson had just returned from touring the Isle of Youth, just south off the mainland, and the largest of Cuba's 1,000 keys. Over 15,000 third world students, mainly from Africa, study there on scholarship.

The event may have marked the first time Fidel Castro had graced a house of worship since the 1959 revolution. Yet, the standing room only religious crowd, after waiting hours for his arrival, chanted "Fidel! Fidel!" as he entered. Perhaps they sensed that the event signaled the start of the thaw in Church-State relations that would culminate five years later when the Communist Party opened its doors to believers, the constitution was amended to make Cuba a lay state, and the faithful plunged into social service and politics with new-found vigor.

An emotional Rev. Jesse Jackson described the Isle of Youth as "the closest thing I've seen to God's work on this earth," as he called for the normalization of relations between the United States and Cuba. Castro stated he believed the basic values and ideals held dear by true Christians and Communists were one and the same, and that he saw no reason why the two shouldn't join hands to build a better world.

I left Cuba seven years later. I had seen Castro speak perhaps 100 times, observed him deep in discussion on every detail of the country's life with residents of dozens of Cuban neighborhoods, at gatherings of students, workers, farmers, administrators, women, journalists, legislators and religious leaders; chased after him as he toured Havana and Cuba with one world leader after the other; and talked briefly with him on several occasions.

The first thing that struck me about Fidel Castro was just how "Cuban" he is. Obvious perhaps, but I had tended to think of him in U.S. and Western terms. Castro's speech, his mannerisms, the proximity of his emotions to the surface and his willingness to express them, his energy and fierce pride reminded me time and time again of many other Cubans I came to know. To watch Fidel Castro in action is to see a man in extraordinary harmony with his country's human environment. Cubans don't expect Fidel Castro to be perfect or always right. Cubans do expect Fidel Castro to be honest, say what he thinks and feels, listen to their concerns, be right far more than he is wrong, put the nation's interests above all else, and never surrender.

In this context, Fidel Castro is exceptionally good at his job. As the First Secretary of the Cuban Communist Party and President of Cuba, he has managed to lead and unite his nation. Castro acts as a symbol of hard work and moral integrity that binds the Cuban Communist Party, government and majority of people together, no matter how many disappointments and headaches the average Cuban encounters in daily life. The Cuban President is also a skilled diplomat. Despite a 30-year U.S. smear campaign against him, Castro remains a popular folk legend throughout the developing world, one who has forged the political and economic ties Cuba needs to survive and develop as an independent nation just 90 miles from U.S. shores. Cuba had normal diplomatic and economic relations with the governments of over 145 countries in 1991, including every developed capitalist country and every major country in the Western Hemisphere, except the United

States. The rest of Fidel Castro's traits everyone agrees on. Famous for his marathon speeches, Castro is a powerful orator and orienter, with perhaps the most experience of any head of state alive today.

Socialist Cuba's 33 years of existence have been ones of continuous crisis and constant U.S. threats to Cuba's independence and national security. Given such an exceptional situation, most Cubans consider themselves lucky to have a man of Castro's caliber at the helm. The Cubans, forced day and night to scramble to survive and defend themselves against all odds, have never felt the time was right to replace Castro. By 1992 socialist Cuba faced the gravest crisis and most serious threat to its existence ever. The general sentiment in Cuba remained "if anyone can, Fidel will get us through this one."

There are no new "Fidels" waiting in the wings to take Castro's place. There are, however, a number of people capable of running the nation, especially under normal circumstances. The Cuban Party and government are made up of much more than those 12 young men who were the core of the "Rebel Army" that drove Fulgencio Batista from power back in 1959. There is a pool of experienced Cuban leaders on the Party Political Bureau and Central Committee, in the government and military, leading the Union of Young Communists and Cuba's many national mass organizations. Some of them boast histories that date back to well before 1959, such as Cuban Vice President Carlos Rafael Rodríguez, whose literary and diplomatic brilliance has earned him fame, second only to Castro, in all corners of the world. Others, like party leader José Ramón Machado Ventura, a medical doctor, made their mark after the Rebel Army marched victoriously into Havana. There are also those like Union of Young Communist leader and Party Political Bureau member Roberto Robaina, one of 300,000 "internationalists" who served in Angola, and who were infants when the United States invaded Cuba's Bay of Pigs in 1961.

How does Fidel Castro see his own role? The Cuban President, meeting with a group of Brazilian intellectuals in 1990, described it like this:

> No one ever calls me Mr. President or anything like that. Everybody calls me just Fidel . . . Because I happen to be one more neighbor, close at hand, a fact that they (Western politicians and the media) simply can't understand. They think . . . I live in an ivory tower, removed from the world . . . We have a shared presidency, if you will, just as there is a shared Party leadership. I cannot grant a pardon on my own; that's one power presidents have everywhere. I have to convoke the Council of State to grant a pardon. I can't appoint an ambassador; it's the Council of State that appoints ambassadors . . . The Council of State appoints ministers and must issue a

decree with the support of all of its members. However, none of this means that I don't have authority, that I don't have influence, that I carry no weight in the life of the country . . .

"What I do is talk," continued Castro. "I don't issue orders. I talk to people to persuade them to do what should be done—and I'm good at persuading people . . ."[2]

THE PEOPLE

During my seven years in Cuba I developed a deep respect and great warmth for Cubans, for their fierce independence, and the courage and values backing that up. Washington's effort to force a propaganda TV station on the Cubans, even naming the station after their National Hero, José Martí, best illustrates how Washington has internalized its own disinformation about public opinion in Cuba, a vision further skewed by wealthy Cuban American advisers.

Twenty million dollars was spent the first year to transmit a TV signal that, after it went on the air on March 27, 1990, was jammed at a fraction of the cost. The use of José Martí's name deeply insulted average Cubans. Further, the attempt to impose TV programming on the island proved Fidel Castro was right again when he warned the nation to prepare for stepped up U.S. hostilities. But the Cuban government didn't only erase TV Martí from the screen: Havana also delivered a psychological blow. In July, 1991, Cuba revealed a top TV Martí programmer, José Fernández Brenes, who had "defected" in 1988, was actually working for Cuban intelligence.

Public reaction to TV Martí—dubbed an "Electronic Bay of Pigs"—was swift. Twenty-four-year old José Miguel Ruiz, on the construction crew building Cuba's first five-star hotel, told me: "We have news here; I don't need to see what the U.S. government decides I should see. They say they are broadcasting to provide us with information but that's bull . . . like all other U.S. hostilities, TV Martí will end up as one more embarrassment for Washington."

Ida Estrella Cuellar worked in the Havana underground to topple Batista. The retired seamstress and mother of four adult sons said she worried about the impact the U.S. station could have on "the sector of our youth who are not politically prepared for the poison they are going to try to put in their heads . . . We are trying to give our young people a healthy foundation that teaches them to study and work together; not one that leads them to selfishness, vice, drugs and corruption."

Mario Victorio Varela was a barber for 41 years, and he was mine for seven. This father of three sons called TV Martí "a big mistake" that the U.S. people would end up paying for. "Martí predicted a century ago that the U.S. would use force to dominate Cuba; then pounce on Latin America. We Cubans know Martí and his work, and we know Washington's motives. Americas' tax dollars should be used more constructively."

University English students Jorge Cancanon, Migdalia Caballosa and Ileana Jorge Cobián said they feared Washington and Havana were headed for confrontation over TV Martí. The students, among the ten to fifteen that came to my apartment one night a week for two years to study English and fill me in on the "real Cuba," lamented over the U.S. plan because they wanted better relations and more contact with U.S. students.

"What does your government expect ours to do?" asked Jorge. "Sit here and allow it to broadcast whatever it wants into our homes? What would you do if a country that always attacked you tried this? What would you think of your government if it couldn't protect your airwaves from foreign interference?"

THE YOUTH

Washington designed TV Martí and its predecessor, Radio Martí, to attract Cuban youth, reasoning that the island's under-thirty generation is rebellious, anxious for change, and susceptible to the glitter shining across the Florida straits. It's true that Cuban youth, like all young people, are critical of their parents and the world they have built. It's only natural. Each generation's critique of the last is what moves civilization forward. However, from my experience, Washington's politicians and think tanks miss the mark when it comes to Cuba's young people.

There is a daily focus in Cuba's media on the feats of young construction, factory, farm and other workers, young doctors, scientists and rising Cuban leaders. The coverage, and the young people themselves, stand in sharp contrast to articles on Cuban youth in the Western press. These tend to picture Cuban young people as bored, unhappy, hypercritical, starved for consumer goods and on the fringes of an oppressive Cuban society. If that were true, Cuba would indeed be in serious trouble.

A spate of articles appeared in the Western press in 1988 about

Cuban "freakies," a "sure sign" that Cuban socialism was crumbling. I was startled when I first read about the freakies because I had never noticed them. I immediately set out to find some, and sure enough I discovered a group of about 12 teenagers, devoted to punk rock, who hung around a local park a few blocks from my apartment in downtown Havana. I found these freakies a bit lost and alienated to be sure, but no more critical of Cuba than many other young people I knew and certainly not in favor of returning Cuba to the U.S. fold. During a November 1989 interview with Mirtha Caridad Cardona, Secretary of Havana's provincial government and President of its Social Concerns and Prevention Commission, the freakies happened to come up. We burst out laughing upon discovering that we were both taken by surprise at their very existence.

"Well," exclaimed Cardona, "we saw all this information about the freakies in the international press and didn't know anything about them. So a team of educators and psychologists went out to find them. We discovered there were perhaps 200 freakies in Havana. We came to the conclusion that most of the freakies are young people with family problems, divorced parents, kids who are not well taken care of in the bosom of the family. This lack of family warmth and love leads them to search each other out. Its interesting to talk with them, because they will tell you how they take care of each other to escape problems at home.

"These are very peaceful kids," she went on. "They don't commit crimes, but just like to get together to talk and listen to music. Their long hair and dress is to attract the attention they never received at home. They certainly are no problem for us. We can only hope to help them make their lives better." A month later, the freakies turned out for youth-led protests against the U.S. invasion of Panama. Their presence, captured by Cuban TV, was hard to miss. They carried banners and posters proclaiming "The Freakies Support Our Panamanian Brothers and Sisters" and "Freakies Say Socialism or Death—We Will Win!"

"Take a poll of the young people and you will find that most are eager to go on internationalist missions abroad in other developing countries, under difficult conditions. I'll take you on: my ten cents for every 'no' to your one cent for every 'yes,'" challenged Roberto Labrada, a 30-year-old Angola veteran, steel worker and judo champ. Hundreds of thousands of Cuba's youth have done just what he described, and the shock of spending time in other Third World countries goes a long way in consolidating their support for Cuban socialism.

"Young people need to be heroes here at home, too," continued Labrada. Referring to Cuba's current state of economic emergency and increased U.S. hostility, he noted that "today's events have provided us with the opportunity to write a new chapter in Cuba's remarkable history. Most of us want those pages to show that we are just as courageous and intelligent as our parents, grandparents and great-grandparents. We don't want those pages to reveal that it was our generation that lost Cuba's long-fought-for independence, and submerged the country once more into the capitalist dependence and misery of other Latin American and Caribbean countries."

Labrada, a member of the Executive Board of Cuba's 600,000-strong Union of Young Communists (UJC), was responsible for political work among Cuba's young workers, now close to 40 percent of the labor force. "Young people need a chance to make history, too," said Labrada. "When they are given responsibility they also develop moral strength. Their attitude changes, and they become strong enough to say this leader is poor while this one is much better. The country is no longer a gift. It becomes theirs, because they earned it. They have built it, too. Getting people to understand this is what my job is all about."

A similar view, applied to the entire society, was expressed in 1986 at the Third Congress of the Cuban Communist Party when it assailed the older generation for not making space for the new and not encouraging their initiative. "After all" said Fidel Castro, "most of us were under 30 when we made the revolution." The Party Congress replaced a full third of the Central Committee with mainly younger faces.

Marta Carreras, a 33-year-old Party member who works with young people, said this was a necessary step. "The majority of Cubans are young. Soon the majority of workers will be under 30. Youth are Cuba's future. If you want to educate this future and work with this future, you need to be close to young people. You have to be able to understand what they are thinking. Times change; the years go by. The thinking and concerns of my parents at the time of the revolution are not the same as ours. You can't apply the same old formulas." Based on this conception, said Carreras, the Party began to look towards younger people at all levels, and even changed its admission policy so that people in their twenties could become members.

Labrada said the Party is insisting that leaders of government enterprises and national mass organizations promote young people into responsible positions and train them to take over the reins. "Our job is not to tell the older cadres to step aside because the young people are coming in," explained Labrada. "But, wherever we have someone who is more capable, young or old, that's the person who should have the job."

I could see the excitement in Labrada's eyes as he spoke about what was happening with young workers in general. He described the UJC's skepticism when the first "youth shift" sprang up. "We heard that the UJC at the Antillana de Acero steelworks had gone off on their own, packing a shift with young people, then challenging other shifts to match its efficiency and production. I was really mad. I went right over there and told them they were putting our prestige on the line and that, if it didn't work, they'd have hell to pay. But they insisted. So we supported them and it's been a remarkable experience. They are the best shift at the plant . . . and now everyone wants to try it."

The picture Labrada paints of Cuban youth is certainly more in line with my own experience than that drawn by the Western media. For every lost kid who approaches a foreign reporter or tourist to change pesos for dollars, and in the process becomes an "unidentified source," there are 10,000 "invisible" ones who are taking up the challenge of everyday life and making something of themselves in the process. I told Labrada it was a shame that such a distorted picture of Cuban youth prevailed in my country. He shrugged his shoulders and asked, "What can we do?" Labrada pulled out a stack of computer print-outs. "Marc," he said, "you see this. This is a list of most of the kids involved in changing dollars and other black market activities here in Havana. What should we do? Arrest them? Put them away to protect our image? What good would that do? What we do is try to work with them, their families and communities. We try to get them back in school or find them a job. Just a few days ago I had five of them in my office. I tried to convince them to go to work. Three took jobs and now we'll see if they last."

The Third Party Congress of the Cuban Communist Party was followed by the 1987 Fifth Congress of Cuba's Union of Young Communists (UJC). Scheduled for three days, it stretched into five as the young people debated how best to shoulder their new responsibilities. Many of Cuba's national leaders, including Fidel Castro, were on hand, and much of the proceedings was nationally televised.

"We made a number of important decisions at the Congress," 30-year-old UJC leader Silvio Gutierrez told me. "First we decided to change our style of work. We were too closed, and looked at ourselves as marching out in front of Cuba's youth instead of being at their center. Second, we decided that economic education is the UJC's primary job. For some time now, all of us to some degree have felt that the revolution was a gift from our parents. Our most important task these days is to make sure that young workers maintain a profound and responsible attitude towards their work." As part of this effort, he said, young people had taken on some of Cuba's most important development projects, called "crash tasks," including new hotels at the Varadero beach resort, Holguin's nickel refining industry, and in 1992, the construction of defense works across the island.

A CRASH TASK

The 515,000-square-meter expansion site of the Antillana de Acero steelworks dwarfed the 2,400 people at work there. A web of black wires, hung loosely between dozens of different structures taking shape, was the source of the salsa blaring from loudspeakers nestled amid the cranes, bulldozers, steel girders, cement blocks, dust and din.

"They're our idea," said 26-year-old José Ferro, a medium built electronics professor-turned construction worker-turned UJC head of the Antillana de Acero Crash Task, just outside Havana. "Every morning we broadcast what we did the day before and what's planned for the day ahead. What's on schedule, what's not. People want to know what they've accomplished, where they're bogged down, and what's coming up . . ." The music," he grinned, "was an important afterthought."

I spent a day walking around Antillana de Acero in March of 1989. I spoke with dozens of the 1,500 young people working on the expansion project. Ferro said they were volunteers: "We work from seven in the morning to six at night, 10 hours a day with an hour off for lunch. We are responsible for our own discipline and maintain it through peer pressure. We can sanction and even remove people from our crews."

Half a dozen conversations later I asked Ferro to square what he said with what everyone else was telling me: that they worked 12 to 14 hours a day, three out of four Saturdays a month, six hours the following Sundays, with one full weekend off for rest each month. "That's our crash task within the crash task," he said. "The UJC's 14 branches here decided to form volunteer brigades to work on the most strategic parts of the project or ones that are falling behind schedule. Right now, many of us work after hours over there at the two continuous casting plants being added to the old plant. Our goal is to finish them this summer, and together they'll start by producing 100,000 tons of steel rods needed for construction."

At 7:30 p.m. on March 12, 1989, I stood inside the foundation of the crash task within the crash task at Antillana de Acero. There were a few hundred young people working around me. The spotlights caught them fastening the building's girders, working on the roof, laying the cement to mount the big continuous casting machines that had already arrived at the site. The salsa music still blared away. "I'm a Yankee at heart," I told one after the other. "I can't believe that there are no personal and economic motivations behind all this." Time after time I got the same response. Juan Carlos Amador's baby face broke into a laugh behind his beard. The former Ministry of Trade employee, just thirty, said he did have a personal motive: "I'm a candidate for Party membership. But really, the material and personal incentives are secondary to our understanding of what we are doing. Spare time is precious, especially for young people. We like to enjoy ourselves. We don't give this time away for money. It doesn't interest us. What interests us is our investment in our country."

Mario Hill was the 1988 "vanguard" worker at the Antillana crash task: he put in thousands of volunteer hours. Obviously shy, he nevertheless told me he liked the honor and national recognition of being "vanguard" and was happy about the color TV he was given. "Why do I do it?" he pondered. "Because I know the country needs it. Because the work makes me feel good."

I found the enthusiasm of the young people at Antillana extraordinary. I asked Ferro how he managed to keep spirits high, despite the gruelling hours. "I'm not sure . . . ," he said. "I guess its because we are committed to our country and its policies. But also because we sense our country is committed to us. Emphasizing development means putting the future of Cuba's young people above all else."

HISTORY

The history of socialist Europe differed radically from Cuba's. All, with the exception of some of the USSR's republics, were fairly developed industrial or agrarian capitalist societies within a pre-World War II context, compared to what were then the colonized and neocolonized countries of the Third World. East Germany was part of imperialist and then fascist Germany. Czechoslovakia boasted one of the most developed capitalist economies in the world. Poland, Hungary, Romania and Bulgaria were fairly backward agrarian capitalist countries where, with the exception of Bulgaria, fascism rallied widespread support. Czarist Russia, no matter how backward, was a European power to be reckoned with.

War played an important part in forming today's Europe. Within the borders of many countries, including the former USSR, many nationalities existed side-by-side, atop a volcano of longstanding tensions. Socialism in Eastern Europe and some Soviet republics was at least partially superimposed on this uneasy picture, during a very complex and tragic historical moment, tending to run counter to national aspirations and real independence.

It was during and after the Second World War that Eastern Europe came under the Soviet wing as the Red Army consolidated socialism on lands liberated from fascism. Those were frightening times. Capitalist Germany had unleashed a terrible war, amassing human rights violations on a scale never before known to humanity. The big capitalist powers hoped to direct Hitler against the Soviet Union. And the people of the USSR, who played a key role in defeating Hitler and fascism, suffered 27 million dead, millions more wounded and the destruction of their homeland.

There is no doubt that the Soviet Union wanted to create a buffer zone between its borders and capitalist Europe, to insure that the Soviet people would never again be the victim of capitalism gone completely mad. So amidst the rubble, the massive destruction from the world's first atomic bombs, the horror and suffering of capitalist-inspired fascism and war, the Soviets used their armed forces and political clout to push communist and socialist parties into power in several countries—parties whose most courageous and competent leaders had been all but wiped out fighting fascism. The alternative was to leave liberated Eastern Europe and the Baltic republics in the hands of the USA and its allies, to completely encircle the war ravaged Soviet Union.

Postwar socialist Europe scored important economic and social gains, rebuilding over the psychological, social and material rubble left by the war. It also played a pivotal role in the international struggle against imperialism and for national liberation, a process that freed so many countries from direct colonial rule and some from neocolonialism as well. The socialist camp did not prove an economic match to imperialist economies, built as they were on the back of slavery, Third World poverty and the growing gap between rich and poor on the domestic front.

Grave errors were made throughout socialist Europe that included criminal repression, corruption and the development of a bureaucratic and inefficient administrative and economic system. In the end, the ruling Communist Parties failed to ideologically, and thus morally, fully develop their own members and people and to link their national identities solidly with socialism. National identity and socialism, far from merging, became ever more at odds in many East European minds and among some people in the Soviet republics as well.

The history of socialist Cuba is different. From the moment Carlos

Manuel de Céspedes decided to free his slaves and battle against the Spanish crown in 1868, the island's fight for independence was a completely indigenous process—against all odds and without outside help. For close to a century, the island waged a truly remarkable struggle for freedom: first against Spanish colonialism and then against Washington's neocolonial protectorate status. Since the 1959 revolution, Cuba has fought to maintain its independence and right to develop in the face of constant U.S. hostility.

Cuban calls for freedom have always had at their core a strong anti-imperialist and anti-racist content. Since the revolution, national identity, anti-imperialism and socialism have merged as one, and the national question (or more properly stated, the "ethnic question" as most Cubans are of mixed ethnicity with either a predominantly Spanish or African ancestry) has been largely overcome in the struggle to create one independent multi-ethnic nation with equal opportunity for all.

NATIONAL IDENTITY

People find their bearings and measure their success by comparing their current lot with the past and that of others. Entire nations do this too. Many East Europeans and people in the Soviet Union have a European identity. They gaze longingly at the developed capitalist countries, blind to imperialism. They believe that this tiny minority of the world community owes its wealth to the private property relations and market economies of the 1800s, and not to the development of monopoly capitalism and an international economic system in which 20 percent of our planet's population consumes over 70 percent of its resources.

Cuba identifies with the world of Latin America, the Caribbean, Africa and Asia. When Cubans speak of what they do or don't have, most use the "developing" world as their yardstick. Cubans see that their standard of living and general social tranquility and peace put them light years ahead of most Third World peoples. And they believe their brand of socialism has brought them an independence and national dignity unequaled in the lands of their Latin American and Caribbean neighbors.

Over half a million Cubans have worked abroad, in many of the world's more than 120 Third World countries. As some Europeans focus on the marvels of capitalism, market economies and private property, Cubans see the hunger, illiteracy and disease in countries like Angola, Ethiopia, Nicaragua, Bolivia and Brazil.

Two internationally recognized indicators of a nation's social and economic well-being are infant mortality and life expectancy. Cuba's infant mortality in 1958 topped 60 per one thousand live births, with a range upwards of 100 in rural areas. By 1991 infant mortality had fallen to 10.64 with no significant difference between urban and rural areas, with child mortality (from one to five years of age) at 13 per 1,000 children. Compare these figures with the Latin American region's infant mortality rate of 65 per 1,000 live births and child mortality of 85.[3]

James Grant, who heads up the UN's Children's Fund, UNICEF, commented in 1989 that "if every Latin American country had a health care system like Cuba's, we would save the lives of 700,000 Latin American children under five, each and every year." To look at this in the reverse is to see the seven million children who will die in the capitalist-dominated region by the year 2000, as these same countries are drained of life-giving resources by the transnationals, monopoly banks, the foreign governments whose flags they fly and the domestic elites that collaborate with them.[4]

Since the 1959 revolution, Cuba's life expectancy has risen faster than any other nation's. By 1990, Cubans lived to an average age of 75—13.2 years more than in 1959. That same year, worldwide life expectancy stood at 60.4 years. For the developed countries it was above 70; for the Third World, 58.2. In Africa 51.8; in Latin America 65.6.[5]

Perhaps more startling is a comparison of Cuba's basic social indicators with the more developed ex-Soviet Union and East European countries. According to UNICEF's 1989 Report "On the State of the World's Children," **at the end of 1987** Cuba's infant mortality rate stood at 15 per 1,000 live births, Mongolia-46, the USSR-25, Romania-22, Poland-18, Hungary-17, Bulgaria-15, Czechoslovakia-10 and Democratic Germany-9. Cuba's life expectancy had reached 74, Mongolia-64, the USSR-70, Romania and Hungary-71, Bulgaria, Czechoslovakia and Poland-72, with only Democratic Germany on par with Cuba at 74.

There is no other country in the world that can match Cuba's commitment to the struggle against racism. Institutional racism has been wiped out. You won't find jobs, medical care and education being made available along the color line. There are no differences in nutrition or housing. There are no segregated neighborhoods; There is absolutely no racial violence in Cuba. Events that have become commonplace in the United States and many other countries, just one incident of racial violence, would provoke a national crisis.

But that doesn't mean all prejudice has disappeared from the hearts and minds of every Cuban. It hasn't, so the struggle continues, with the government and Communist Party in the forefront. Cuba has a strong affirmative action program that aims at proportional representation in all the leading bodies of society.[6]

There is a similar affirmative action program for women, who now make up some 40 percent of Cuba's labor force and more than half of all professionals. In 1991, women made up 20 percent of Cuba's Party members and about 17 percent of elected government officials. They were better represented in Cuba's national mass organizations. Their numbers tapered off the higher one went in Cuba's superstructure.

Women workers have access to day care and receive equal pay for equal work. They also enjoy many other benefits, such as free health care, six months paid maternity leave, priority service at stores and control over their own bodies, with the right to free abortion on demand. The fight against sexism in Cuba today centers on convincing men to do their share of the housework, freeing up women to lead, and improving women's image in the mass media. Promotion of women into management has been identified as a key battlefront in the continuing fight for full women's equality.[7]

Peace of mind is a less tangible but just as real change for women in post-revolutionary Cuba, and indeed for men. The peace of mind to walk down the street day or night and live in their homes, old and young, with relatively little fear of violent assault. There is no pornography in Cuba, no topless bars, organized prostitution or child kidnappings.

Cuba's record against violent crime and drugs is impressive. I spent three weekends observing emergency room traffic in three different Havana hospitals. No hard drug cases came in, no bullet wounds, no rape victims and just a few knife wounds. Over a dozen doctors told me they hadn't seen an intravenous drug user in more than 25 years and that gunshot wounds and rape cases were rare.

At the 1990 United Nation's Congress on Crime Prevention and the Treatment of Offenders, held in Havana, the main report warned that worldwide "crime is rising at an average five percent annual rate," and "becoming increasingly violent." The report pointed to a jump in organized crime, police abuse, excessive use of lethal force and poor prison conditions.

"The predatory traffic in drugs," it continued,

has become a global tragedy: it has ruined the lives of its victims and forced millions of citizens to directly face unprecedented violence. In a developed country with a high crime rate, 1 of every 133 citizens will become a murder victim; 8 of every 10 citizens will be attacked, and of these, 50 percent more than once in their lives; practically all citizens will be robbed and 9 out of 10 people will be robbed three times or more . . . In a developing country with ten million residents there will be tens of thousands of violent crimes every year and hundreds of thousands of crimes against property.

Compare these figures with Cuba's. Attorney General Ramón de la Cruz delivered a special crime report to Parliament in July, 1990. There were a total of 186,688 criminal acts reported in 1989. Of these, 70 percent were robberies, 57 percent against property and the vast majority petty thefts of under 100 pesos. Only 8 percent of the robberies involved more than 500 pesos. Violence was used in only 2,385 robberies and force (breaking and entering) in 21,058 cases. There were 401 murders and 368 manslaughter cases in Cuba during 1989. Ninety-five percent stemmed from personal grievances with just five percent for financial gain. Most were committed under the influence of alcohol; 3,606 people were seriously hurt in various attacks and there were 1,530 rapes reported. In all of Cuba there were only 948 drug cases, almost all of which involved marijuana or pharmaceuticals.

The United Nations Economic and Social Council states that in the 1980s developing countries had an annual rate of 1,600 robberies per 100,000 citizens and 10.7 murders. The figures for Cuba were 857.12 robberies and 3.28 murders.[8]

SOCIALIST DEVELOPMENT MODELS

From the start, the Cuban revolution looked for its own path of socialist development. Fidel Castro, Che Guevera and other Cuban leaders criticized the European socialist model as relying solely on economic methods, including capitalist methods, to develop socialism. They criticized socialist Europe's bureaucratic and undemocratic style, insisting socialism encompassed more than economic development. They argued for changing society's thinking and consciousness through consistent political work, by actively involving the public in policy formation and socialist construction. The struggle for socialism, they argued, meant first and foremost bringing out the best in each individual: nurturing what Che Guevara called "the new person," an individual with the morals, values and intelligence needed to give birth to and sustain socialism in the face of an extremely powerful and aggressive old order.

After touring Eastern Europe, Che Guevara, the Argentinean doctor who made the Cuban revolution his own, wrote in a 1965 essay entitled "Man and Socialism in Cuba":

> The danger lies in not seeing the wood for the trees. The illusion of building socialism on the legacy of well-worn weapons of capitalism (commodity, profitability, individual material interest as the lever, etc.) can be a dead end alley. After travelling a long distance, paths may have often crossed and it may be difficult to see where a wrong road was taken. Meanwhile, the adapted economic base has undermined the development of consciousness. To build communism, along with the material base there has to be a new man in the making.
>
> That is why it is so important to choose the right tool for mobilizing the masses. That tool has to be basically moral, without obviating a correct use of material incentives, especially the social kind.
>
> In moments of extreme danger it is easy to invoke moral incentives; for them to remain relevant, there needs to be developed an awareness that has the values of a new category. Society as a whole must become one huge school.[9]

In the 1960s, the Cubans tried to forge their own model of socialist development that stressed consciousness raising and grassroots participation in the political, social and economic life of the country. A number of factors made Cuban socialism unique: the literacy campaign and emphasis on health and social well-being through the development of extensive and free social services; the systematic struggle against racism and sexism; the national mass organizations; linking study with work; promoting voluntary work; agrarian reform; and the consistent struggle to instill a deep sense of anti-imperialism and internationalism in Cubans of all ages.

Speaking on March 17, 1990, with liberation theologians in Sao Paulo, Brazil, Fidel Castro illustrated some of the differences between how Cuba developed socialism and what happened in the USSR and other countries. Pointing to Cuba's different history, its geographical proximity to the U.S., and even to the Cuban "character," he asserted, "We didn't make the same mistakes they made. We made other mistakes, of a different kind, and we had to rectify them . . ." Castro said Stalin bred an "abuse of authority" and violence in the Soviet Union. In contrast, he argued, "we have never used violence against our citizens; not even tear gas. We would never stoop to that . . . Even the spies and terrorists who were executed were tried with due process; and we have never used force to make anyone talk or confess."

Referring to agrarian reform, the Cuban leader continued: "We never forced anybody to join the state farms or cooperatives . . . We never pressured anyone . . . So we don't have to rectify anything on that score . . ."

And on the development of a privileged elite and corruption he noted,

> We've also been careful to avoid as much as possible privileges for our leaders, officials, cadres—we struggle against that. Above all, we have made great efforts to uphold the unity between our Party and people, between the revolution and the people. Because what has happened in several of these countries is that there was a gap between the Party and people, the government and the people, the leadership and the people. If we were to commit those mistakes, we wouldn't last two minutes next to the United States, a powerful country that blockades us, pressures us, harasses us, wants to destroy us. Without a united, organized and armed people to defend the revolution, we couldn't exist next to the United States, and so reality shows that we haven't made those types of errors.[10]

The Cubans are the first to admit that they committed serious, mainly idealist errors in the sixties. By the early seventies, the pendulum had swung strongly in the opposite direction. Forces who advocated a more orthodox European model of socialist development gained strength. Cuba joined the Council for Mutual Economic Assistance (CMEA) in 1972. The first Congress of the Cuban Communist Party, held three years later, voted to adopt shadow economic planning and management models like those in place throughout socialist Europe.

Cuba began to slip more and more into relying on administrative means and purely economic incentives to build socialism. Political work declined. Eastern Europe's decades-old approach began to take hold in Cuba. Grassroots mobilization methods that had paid off in Cuba, like voluntary work, were abandoned. Money, and central planners sitting in their Havana offices, became the answer to everything. Strategic growth and the rational use of resources were replaced by growth-for-growth's-sake and the squandering of resources. The bureaucracy mushroomed, as active mass participation in the revolutionary process faltered; mismanagement, corruption and stagnation spread; social problems grew. Less attention was paid to people's needs and views. Problems went unresolved and grew in number and urgency. It's interesting to note that the Cubans, by early 1986, were saying the errors they committed between 1975 and 1986 were so grave that these had threatened to destroy people's spirit and consciousness and thus the revolution.[11]

Less than ten years after the first Congress of the Cuban Communist

Party and well before Mikhail Gorbachev came to power, economic disorganization and popular discontent were forcing Cuba's leaders to take stock and act. In November 1984, the Communist Party's top leadership stripped the bureaucracy of its power, taking over national planning and management policy. This drastic move, which placed the Party and politics back at the center of Cuba's economic life, marked the unofficial start of what would become known as "Rectification," the reshaping of Cuban socialism from top to bottom.

PART I: PERESTROIKA CUBAN STYLE

Chapter One
WHAT'S RECTIFICATION?

In the Beginning

Cuba's leaders insist their country's "rectification" began well before the advent of Mikhail Gorbachev on the Soviet and world scene. The Cubans state they began to analyze their system and take corrective action for three reasons: growing domestic problems and popular discontent; the need to cope with a mushrooming foreign debt and hard currency crisis; and new saber rattling from Washington under President Ronald Reagan.

In fact, rectification's roots can be traced to before March of 1985 when Gorbachev came to power in the Soviet Union, the process taking shape during 1986, before Perestroika and Glasnost had become household words. The year 1986 began with the Third Party Congress and a blistering critique of Cuba's status quo. The year ended with a second deferred session of the Congress in early December, which summed up a year-long debate over Cuba's problems and how to solve them.

Cubans point to Fidel Castro's April 19, 1986 speech, delivered on the 25th anniversary of the proclamation of socialism in Cuba and the victory at the Bay of Pigs, as rectification's official kickoff. Castro challenged the well-entrenched notion that the U.S. economic blockade was to be blamed for all of Cuba's shortcomings. He argued against the taboo on people openly identifying and debating problems for fear that Cuba's foes would use the information against the country. But what makes the April speech a landmark is that it represented the first public call to tackle the country's difficulties, and the start of the Cuban Communist Party's drive to mobilize the country in a struggle to further democratize Cuban society.

Castro, speaking at Havana's Karl Marx Theater, reviewed Washington's long history of bullying Cuba and other Third World countries. He warned that Ronald Reagan's Washington was more aggressive and warlike than any previous U.S. administration. Castro then analyzed the difficult economic situation facing the country and asked: "Why talk about such issues today, during celebrations marking the defeat of the U.S. mercenary army at the Bay of Pigs?"

Because, answered Castro, "today's enemy isn't mercenaries or mercenary invasions but . . . people who act like them." The Cuban President cited the example of artists and interior decorators who earned up to 200,000 pesos a year beautifying state buildings. The issue wasn't just that these individuals made twenty to forty times more than a heart surgeon but that government officials wasted such enormous sums of public monies.

The Cuban President gave the example of a government company that billed a hospital 5,000 pesos to install stainless steel sheets in its elevators. The company had wanted 10,000. The hospital provided the materials, and the company two men who did the job in 15 days. Castro charged that the company paid the workers no more than 300 pesos and the rest went down on the books as profit, when it was really money stolen by a state company from a state hospital, and did not reflect new value produced. "Some people," charged Castro, "put their company's earnings, profits and bonuses, above the interests of society," and thus "have become capitalists in every sense of the word."

Castro next recounted how he had come across a 40,000 peso house being built for a warehouse manager who earned 199 pesos a month. The man had "borrowed" a state-owned 16-ton crane, a cement mixer, two trucks, building materials and an ample supply of pork and beer for the group of men helping him build the house. Castro termed the example a case-in-point of the widespread practice of diverting public resources for private use and gain. He questioned if such a diversion of resources could take place without a wink and a nod from the people in charge of them.

"Things aren't functioning well and consciences aren't functioning well," Fidel Castro told his people. "There are managers who are not doing their jobs properly, since they do not keep records of the money and resources they administer . . . There are those who feel socialism can be built without political work, and even some who think it can be built without physical work." These weaknesses, said Castro, were Cuba's "new enemy." He blasted those looking for "privileges and cushy jobs, who divert resources, who seek to pocket money that they haven't earned by the sweat of their brow, who are racketeers."

The Cuban President cautioned that he wasn't calling for a "cultural revolution" but a "persistent struggle" by the Cuban people. He criticized the Party and Union of Young Communists, whose combined one million members (one out of every ten Cubans) had to be aware of what was going on, but who did nothing—or worse. "This struggle will last longer than just a five year period," he said. "All our lives we will have to fight against this tendency, because there are always two factions, as José Martí said: 'those who build up and those who tear down.' There is a large faction that builds up. But there is another one, where the lazy and irresponsible sit. And they don't have to be counterrevolutionaries. These are people who don't realize that they are acting like mercenaries."[1]

Over the next eight months, an extraordinary series of national meetings took place, each involving a different sector of society and each following extensive public debate at the local and provincial levels. The leaders of Cuba's 1,600 farm cooperatives met; then the directors of Cuba's major companies; so, too, the leaders of various national mass organizations, from the labor unions to high school and university students. Scrutinizing stagnation within each sector, the debates received broad media coverage with special focus on the measures adopted to correct the most glaring problems that came to light.

Three broad negative tendencies emerged. First, unearned income, be it a worker collecting for two jobs in an eight-hour workday or a company overcharging other state companies to jack up earnings. Second, lack of discipline, be it teachers not teaching, workers not working or managers staying away from the job. Third, outright corruption, be it Party functionaries taking advantage of their position, doctors selling work disabilities or early retirement, students cheating on exams or workers and managers helping themselves to public resources.

An identical series of meetings followed in 1987 and 1988, checking up on the 1986–1987 agreements, deepening the analysis of the systemic causes of Cuba's problems and coming up with proposals to restructure, in particular, the Cuban economy and management-labor relations. Fidel Castro, along with most other national leaders, attended all the meetings. At each, Castro, in his role as point man for the Party's political work, hammered away at the question of moral decay, arguing that uncontrolled economic mechanisms and material incentives lead to the degeneration of socialism from within. "In the search for economic efficiency, we have created the breeding ground for a heap of vices and distortions," Castro told the leaders of Cuba's Cooperatives on May 18th in Havana. "And what's worse," he continued, "is corruption. That hurts! Corruption that can dull the revolutionary consciousness of our people . . ."[2]

On June 25th and 26th, the top managers, Party and union leaders from Cuba's state-run companies met in Havana on the Cuban economy. They concluded that companies were losing sight of the nationwide picture, as they raced to top production goals and collect the bonuses that followed. "What concerns us most is the increase in the ambition for money, the spirit of profit that is invading our working class," Castro told the gathering. "We fell prey to the misbegotten dream that an economic management and planning system would solve all our problems . . . That we could forget and do nothing about political work."[3]

The deferred session of the Third Party Congress focused on the year-long discussion that was coming to a close and the need for Party members to take the initiative in identifying and solving problems, combatting personal and public corruption; and to lead by example and accomplishment, not rhetoric and dictates.

Summing up the debate on December 2, 1986, Castro warned

> . . . the Party was starting to go to pot . . . When mistakes are not energetically fought, the people start to become skeptical, discouraged and demoralized; the revolution's ideals are discredited . . . The construction of socialism is essentially a political task, a revolutionary task. It must be fundamentally the fruit of the development of a social awareness and of educating people . . . This doesn't deny the usefulness and necessity of economic mechanisms. But to me it's clear that economics is an instrument of political and revolutionary work. [4]

CHE GUEVARA

As Cuba's rectification process got off the ground, there was a Party-inspired revival of Che Guevara that peaked in 1988, though an increased interest in his life and work continues as of this writing. Actually, the Argentinean doctor's example was already very much alive when rectification began. Cuban children, from their first day in school, are taught "to be like Che."

Che Guevara played a critical role in Cuba's "July 26th Movement," the political leadership responsible for toppling Fulgencio Batista in 1959. Che became Cuba's most important economic leader during the first years of the revolution, and he struggled to adapt Marxist-Leninist theory to Cuban conditions and those of the Third World in general. The Cuban and Latin American hero, who was a severe critic of what he saw as an authoritarian and bureaucratic European socialist model, was executed by the Bolivian military under orders from the CIA in 1967. At the time he was trying to conduct a Cuban-like revolution in the Bolivian mountains. Today Bolivia remains one of the poorest countries in the hemisphere, second only to Haiti, with social and economic indicators far lower than even pre-revolutionary Cuba.

The increased Cuban interest in Che's work culminated with the 20th anniversary of his death on October 9, 1987, and the 60th anniversary of his birth, the following year. Some U.S. Cuba experts drew the erroneous conclusion that rectification was a mere return to Che's political and economic thought or, worse still, to that brief period in the late 1960s when Cuba tried to leap directly to communism, abolishing all economic incentives.

U.S. Cuba expert Saul Landau wrote in the August, 1989, issue of *Mother Jones*

When Fidel urged people to think like Che and model their lives after him, it was more than exhortation. This was Fidel's answer to Glasnost and Perestroika; Cubans would "rectify" their mistakes by resolving to "be like Che," an answer that required transporting themselves backwards.[5]

Nothing could be further from the truth! What Landau was referring to was the Cuban leadership's efforts to strengthen rectification's ideological content. And why not Che? Landau states in the same article, "Che accurately symbolizes spiritual integrity, hard work and commitment to the collectivity." All traits Rectification seeks to promote.[6] In addition, Che Guevara was indeed an internationalist, an independent thinker and a man that insisted on applying Marxism-Leninism creatively to a country's concrete conditions. What's more, Che believed in political and social consciousness as the moving force behind socialism. He repeatedly warned that socialist Europe's failure to realize this could lead to its downfall.

So, while socialist Europe rushed headlong into the market economy, and with rectification picking up steam in Cuba, the Cubans highlighted the following theoretical contribution of Che's: *the organization of socialist production and distribution is much more than a short-term economic question and must be looked at in terms of its impact on each worker's consciousness. How an economy is organized is fundamental to each person's ideological development, to the formation of their social consciousness and thus a strategic question for socialism.*

"In essence Che was radically opposed to using and developing capitalist economic laws and categories in building socialism," Fidel Castro told his people on October 8, 1987, at a national ceremony on the eve of the 20th anniversary of Che Guevara's death. "He advocated something which I have often insisted on: building socialism and communism is not just a matter of producing and distributing wealth but is also a matter of education and of awareness. He was firmly opposed to using these categories which have been transferred from capitalism to socialism as instruments to build the new society."[7]

RELYING ON THE PEOPLE

The seeds of rectification can be traced to 1981 when Cuba adopted a new defensive strategy called "war of the entire people." In the late 1970s, the U.S. Carter Administration began a brief thaw in the USA's Caribbean Cold War. However, the process quickly succumbed to Ronald Reagan's big chill, and he began the 1980s with a spate of McCarthy-era rhetoric directed at the island. Cuba felt threatened like never before, and set about reviewing defense preparations. The nation's political leaders discovered that Cuba's defense had become ossified, relying increasingly on the professional military and its hardware. They decided to turn this strategy on its head, relying first and foremost on the willingness of millions of Cubans to defend their country. With help from the Vietnamese, the island's military leaders designed a 20-year defense plan based on Cuba's terrain and real strengths, improved leadership and massive grassroots participation. The preparations were blocked out in four stages through the year 2000. The ultimate goal: for every willing, able-bodied man and woman to know their spot in case of attack, and how to defend it. Militia training takes place one Sunday a month, and many people are mobilized each year for weeks on end. Training as a weekend warrior is strictly voluntary and the national program is partially funded by union members' annual donation of a day's pay.

Since the early 1980s, the average Cuban has learned how to handle a rifle stored at factories, farms and in neighborhoods: how to evacuate children, the disabled and the elderly; and how to keep factories, farms, hospitals and schools running if the nation is attacked. Each province regularly practices defense maneuvers; and once a year, national maneuvers unfold. Vast tunnel networks and underground production, storage and living facilities have been dug in the 1,400 defense zones covering the island.

The United States launched three simultaneous war games aimed at Cuba in May, 1990. They came right after the invasion of Panama, the fall of the Sandinistas and amidst the ruins of European socialism. The U.S. had just launched TV Martí broadcasts and the Presidents of Venezuela and Spain were openly warning Cuba that Washington was considering military action against the country. Cuba declared a national alert and mobilized the entire population.

I spent most of those ten days in Havana, with a ground to air missile battery in my backyard, waiting for word to evacuate my 3-year-old daughter. I also toured a number of Havana communities and watched hundreds of thousands of Cubans take up position and drill. On May 3rd and 4th I travelled to Pinar del Río, considered one of the most defense-ready provinces. Visiting a parts plant eighty miles west of Havana, an air raid siren blared. Within five minutes 200 employees shut down their machines, gathered their weapons and took up positions in and around the factory. Outside, others scrambled to move anti-aircraft batteries into position.

"The plant opened in 1983, and ever since we have been practicing how to keep it running and defend it if your country attacks us," factory director Felipe Pérez told me. "The average age of the workers here is 27; many of them fought in Angola." The head of the Communist Party committee at the plant, 32-year old José Hernández, was comfortable running a metal lathe or holding his AK-47 as we spoke. "Most people here aren't Party members, but they all have a gun," he said.

The Communist Party First Secretary in Pinar del Río, Fidel Ramos Perera, met with foreign journalists that same Friday afternoon.

"I want to explain why we are dressed in military uniforms," began Ramos Perera. "There's a nationwide defense alert and I'm head of the provincial Defense Council. For three days we have been mobilizing our artillery, tanks, pilots—practically all our forces. I just came from a tour of our anti-aircraft batteries in one of the province's 110 defense zones. The American exercises may be a cover for a surprise attack on Cuba. We're not taking any chances. The province is on alert, our combat units are in place. The general population will be mobilized over the weekend."

Practice is one thing, war another. "What makes you think you can rely on these civilian volunteers in case of a real attack?" asked one reporter. "Pinar del Río was once one of Cuba's poorest provinces," began Ramos: "Our infant mortality rate was 70 per 1,000 live births in 1959 and so far this year it is six. Back then, more than half the children never went to school; today they all are in class through the high school level. There was no child care; now we have 54 centers with seven more under construction. We are building three special schools and over 4,000 apartments this year. Before the revolution, there was no higher education here, and only 10,000 university students on the entire island. Now there are 10,500 university students in Pinar del Río alone, with 15,000 professionals and 30,000 specialists already hard at work. This is what all of us are defending."

SETTING PRIORITIES, WORKING TOGETHER

On November 22, 1984, Cuba's leaders gathered in Havana for an emergency meeting. Those present included the Party's Political Bureau, the Central Committee Secretariat, Council of State Vice Presidents, the country's Ministers, provincial Party and People's Power officials and the leaders of Cuba's national mass organizations.

The Cuban economy was booming. Gross National Product had grown an average 7 percent annually since the decade began, with a 7.4 percent growth in 1984. Ironically, that very fact now threatened to undermine the economy. Cuba's leaders agreed the question was not how much the economy grew, but what sectors grew and on what basis. To sustain high growth rates, more and more imports from the West were needed, bought with hard currency earned from exports. But the island's exports were faltering. The 1984 sugar harvest, Cuba's key export, came up 700,000 tons short; production of nickel and citrus, two other top earners, declined; tobacco yields seemed to have grown dramatically, but only compared to an earlier crop which was wiped out by a hurricane.

Fidel Castro told the year-end session of the Cuban Parliament that the November meeting resulted in a number of ideas on how to stem the growing trade imbalance and mounting foreign debt. A central working group was set up on an emergency basis to rescue the 1985 plan. Castro reported that the plan was being redrafted to prioritize hard currency exports, import substitutes, exports to socialist countries, key development projects and essential services.[8]

To carry this out, Cuba's planning process was dramatically revamped from top to bottom. In fact, an entirely new process began to emerge. Fidel Castro explained it as a strategic change in economic priorities, a "conceptual revolution that revolutionized the way the plan should be drawn up, how it should be implemented and how it should be supervised—a task involving all sectors of the economy and government."

The 1984 meeting also targeted a negative tendency that had existed from Cuba's first stabs at central planning. With a limited amount of resources available, the country's agencies, ministries and state institutions began vying for the scarce funds and supplies. "Decisions," Castro said, were not "necessarily rational or optimal" as a result. "We overlooked the fact that we were not applying one of the fundamental principles of socialism," he stressed. "Socialism is not only nationalizing the factories, the land, the mines, the banks, all the resources and means of production. Socialism is coordinating efforts, and making optimal use of the country's resources as a whole, with everybody pulling at the same time and in the same direction . . ."[9] The plan, until now the conglomerate result of turf wars, must be a comprehensive plan from the start.

FROM QUANTITY TO QUALITY

During the first 30 years of the revolution, despite ups and downs, there was a tremendous quantitative build-up in all areas of Cuban society. Hundreds of factories and social facilities were built, hundreds of thousands of professionals, specialists, technicians, teachers and nurses trained. Development, fueled by the Cubans' efforts, massive support from socialist Europe and loans from the capitalist world proceeded at a pace that was faster than Cuba's ability to make the best use of it. This contradiction had come to the fore by the mid 1980s and played an important part in sparking and molding the rectification movement. Cuba had reached a point where it was possible and necessary to shift the emphasis to quality.

Castro, closing the deferred session of the Third Party Congress on December 2, 1986, placed this dilemma on the rectification agenda. "Our problems are new," said Castro, "not what we faced in 1959."

Our problems in education are different. We don't have illiteracy. We don't have a teacher shortage. We have problems in education because we have built thousands of schools and we want these schools to function in the best possible manner. We have problems because we have 260,000 teachers, and we want these teachers to provide quality education. We have problems because we have built and expanded many hospitals. We have problems because we have more than 25,000 doctors, not the 3,000 left by the imperialists, but 25,000 and all trained by the revolution. Tens of thousands of nurses, and health specialists: and what we want is that they do the best possible job. We have problems because we have built thousands of industrial and agricultural facilities, because we have tens of thousands of tractors and pieces of construction equipment; and we want all these resources to be efficiently utilized . . . We have problems because we have huge resources compared to what we had in the past, and we are waging a battle to make the best use of them . . . We have had the privilege of having . . . extraordinary foreign cooperation, satisfactory trade with the socialist countries. We have had many resources available to us and we are to blame for not having known how to use them more efficiently.[10]

Cuba's strong points, education, science and health care provide good examples of the breadth and depth of the rectification process and the shift from a quantitative to qualitative approach.

EDUCATION

One of the revolution's first goals and achievements was to provide schooling for all children, and teach every Cuban to read and write. Literacy, reasoned the Cubans, was not only a basic human right but the key to real democracy. However, in 1960, 89.1 percent of all of Cuba's students were enrolled in the primary grades, 8.5 percent from secondary through high school; and just 2.4 percent in higher education. At the same time the country had a serious teacher shortage. "To teach or not to teach everyone" was the question of the day. For Cuba's new leaders there was only one answer, and seventh graders began five-year teacher training courses, even while teaching primary school children. A primary school teacher's qualifications moved up to ninth grade by the mid 1970s, which was also when they began their pedagogical studies. Those who taught secondary school had at least the equivalent of a high school diploma. Due to the 1960s baby boom and lower infant mortality, demand at the primary school level remained high, at 71.6 percent of total national enrollment. The secondary and high school level share of enrollment had grown to 25.1 percent, and higher education's to 3.3 percent. The picture was quite different by the 1990s. Just 39.7 percent of all students were in grade school, and 48.1 percent in secondary and high school. University and post-graduate enrollment climbed to 12.2 percent. Cuba was finally able to turn to improvement in teacher training, with the resulting impact on the classroom and society as a whole.[11]

"The panorama we have now is very different from that in the 1960s and 1970s," Magaly García Ojeda, National Primary Education Director, told me in a 1990 interview. "For one thing, today every primary school teacher has a degree. This year, we began enrolling students in pedagogical school after they graduated from 12th grade, so they will begin teaching with a university degree. In addition, most of our teachers who are already working continue their studies towards a university degree on the job. They take night courses for four years and then are given a two-year sabbatical to complete their degree."

Rectification in education also meant a conscious shift from learning by rote to learning how to use your head. The Cubans say: from instruction to education. National education seminars began in 1987. They combed through the education system, adopted measures to improve it and sent delegates back to the base to share results with everyone from principals, teachers and school workers to the students and their parents. Curricula, previously changed every five to ten years, are now continuously updated. There is a new emphasis on the special education needs of some children, creative thinking and motivation, staff discipline and parent-community involvement. Rectification has also resulted in better pay and more public recognition for teachers. Standardized testing began in 1988 to evaluate administrator, teacher and student performance.

I asked Magaly García Ojeda about charges that Cuba's education system encouraged teachers to pass students regardless of merit. "Our system did encourage this, and it was a mistake," she responded. "Sometimes, to attain a high percentage of passes, which in turn was rewarded by the system, teachers would damage quality and also the students themselves . . . Now there is a strong orientation that real learning doesn't happen by making everything easy, from classes, to tests and standards. It only happens through high standards and great efforts by teachers, students and everyone involved in the education system."

Combining study and work is the hallmark of Cuba's education philosophy. But the policy didn't take hold in higher education (with the exception of medical school); many trade and technical schools, nor in the capital's schools at all levels. One of rectification's first fruits was to link higher education to production. For example, engineering and agricultural schools are now tied directly to some of Cuba's most important factories and state farms. The dean sits on the workplace's board of directors; and the manager on the school's faculty council. Professors work; and the best engineers, specialists and skilled workers teach. Students spend increasing amounts of time on the job and their theses must address issues they've confronted. New graduates spend their first two years rotating from department to department at their workplace before beginning a specialized career. And on the other end, experienced workers can go back to school for their degrees.

Trade and technical schools have also been linked to over 250 major industrial and agricultural centers and follow the same system of interlocking leadership and on-the-job training. And in the capital, many junior and senior high school students now go to school in the countryside while others spend at least a month in the fields.

SCIENCE

Cuban science provides another good example of the quantitative to qualitative shift during rectification. Noel Toledo, first Vice President of Cuba's Academy of Sciences told me: "Before we could develop our science program we had to eliminate illiteracy, bring education to all corners of the country and develop a thorough university reform aimed at providing a wide range of majors. Only two technical science majors were offered in 1959, and now there are 80. So today we have a pool of skilled specialists, scientists and technicians who are destined to play a leading role in Cuba's economic and social development."

In the early years of the Cuban revolution, many scientists and researchers employed by U.S. companies left home, lured by higher salaries in the industrialized showcase to the north. The scientists who remained were brought together to share their experiences, conduct research and, most of all, teach. The National Commission for the Cuban Academy of Sciences was formed in February, 1962, and the first research centers opened. "There was no brain drain to the socialist countries," said Toledo. "Just the opposite. We couldn't have developed our sciences without the help of the socialist countries. They provided most of the equipment for our centers, and Cuban scientists began travelling to the Soviet Union and elsewhere for advanced training. In addition, many of their scientists came here to work and teach."

By 1985 there were 185 research centers in Cuba. But rectification pared down the number. "There was a boom, and we lost our sense of priorities," Toledo said. "Some centers were duplicating work and needlessly purchasing similar and very expensive equipment. What is important is not the number of scientific centers and personnel, but the quality of their training and their work."

Cuba had 40,000 people involved in research and development work by 1987. Just 177 of them held Ph.D.s, plus another 2,524 doctoral candidates. Of the Ph.D.s, 25 percent were in social sciences, 20 percent in technical sciences, 19 percent in natural sciences, 18 percent in biomedicine, 17 percent in agriculture and one percent fell under the category of "others." But if the newer crop of doctoral candidates is added, there is, a radically changing set of priorities: 34 percent worked in agricultural sciences, 24 percent in technical sciences, 22 percent in biomedicine, 10 percent in social sciences, 6 percent the natural sciences and 3 percent in technical services.[12]

At 43 years old, Dr. Rosa Elena Simeón was named to head the Academy of Sciences in 1985. One of Simeón's first efforts was to reorganize. A number of research centers were merged. Qualifications for researchers and scientists were tightened, and the nation's top scientists formed experts' committees to review work, decide promotion, demotion and firing. As a result of the streamlining, the number of scientists and researchers at the National Center for Scientific Research was reduced from 1,084 in 1985 to 600 by 1987, with improved results. The Center had 146 supervisors and just half the staff was directly engaged in research. By 1987, only 27 supervisors remained, and the rest of the scientific personnel dedicated their time to research.[13] Dr. Simeón reoriented research and development efforts to coincide with the country's new priorities. Thus, major programs focused on increasing exports, substituting for imports and putting natural resources to better use, especially energy resources.[14]

Perhaps the biggest problem for Cuban science was translating research findings into practice. Two factors hampered the effort: poor planning, management and organization, and the lack of resources. In 1986 the Academy began a systematic review of the large backlog of scientific discoveries never put into practice, as well as a crash program to implement them. All new research proposals had to include how, if successful, they would be implemented and paid for.

The Academy's 1987 plans called for implementing the findings of 22 important scientific projects. Only nine made it on stream; another 11 were partially implemented and two not at all. The Academy estimated its research contributed 6.7 million pesos to the Cuban economy.[15] The Academy's 1988 plans called for implementing 89 discoveries, many dating from the early 1980s. 22 were implemented, another 18 partially and 39 not at all, for an estimated contribution of 24.9 million pesos—half of that year's plan.[16] For the first time, in 1989, plans to introduce scientific advances were met to the tune of 120 million pesos.[17] A year later, another 440 discoveries had contributed 819 million pesos to the economy.[18]. The Academy and Cuba's scientists, engineers and researchers were now in the thick of all major economic and social efforts and at the center of the nation's attention. The country initiated an annual science day to review and honor scientific efforts and at the 1991 Fourth Party Congress more time was spent on research and development than on any other topic.

PUBLIC HEALTH

Dr. Osvaldo Castro is a man with big responsibilities and a tiny office. Fifty-five years old at the time of our 1991 interview, he was the father of three children, grandfather of a growing flock and chief of the public health system's planning and development. I found him in a back room on the second floor of what was once a private mansion in Havana's Vedado section.

Dr. Castro told me Cuba's health care system developed through three stages. The first brought basic health care to rural Cuba and launched public health campaigns against various diseases prevalent in the Third World. The second stage, which began in 1968, was marked by the expansion of Cuba's health care system and development of modern facilities and technique. The third is now underway, aimed at perfecting what has been accomplished to date.

"Rectification has had a big impact on the entire health care system," Dr. Castro said. "Directly, in terms of health worker's attitudes and indirectly, in terms of the new mentality it has brought to all Cubans." An important political movement has developed in the sector that emphasizes the special character of health workers' jobs. "Health care is a special type of job that demands a high level of attention and sacrifice," said the doctor. At the same time lower paid health workers were the first to receive raises when rectification began. A new system to evaluate institutions, departments and individuals emphasizes quality and costs and includes feedback from the public.

In the early 1980s, Cuba formed a national commission of medical professors to revamp its medical school curriculum. The commission visited prestigious medical schools around the world, and then designed a new curriculum that sought to train doctors not just in anatomy, physiology and other hard sciences, but also in sociology and psychology.

"We wanted medical students to graduate with an integral view and knowledge of health care that would then be strengthened by their residency as community-based family doctors. After that, they would go on to specialize," explained Dr. Castro. He asserted that rectification has brought important changes to the selection process of medical students as well as the curriculum. Medical students are now selected not just by their grades, but also by their character, ethics and general vocation. For the first time all applicants must take an entrance exam which carries a 50 percent weight in the acceptance decision.

The training of other health professionals has also been revamped. Dr. Castro pointed to nurses as an example. In the 1960s, basic health care was spread throughout the country, and there was a serious nursing shortage and a low national educational level. "So we began nurses aides' training at the seventh grade level," recalled Dr. Castro. By the 1970s, nurses with a ninth grade education took over. A decade later, a nursing education was the equivalent of a high school diploma. Today, more and more nurses have university degrees. Dr. Castro told me he expected all nurses to be college graduates by the year 2000.

That same upscaling is taking place among Cuba's medical technicians. Adapting to today's high-tech, complex medical world, the Cuban health system is employing more degreed scientists, biologists, chemists, and physicists; as well as electronics, computer, nuclear and laser specialists.

The most important change taking place in Cuban health care can be found in a rural health outpost, a large factory, on a fishing boat or in a city neighborhood. It's the country's growing network of family doctor-nurse teams, which Dr. Castro termed a "revolution in Cuban health care." Dozens of Cuban officials, doctors and medical students told me over the years that the family doctor program was changing the entire health care system from a passive one that simply treated the sick to an active system aimed at prevention and the early diagnosis of illness.

Each family doctor-nurse team cares for around 500 people, giving a personal touch to health care within the framework of socialized medicine. The teams also free up neighborhood health clinics and hospitals for more specialized services, cutting down on long waits at these facilities.

Cuba's neighborhood health clinics are being transformed into post-graduate resident teaching centers and coordinators for the 20 odd family doctor-nurse teams attached to each one. Every clinic now boasts a specialized team that includes M.D.s in internal medicine, obstetrics and gynecology, and pediatrics; as well as a psychologist, social worker and nursing administrator, that supports the family doctors and nurses in the field. A 1991 study of the Family Doctor Program undertaken by the United Nations Children's Fund, the Pan American Health Organization, the Cuban Public Health Ministry and the United Nations Population Fund gave high marks to the program. It states: "The family doctors carry out actions aimed at promoting the adoption of adequate health practices, prevention of disease, the timely diagnosis of health problems and their treatment and the rehabilitation of those afflicted with disease."

The report describes the family doctor-nurse team goals as follows:

1) To promote health by disseminating relevant and useful health information and the adoption of appropriate health and hygiene habits on the part of individuals and the community at large.

2) To prevent the outbreak of disease and damage to the health of the population.

3) To guarantee the timely diagnosis and integral treatment of disease through the system of direct consultation and hospital health care.

4) To provide community based rehabilitation for the physically or mentally ill community members.[19]

Indeed, these days, senior citizens can be seen exercising in city parks every morning under the watchful eyes of their family doctors; young people gather at night to talk about personal hygiene, sexuality, birth control and AIDS. Family doctors are making life difficult for smokers, the sedentary and over-eaters. There's now a family dentist program, and by the year 2000 Cuba plans to have psychologists assigned to most workplaces and communities.

But primary health care is only one level, as Dr. Castro pointed out. "We also have important programs underway to improve the treatment of heart attacks, strokes and cancer; we are developing ultra-modern child and adult Intensive Care Units, trauma and burn centers; and improving emergency room care and rehabilitation for the heart attack, cancer, stroke and accident victim. Our transplant program is expanding and improving. Its already by far the best in the Third World. As the population lives longer, there is increased emphasis on geriatrics."

The 1990s promise to be truly spectacular years for Cuban public health, despite the country's economic difficulties, insisted a confident Dr. Castro. "Our goal for the year 2000 is to be equal to or better than the best medical systems in the world. We're working to meet Fidel's 1981 challenge to become a world medical leader." He said that meant doing four things: "relentlessly improving the population's health; sharing our knowledge and achievements with the Third World; developing new medical equipment both for our use and export; and advancing Cuba's pharmaceutical industry."

Chapter Two:

TRANSFORMING MANAGEMENT/ LABOR RELATIONS

Rectification and the Economy

The Cuban people have a wonderful, wry sense of humor, swapping jokes about everything from international events to Cuba's domestic shortcomings. This made the rounds in 1985:

> A group of Japanese trade unionists, in Havana on an exchange between the Cuban and Japanese labor movements, begin work at a factory. The first day, they arrive on time only to discover that people straggle in over the next hour. Many workers never show up at all. Thirty minutes after the assembly line finally starts up, it's break time. Forty-five minutes later, everyone is back at work until lunch time, an hour later. Two hours go by before the line starts up again, only to be shut down for the afternoon break. No one returns! Day two is a repetition of day one. On day three, the plant closes down after lunch for the monthly production assembly. The Japanese workers are introduced and given the floor. Their spokesman stands up and says "We discussed the situation here at the plant last night, and in solidarity with our Cuban brothers and sisters, voted to back your job action.

There are many ways to judge a social system, but one certainly must be economic performance. The most realistic critique of Fidel Castro's leadership and Cuban socialism has been in the economic realm. Yet, the Cuban socialist system produced through 1990 at a rate equal to any other country in the Latin American region and most of the Third World. Cuba's far more equal distribution of what it produced gave its people a much higher standard of living than their Latin American and Caribbean neighbors and the overwhelming majority of Third World peoples.

Various sources put socialist Cuba's annual economic growth through the 1980s at between 3 and 5 percent and per capita growth at between 2.5 and 3.5 percent. U.S. economist Andrew Zimbalist writes that between 1965 and 1984, industrial growth averaged about 6.5 percent a year. Cuban sources estimate the country's industrial growth between 1959 and 1988 at an averaged 4.5 percent in constant prices.[1]

Average annual economic growth in Latin America and the Caribbean stood at 5.75 percent in the 1970s and 1.8 percent between 1980 and 1988.[2] Average annual growth in Cuba hovered near 4 percent in the 1970s and at a little over 3 percent during the 1980–88 period.[3]

Economic statistics mean little if they disguise huge differences in income, wealth and foreign control over a nation's industry, resources and wealth. Over half the Latin American region's labor force was unemployed or underemployed, and over sixty percent of the region's 450 million people lived in absolute poverty as the world entered the 1990s. Twenty million homeless children wandered the region's streets. Latin American and Caribbean workers' real wages fell over fifty percent during the 1980s. Few dared even think of the fate of the region's unemployed, disabled, handicapped and elderly with no benefits, medical care or education, when they were hit by an average 1,000 percent inflation rate in 1989 and 1990.[4]

Cuban workers' real wages remained stable during the 1980s, as unearned income was cut and raises were granted to the lowest paid workers. A worker's average salary in 1958 was 82 pesos per month, in 1985, 188 pesos and in 1988, 187 pesos. The pre-revolution statistic did not take into account huge income gaps, while the post-revolution data does not figure in the social wage which includes complete social security coverage, free health care and education, subsidized arts and entertainment, rents and mortgages of no more than 10 percent of income, no taxes, subsidized food and special services for the elderly and handicapped.

While Cuba is dumping economic models imported from former socialist countries, Cuba's leaders equally reject their former allies' present course of eliminating planning, privatizing the means of production and embracing market economies. They see this as nothing less than a return to capitalism, stripping workers of all power over their economic lives. Cuba's approach to economic reform, says Fidel Castro, is aimed at not throwing the baby out with the bath water, and searching for increased worker participation. At stake, the Cubans believe, is their children's right to an adequate diet, decent health care, a quality education, a job, social justice and independence.

Between the opening of the Third Party Congress in February 1986 and the closing of its deferred session on December 4, 1986, Cubans from the rank and file on up analyzed the country's economic problems. The National Commission on the Economic Direction System, linked to the Party Political Bureau, was formed to guide efforts to revamp the Cuban economy. Castro, speaking at the 1986 meeting of company directors, termed the system an "old mule that hasn't been properly ridden or steered."

A year later, on October 8, 1987, at ceremonies marking the 20th anniversary of Che Guevara's death, Castro said there was no doubt a better system had to be developed. At the same time he warned that economic problems "are serious, complicated matters," that Cuba couldn't "afford to take shots in the dark," and that "there's no place for adventures of any kind." He asserted Cuba's "accumulated experience had to be worth something. And that's why we say now, we can't fulfill the plan in terms of its peso value, we must fulfill it as to stock . . . We maintain that all projects must be started and finished quickly, so that we never repeat what happened when the mule bucked and kicked . . . that tendency to say, 'I met my work plan in pesos but never finished a single building,' which was the same as burying hundreds of millions, billions . . . "[5]

Pedro Ross, General Secretary of the Central Organization of Cuban Trade Unions (CTC) and a Party Political Bureau member, was deeply involved in the initial efforts to rectify Cuba's economy. Ross told me in January 1990 that at the heart of Cuba's economic mistakes lay the "illusion that certain economic mechanisms would allow socialism to develop spontaneously." He said the Cuban Party, government and unions had "neglected the struggle to develop people's revolutionary spirit, solidarity and altruism, to educate and empower workers at the point of production and services."

Ross asserted that economic planning and management was burdened by wrong concepts, economic performance measured superficially: "State companies showing profits because they charged bloated prices to other state companies . . . The construction industry claiming to have built millions of pesos worth of projects, but actually only starting thousands and finishing none. State farms planting their quota but showing no interest in the final crop or even if it ever got to market."

Community projects, continued Ross, like housing, childcare centers, health clinics and schools—seen as having no economic worth— were neglected. "There was a growing tendency to want to resolve all production problems by throwing more and more money at them," said Ross, "when what we should have done was empower the workers to solve them. The system was promoting selfish 'me-first' thinking," he insisted, "and the idea that you could make easy money without really working very hard. At the same time workers' participation waned, becoming more and more a purely formal affair, destroying their motivation."

Rectification brought with it a more centralized investment policy aimed at increasing exports, replacing imports, accelerating the development of Cuba's infrastructure and meeting basic consumer needs. At the same time, a Herculean effort got underway to improve management, decentralize day-to-day decision-making, save resources and increase productivity through better organization and more rank and file participation. The effort, which was the centerpiece of rectification between 1986 and 1990, took the form of a series of experimental initiatives. The two most comprehensive were the contingent form of management-labor relations, and what is called the Revolutionary Armed Forces Economic Initiative.

THE CONTINGENTS

As rectification got underway and investment guidelines tightened, Cuba's leaders discovered that construction had essentially ground to a halt. Hundreds of important projects begun between 1976 and 1986 were never completed. Ground was broken, foundations laid, sometimes walls built and less often a roof! Bridges went up without connecting roads; housing was built miles from jobs, public transportation and services. Productivity was abominable.

The Party identified three basic errors. Construction projects were bogged down by a bureaucratic nightmare. Dozens of ministries and companies were barking differing orders tailored to meet their own quotas and bonuses; success was judged by abstract figures entered on the books, divorced from the actual completion of any given project; and productivity was embarrassingly low because management paid too little attention to forming healthy labor relations and working conditions.

What was needed, reasoned the Cuban Party, was a streamlined and integrated industry with a new evaluation system based on actual production costs, quality, and blueprints turned into fully functioning economic and social units. Management had to don hard hats and get their boots dirty as blue collar workers were given back their say on every aspect of the job. All were encouraged to be aware of the importance of the construction industry for a developing nation and for the individual's longer-term welfare. The Cuban Party decided to form construction contingents as an end run around the almost paralyzed

Construction Ministry and to trigger, by example and shame, the Ministry's reform.

THE BLAS ROCA CONTINGENT

On October 1, 1987, the country's first construction contingent was baptized. It was called "Blas Roca" after one of Cuba's most important communist leaders who had died a few months earlier. At the time, it was made up of just 174 men and women.

"The contingent marks the biggest revolution ever in the history of Cuban construction," Castro would remark 20 months later as he launched five of the then 17 Blas Roca brigades comprising 2,000 members.[6] A year later, Blas Roca's numbers had doubled to 4,000[7] and, by late 1990, to 36 brigades with 6,000 workers.[8] Sixty-one other contingents with some 25,000 members operated across the island by 1989.[9] Their number rose to seventy-two with 37,000 members in 1990, and there were a similar number of workers organized into brigades aspiring for the honor and material benefits of becoming contingents.[10]

The average Cuban construction worker was paid 4,000 pesos a year and produced some 7,000 pesos in value in 1989. Contingent members earned between 5 and 6,000 pesos while producing 16 to 20,000 pesos per year. Cuba's construction cost per-peso-produced ran well above a peso-per-peso ratio while the contingents averaged 70 to 75 cents per-peso-produced. Today most major construction projects are finished on or ahead of schedule and with guaranteed quality.[11]

The head of the Blas Roca contingent, Cándido Palmero, who became a member of the Party Political Bureau in 1991, explained to me in 1990 how the crash teams in Havana, Havana Province and adjoining Pinar del Río Province were brought in on key development projects such as building highways and bridges, carving out reservoirs, laying Cuba's first high-speed, double-track railway, erecting the country's first five star hotel, cleaning up rivers, etc.

The contingent was put in charge of each project—from breaking the ground to putting on the last coat of paint. "We bring in the equipment and supplies," he said, "while each brigade, operating like a separate company, is assigned a particular project, from start to finish, and is free to make decisions as it sees fit." After explaining how a brigade's performance is based on strict cost accounting, maximum use of equipment, job completion and the quality of the work, Palmero, 42-years-old at the time of our interview, insisted:

The most important thing about all this is not the work itself. Fidel spent a lot of time with us designing the contingents, trying to find a higher communist way of working. He says we are a kind of laboratory for the entire country, and we have changed all the rules. First, everyone here has volunteered for the job. People apply at their workplaces and then we select the best. Eighty-five percent of the contingent's members had never worked in construction before, but qualified because they were motivated to help the country and society, not simply to earn more money.

In fact, the first brigade found itself in a head-on collision with the Cuban President over the issue of overtime pay: "We told Fidel that we would not collect pay bonuses of any kind, including overtime pay after 8 hours." Castro rejected this on the grounds that, under socialism, workers should be paid according to what they produce. "When we work 14 hours we are paid for 14 hours," said Palmero "but don't think that anyone works 350 hours a month for the money. We do it for honor, pride and our country. We are motivated by politics. We work 14-hour days, six days a week and every other Sunday."

The Blas Roca Contingent was the first to scrap the national labor law as paternalistic, a law those same workers helped draw up in 1984. "When disputes arise, we don't apply the national labor law," said Palmero. "The collective of workers as a whole resolves them, including discipline problems. We talk about the issue and vote on a course of action. There's no appeal."

The contingent also pioneered experimenting with a new formula for worker motivation based on a mix of economic incentives and personal attention to each worker's needs. Palmero said "workers with the best records are rewarded on the job and in the community. Their neighbors, family, and children hear about what this person has done for the country and special recognition is paid to them at block association meetings." In fact the entire Blas Roca Contingent has been promoted in the media and by Cuba's leaders as heroes on the same scale as those volunteering for internationalist missions.

Palmero emphasized that the contingents are not "an enthusiastic one-shot deal, but represent a new labor-management system. For the last three years, we've tripled the national productivity rate." Workers, he said, have direct say in planning: "They know the costs down to the last penny. They know and discuss what they've produced each day, and make plans for the next. Furthermore, nobody has just one skill and sits around if his equipment has broken down. We've all mastered more than one job, so not a minute is wasted."

Palmero is an example of contingent-style management. Like those under him, the construction site is his office, his hands are calloused, and he has no time clock. "Management, pared to the bone, is out there working like everyone else 14 hours a day. We've lowered the average management-worker ratio by well over fifty percent, and the ratio of those directly versus indirectly involved in production by over 60 percent."

The contingents receive the best medical care Cuba's socialist medical system can provide and this personal attention to each individual's well-being, said Palmero, "is key to our efforts to motivate workers." A doctor-nurse team is assigned to each brigade. All members are registered at one of Havana's best hospitals for regular check-ups and dental care. In addition, said Palmero, "we provide hot lunches and dinners, air conditioning, color TV's and videos in the workers' lounges; and we draw people's families into the contingent's social life through parties, birthdays and even weddings."

A CONTINGENT WITH PROBLEMS

On September 13, 1989, I attended a meeting of the Seventh Brigade of the Sixth Congress Contingent, named after the 1988 Sixth Congress of the Construction Workers Union. The Brigade was hard at work a few miles east of Havana on facilities for the 1991 Pan American Games. Cuba's labor movement, preparing for its 16th Congress, had the rank and file scrutinizing documents in small groups before debating them and proposing amendments at local meetings.

The preparatory document, which in essence reviewed rectification and made proposals to strengthen the labor movement's role in the process, began with an analysis of the Contingents, "the main protagonists of a new labor education and ethic based on unquestionable socialist principles . . .". It stated: "What has emerged is a new type of management and labor organization where completing and surpassing plans, reducing completion calendars, paying attention to workers' well being, quality, labor discipline, better use of the work day, care and maximum use of equipment and strict cost control have all become something normal—everyday occurrences, not exceptions."

But at the September 13th meeting of the Sixth Congress Contingent it quickly became clear that something was definitely wrong—and it wasn't the workers. They had been laboring 72 hours a week, sleeping in construction site dorms and returning home only every other Sunday and holidays. Grueling, but the work was ahead of schedule.

Construction worker Reynaldo Sánchez took the floor first to tell Pedro Ross and other union officials that the air conditioning was broken down in many dorms, while it was working just fine in the offices.

The dorms were overcrowded with workers who did not belong to the brigade, disrupting morale. Orlando Castillo followed Sánchez and charged that "the food served in our cafeteria has deteriorated to the point that it's the same day after day, usually rice and beans. Many times, there's no milk and other necessities. We've raised this over and over with the administration, but things have only gotten worse. We're out there working 14 hours a day under the sun, without even a glass of cold water!"

Charging violations of contingent rules, an angry Pedro Ross demanded to know where the special food supplies earmarked for the contingent were. But not one top administrator could be found to explain. The management of each workplace was supposed to be present and actively participate in the local CTC Congress discussions. At other meetings I covered, they were.

A young woman, Maria Hernández, rose to tell Ross that, despite the problems, they were keeping up the intensive 12-to 14-hour days on a six-day-a-week schedule. "We plan to finish the job by July 26th, six months ahead of schedule," she said, to a round of applause. She also noted that the brigade had surpassed August's production plans of 90,000 pesos by 211 percent, producing 197,000 pesos worth of construction.

"But what is your cost per peso produced?" asked Ross. Hernández said she didn't know. The local union president rose to say it was 1.14 pesos per peso produced. The room fell silent. "We can't just build to build," said Ross. "We have to build efficiently. That's what the contingents are all about. Efficiency is the responsibility of all of us and everyone should be fighting anything that works against it."

Several times during the meeting, it was pointed out that the contingent and brigade took a turn for the worse when it was placed under a new administration: Department Six of the Construction Ministry. "Obviously," said Ross, "rectification hasn't come home to them." The workers and Ross pledged change by October 19th when a second meeting would take place.

The October 19th meeting was held outdoors to accommodate the 500 workers present. The podium had also grown, to seat a host of Party, government, union and Construction Ministry officials. Encircling the open-air meeting were flags flying Cuba's and the contingent's colors. Behind them were rows of construction equipment, supplemented by the tractors and other heavy equipment that continued to roll in.

There followed a three hour debate on the pre-Congress document. This time it was obvious that the workers had done their homework.

From the broader questions about rectification, the economy and unions, the discussion finally got around to conditions at the work site. The head of Department Six, Orlando Medina, was put on the spot to explain what had been done about correcting the complaints raised a month earlier.

"Efficiency is still poor," Medina admitted, "but a plan is being worked out that will allow workers to monitor costs on the job. The goal is to have costs fall below a peso-per-peso produced by the end of the year." Meanwhile, the work itself continued way ahead of schedule.

"All outside workers have been moved or will be moved out of the dorms by the end of the month," promised Medina. "And the air conditioning has been fixed." The administrator explained that the food situation had improved, but the contingent's quota was also used to feed volunteers and a large group of workers pitching in at the construction site while their plant underwent repairs. "No good," said Ross. "They are supposed to be fed by their factory. They should not be eating the contingent's food." Medina agreed to find a solution.

The administrator reported that a worker-led quality control commission was now monitoring meals. "At a weekly meeting, we plan the menu, but it still leaves much to be desired," Medina said, to shouts and nods of agreement from the workers. "It's ridiculous to ruin all the special foods sent to the contingent with a lousy cook," interjected Ross. He suggested that the top Havana officials sharing the platform find a decent chef "even if the person has to be taken from a five-star restaurant." Cheers passed that motion.

More workers commented that conditions had improved, with many now pulling together to solve the remaining problems. Medina added that there were now five cold water trucks at the site, a doctor, nurse, ambulance and a small clinic.

THE CONTINGENTS' RECORD

The contingents, to be sure, have their ups and downs, yet there is no doubt that they represent a serious attempt to improve management and increase worker participation and control. The concrete results of their efforts through 1991 were impressive. Take highway construction, which nearly stopped during the early eighties: between 1959 and 1985 the country built 230 miles of new highway; between 1986 and 1990, another 340 miles were dug, paved, bridged and opened.[12]

The contingents are revitalizing one of the revolution's most important gains: Cuba's vast reservoir and irrigation system. Between 1981 and 1986, just seven new reservoirs were opened with a capacity of 340 million cubic meters of water. By 1988, another eight reservoirs were completed, adding 391 million cubic meters to the national system. Seven reservoirs, with a 488 million cubic meter capacity, came on line in 1989. And by 1991, 18 more reservoirs, with a 790 million cubic meter capacity, were in operation, along with many major canals and hundreds of minor ones.[13] The contingents opened 20 new reservoirs in 1991, adding 800 million cubic meters.[14]

Waterworks construction is linked to a crash program to introduce new drainage and irrigation systems into agriculture. For example, only 20 percent of Cuba's sugar crop was irrigated in 1987; just two years later 30 percent was irrigated, for an irrigation development rate 10 times that of the past.[15]

Tourism is destined to become one of Cuba's key hard currency earners, and in the process it will provide some 250,000 new jobs. In 1987 and 1988 the country was completing an average of 700 new tourist quarters per year. In 1989, with the contingents now involved, the figure jumped to 2,000 and in 1990 4,000 with another 2,000 renovated.[16] 1991 saw an additional 4,000 new quarters opened and a similar number modernized.[17]

As of 1992, the contingent model had been applied to a single industrial company. Havana's Juan Roberto Milán Construction Materials Company, a highly automated complex of seven factories. The contingent was officially inaugurated on November 7, 1989, in honor of the Russian Revolution. The company was a caricature of the joke that began this chapter. It never met its plan, costs ran well over a peso-per-peso produced; and it was plagued by labor shortages, absenteeism and young employees leaving at a rate of 40 percent each year.

In early 1989, the Company's Board of Directors, made up of management, the Party, trade union and the Union of Young Communists (UJC), approached the Blas Roca Contingent for help. Working closely with contingent chief Cándido Palmero, the Havana Party and the Council of State, they reorganized along contingent lines. In six months the place had been turned around. The work force was reduced from 300 to 200, with those unable to keep pace placed at other jobs, costs cut to 62 cents per peso produced, and monthly productivity doubled to 1600 pesos per employee. A single shift worked 12 to 14 hour days and salaries were up by 20 percent.[18]

A year later, on November 7, 1990, the company met its 1990 plan with a payroll of 198 workers, most under 30 years old. Costs remained at 62 cents per peso, but monthly productivity was up to close to 2,000 pesos per employee. Despite the 14-hour work days, 18,000 hours of voluntary work were recorded. The plant sported a remodeled cafeteria, improved health and safety equipment and had organized a small workshop to replace parts on its forklifts and other machinery, many previously imported. Energy use had been cut by 10 percent and a garden started to supply vegetables to the cafeteria. Absenteeism and leaving the job had been reduced to nil.[19]

Contingents specializing in banana production began forming in 1990 after the pilot project success of Villa Clara's Quemado de Güines State Farm. There, they introduced the micro-jet irrigation system, a new seed variety and other scientific advances which, when combined with adequate care of the plantations, can triple and even quadruple yields. Production at "Quemado de Güines" rose from 600 metric tons per 33.5 acres in 1988 to some 1,750 metric tons in 1990. Average pay rose 30 percent to above 300 pesos per month.[20] The Agriculture Ministry announced in late November, 1990, that a similar system would be introduced into livestock raising, dairy and poultry farms.[21]

"The contingent concept has harmonized the communist concept of paying one's social debt with the socialist principle of each person receiving according to his work," Pedro Ross asserts. "Their biggest gain is to have demonstrated that when you pay attention to each worker's needs, not just in material terms, but fundamentally moral terms, they react positively. The contingent's high labor, technological and social discipline comes from the rank and file . . . Discipline becomes a 'family affair'. The worker who falls down on the job affects the work of those around him and, for this reason, is accountable to them. The same holds true for management."

THE REVOLUTIONARY ARMED FORCES ECONOMIC INITIATIVE[22]

Apart from the contingents, the most important economic experiment was the armed forces initiative begun in 1987 at the Che Guevara Industrial Complex in Las Tunas province. Over two years, personnel was cut by 10 percent as production jumped 69 percent and quality improved from a 78 to 96 percent acceptance rate. Cost per-peso-produced fell 15 cents for a two-million peso savings, while salaries rose 2.4 percent.

The model developed at the plant was applied in 1988 to a dozen other companies in the military sector. Over an 18-month period, their production rose on average 30 percent. All companies in the military sector began to restructure along the same lines in 1989; and in 1990, a handful of companies in the civilian run sector. Over 100 companies in the civilian sector, in particular the food processing industry, were slated to adopt the armed forces model by 1993.

Lt. Colonel Armando Pérez Betancourt is head of the commission charged with carrying out economic reform of military-related production and services. In a series of articles in the Cuban Communist Party's theoretical journal, *Cuba Socialista*, and in interviews with the Cuban press, he explained the methods and measures that led to such impressive results.

"Political work and personal attention is the key to success," stressed Pérez, the rank and file must be "part of the process and changes going on. The first step is to make sure that everyone agrees that improving performance is a basic social responsibility and that they themselves can accomplish that goal."

Pérez admits his commission hasn't "invented anything new," but has adopted production mechanisms and procedures from the developed world to the country's "conditions, idiosyncracies and particular characteristics of Cuban socialism." For example, improved productivity and increased profit goes to society, not someone's private bank account.

Pérez emphasizes "the company is the basic unit of the economy and has to run smoothly for the economy to function well. Its main purpose is to produce or provide a service as efficiently as possible, not please central planners and produce value on paper." He said as a rule plans had been made up and a company's performance judged according to 30 or more primary indicators and many more secondary ones. The new system uses just four, with the remaining relegated to a secondary role or eliminated altogether.

"The most important indicator is how you meet your contracts signed with state customers'" explains Pérez. "The next indicators are your rate of productivity, your total production, and your actual earnings. Using these four indicators, we're able to analyze and determine if the company has met its social obligation.

"Annual plans should not be general," insists Pérez. "For example, they shouldn't simply state the company will increase production by 2 percent. They should be more detailed: in this given shop we will increase production by two percent and this is exactly how we plan to do it and what it will cost. That means far more participation by workers in drawing up plans, because they're the ones carrying them out."

Good management is seen as indispensable, and all managers are required to continuously upgrade their skills. The change in planning "is part of our effort to decentralize authority so that management breaks with the culture of waiting for orders from above," says Pérez. "With the new system they have more room to act and have no time to wait for someone else to tell them what to do. Managers have to realize that there are always problems to solve and ways to improve work. They must search for the problems, be bold, take the initiative. No one should be scared of making an honest mistake."

Pérez insists top management must have direct contact with the rank and file. He said its part of the broader concept of personal attention, aimed at insuring each individual is aware of their worth, knows the value of their work, and that their opinions will not just be heard but tried.

Management is also expected to be attentive to the problems workers face both at home and on the job. "These measures," believes Pérez, "help create a socialist climate where mutual aid and cooperation comes naturally."

If a state-run company's fundamental role is to produce a socially useful product, what follows is that the company's various subsystems must take a back seat to the production process and be geared towards facilitating, not hampering it. Pérez warns that some people lose sight of the whole. "Some get lost, operating from the perspective that their small piece is the be-all and end-all. Statisticians live for their numbers. They devise countless forms for others to fill out which end up on the lap of the foremen. Others think meetings and more meetings are what make a company tick so every morning at 8:00 a.m. sharp brigade leaders are in some office meeting with somebody or another when, at that hour, they should be tending to business on the floor. That's why we're insisting that all systems prioritize production and services, and not the other way around."

The military officer also advocates "the principle of collective discussion and a single command. Every process must have someone responsible and answerable for what takes place each step of the way," he insists. "Everything must be discussed in detail by the collective. But in the end, one person is responsible with the authority to act."

Pérez says one of the biggest problems facing the Cuban economy is inflated job rolls and a lack of work for those who make them up. The problem is due, in large part, to a system that defines and details job descriptions at the national level. That's resulted in an excessive division of labor, little flexibility in work content, disorganization and often fiddling away part of the workday. Worker productivity, morale and consciousness suffer.

The questions of production quotas, or what Cubans call norms, has been one of the most difficult for the country to resolve. There were an incredible three million norms in the country in 1986, most of which did not reflect real productive potential.

"Political work must be done to convince workers that under socialism a work norm is a social debt that must be filled in terms of quantity and quality. Further, the norms must be set by technically capable people who have everyone's full cooperation," says Pérez. Part of that political work involves detailing the value of Cuba's free, comprehensive social service system, and food and entertainment subsidies, which double and even triple workers' real wages. Pérez advocates that norms be designed on the shop floor and not by national bureaucrats.

"In the armed forces initiative," he continues, "professional teams made up of engineers, specialists and the most skilled workers design the jobs and pay. We have a team for each area. If a payroll is well-organized, a worker spends most of his time on a stable job. At the same time, he should be capable and ready to do work outside his specialty if time allows or the need arises."

As a rule, in the new system, pay is based on a combination of skill level, time on the job and piecework. Workers are evaluated by the norms of production and undergo a yearly review. "At the Che Guevara plant," said Pérez, "we improved the norms and today workers do in four minutes what they did before in ten. So 75 percent of the norm today equals 185 percent of the norm in the past." If a worker completes 75 to 100 percent of the norm he gets a ten percent bonus. If he does even better he is on his way to a promotion."

In each department a special bonus can be awarded to the best worker. Pérez cautions, however, that the bonus must also be a moral incentive. "When we give a bonus we say it has to come with a heavy moral weight. For example we make a public presentation, explaining why a particular worker received it, how it corresponds with what he has done for society."

If a worker's performance is unsatisfactory, the team leader must discover why. Is the norm too high? Is there a personal or physical problem? If the work continues unsatisfactory, the person involved is demoted. If the work remains poor, he can be dropped another notch or fired. If in a specific area certain indicators of the plan are not being met, management, foremen, and workers can be docked up to 10 percent of their pay. This is done on a monthly basis beginning in April and, if the area catches up, the money is returned. If not, it goes to the state.

Under the new system, seniority has been eliminated with promotion based on ability, which Pérez defines as "skill plus work record." The company's managers, the team leader and what is known as the "Experts Committee" must agree on all promotions. The Experts Committee is made up of a Party member and a UJC member, someone from the union and another from management, along with 3 to 6 workers elected from the shop floor every two years. The body also advises management on evaluations, bonuses and demotions. The Experts Committee plays a key role in enforcing discipline. The brigade leader has the authority to discipline, but any worker can appeal to the Committee. A worker or management can then appeal the Committee's ruling once more to the next highest level outside the company.

With rectification, it became clear that resource control and accurate accounting practically didn't exist in Cuba. That, in turn, meant it was impossible for directors or anyone else to judge a company's performance and that petty theft and more serious corruption ran rampant. Pérez says straightening out the chaos and establishing adequate resource control and a modern cost accounting system are critical and perhaps the most difficult task in each company.

Pérez lists the main objectives of the new system. "It gives management a useful tool for planning, price formation and for accurately determining where problems lie, analyzing them and taking corrective action. The system also helps pinpoint a company's productive reserves and thus improve efficiency and production. Most importantly, it greatly increases the workers' role in day to day operations and planning."

VANGUARD OR MODEL?

An important question has been put to Pérez many times. Isn't it possible that the success described is due to the fact that the companies are in the military sector? He says no. "It's true there is a strong tradition of discipline in the sector, but if you go to a company that produces for the military you can see there are only a handful of military people there, perhaps one percent. Everyone else is a civilian worker. In addition, the Che Guevara plant, for example, gets 80 percent of its supplies from the civilian sector and has no special priority."

I asked Pedro Ross about the view that the contingents are a vanguard formation and that the armed forces companies have received special attention, thus their success and the impossibility of applying either model to the Cuban economy as a whole. Rejecting my hypothesis, Ross said: "If we resigned ourselves to such a fatalistic perspective, we would be negating the profoundly revolutionary character of these new concepts and, what's even more important, we would be forgetting the principle that with socialism, people are both the subject and object of their work."

Ross then cautioned that "we are perfectly aware that it's impossible to apply both experiences immediately to the entire economy. In the first place, we do not have the conditions to technically and materially supply and maintain the high production rates of the contingents and armed forces companies. Nor is it possible to immediately create the living and working conditions that these collectives enjoy. For these reasons, their extension has been and will continue to be limited to the rule that each must be guaranteed basic material conditions before it is formed."

Ross ended our last interview by stating:

"I want to reiterate that these experiences, developed from our own situation, aren't just to satisfy the curiosity of sociologists. We are working to perfect our road to socialist construction—taking into account our condition as an underdeveloped country, the presence of a ferocious blockade that has tried for more than 30 years to destroy our economy and now a complicated international situation.

"We cannot afford to commit strategic errors that damage our economy and, even worse, erode the consciousness forged in our people during years of confrontation with imperialism. With both the contingent and armed forces experiments, politics are in command, though with improved productivity comes a higher salary. And there is a serious effort to improve working conditions. But in the end, consciousness, human solidarity, and putting the interests of society above personal short term gain are the principles on which we base the construction of socialism in our country."

Chapter Three:

TWO, THREE, MANY ECONOMIC EXPERIMENTS

Why Experiment?

Side by side with the contingents and armed forces initiative, rectification brought a dizzying and what often appeared to be anarchistic array of economic experiments to the Cuban workplace. The experiments focused on various chronic problems plaguing Cuba's socialist economy, from planning and resource control to labor discipline. They were subject to greater and greater attention by various ministries and extensive, often critical coverage by the Cuban media, particularly by the trade union daily, *Trabajadores*.[1]

Pedro Ross, General Secretary of the Central Organization of Cuban Trade Unions (CTC), and a member of the Party Political Bureau, told me:

> "The experiments at various companies began as a direct consequence of rectification and sought to eliminate a whole series of errors and negative tendencies outside our real needs, and that weighed heavily on the economy and worker morale. We decided to experiment with different solutions to a series of important questions: what criteria and method should be used to fill new jobs, promote or transfer when a company's work force is reorganized and streamlined? How do you improve labor discipline? How do you evaluate management? How can we improve quality? These experiences haven't meant scuttling existing laws and labor procedures, but we suspend them at certain workplaces on an experimental basis to look for new alternatives."

Ross told me that experimental measures must be reviewed first by various national bodies, including the trade unions. He insisted that before any experiment begins "the workers themselves have to thrash out the proposal."

CONTINUOUS PLANNING

"For the first time our views were heard and respected," Medardo Ferrer told the daily *Trabajadores*, in April, 1989. Ferrer, the director of a state-run farm in Remedios, Villa Clara Province, explained: "Before, the Province would impose its plan on us. They would say plant this many acres of this crop and so many of that. We respected 90 percent of those orders even when we saw disaster ahead."

His state farm was one of 32 Cuban companies picked in 1988 for what was called the continuous planning experiment. In 1989, the number jumped to 177 companies and, in 1990, to 900 companies, representing 48 percent of Cuba's mercantile production and 38 percent of all workers in the productive sector[2]. The companies included all of basic industry, key domestic trade and transport companies and every company in Matanzas province.[3]

"In early 1988, we called a meeting of the farm's board of directors," said Ferrer as he explained the ABC's of continuous planning. The board, like those in all companies, includes management, the Party, trade union and UJC representatives. "Non-board members from all areas of the farm participated, and we designed an initial plan for 1989 based on all our experience. We then began an in-depth discussion with the entire work force.

"By September, our plan was ready, way before any other company could even dream of having one," gloated Ferrer. "In December, we took our plan to the provincial authorities, and they accepted 98 percent of our ideas. We hammered out our differences to reach a full working agreement."

For this state farm manager the most important lesson learned from the experiment was soliciting real input from those who actually till the land. "We listened to and respected the views of the farmers, using their decades of accumulated knowledge . . . "[4]

When Cuba's Communist Party Political Bureau took over direct supervision of the nation's planning and management system in 1984, its first act was to reign in investments so they would dovetail with society's overall priorities rather than the isolated plans of any given sector. A central working group, headed by Political Bureau member Osmani Cienfuegos, oversaw both general planning and its practical implementation until September 1988. From September 15 through the 17th, the Political Bureau met in special session with the Party Secretariat to review the progress of rectification and the economy. At that meeting, it was decided to shift the job of steering the economy from the central working group to the Executive Committee of the Council of Ministers, where it remained as of 1992.

The new structure meant that while one-year and five-year planning continued through the Central Planning Board (JUCEPLAN) and other ministries, a more flexible day-to-day operation of the economy and use of resources would be sought by the Executive Committee. In a sense, the 1988 shift put economic decisions on an emergency basis— a necessity given the serious and growing trade and finance problems Cuba began to experience in its relations with socialist Europe.[5]

It's a difficult battle to make economic day-to-day planning and management a well-oiled operation. Too often, the entire machine begins sputtering as some parts freeze up, and each waits for instructions from above or the arrival of materials and spare parts. In 1988, the Political Bureau announced that "while the government's and Party's general guidelines can be used to begin working out the economic plan, in essence planning should be a collective and continuous process at the ministerial, regional, corporate and company levels. There should be no need for one level to wait for the other to start work on next year's plans."[6]

Cuban Finance Minister Rodrígo García León sees continuous planning as having, for the first time, given management and workers the chance to actively participate in the most important decision affecting their jobs. "Until now, they were simply given directives from above: how much to produce; how much of their profits were to go back into the state budget; their cost projections. Companies and their workers were alienated from the national plan.

"Now," continued Cuba's Finance Minister, "there are general guidelines for the ministries and local governments. But at the company level, they represent only general parameters. The companies have far more room to operate and, during the planning process, must fully consult the workers and gain their approval of the plan."[7]

Cubans will tell you that the philosophical essence of their struggle "to rectify errors and struggle against negative tendencies" lies in the conviction that the task of building socialism has as much to do with the development of the individual as the development of the economy—that the two processes must go hand in hand. Rectification in the economy aims at cementing the unity of the base and super-structure through improved organization and increased reliance on the workers themselves in the struggle for socialist development. That means improving and democratizing the planning process, not throwing it out.

Rutad Gancel Carno, Agriculture Planning Director, told me continuous planning aims at eliminating the initial steps of gathering data from the base, then formulating a proposed plan to be sent down to the companies. "The new process puts both tasks in the company's hands which then negotiates a final plan with the higher bodies. It greatly simplifies the process, gives real weight to the company's criteria, and democratizes the plan through increased worker involvement."

"But why plan at all?" I asked, pointing to what was socialist Europe, where centralized planning has flown out the window and where many say the market does a better job. Gancel Carno scoffed at events in what once were Cuba's economic role models, and insisted that "planning is fundamental if you are to develop a better society . . . it's simply a matter of having goals and objectives, of thinking through how you get from one place to another, deciding what's next—and for that, you need planning."

Columnist José Yarnes writing in the June 21, 1989 edition of *Trabajadores*:

> There has been a decreasing participation of workers in planning. Workers and administrators often speak different languages . . . Management refers to the plan through complex and abstract economic indicators and figures. Workers talk about the same problems and goals, but in concrete terms based on their experience and actions.
>
> At the annual production assemblies the plan is laid out in technical and administrative terms. The workers say little or nothing. The possibility of fusing technical expertise with the workers' concrete experience dies. Everything is reduced to a passive acceptance that freezes shop floor initiative and accommodates the upstairs offices. This deprives the country of the massive resources that lie dormant and could be freed up with an open discussion in a common language.

Yarnes, who, as you can see, doesn't mince words, reported in late August on the continuous planning experiment at 21 companies in Matanzas Province.

> The biggest gain is the ongoing participation of workers based on their concrete knowledge of what's possible. The companies must make their own plans, without waiting for figures from above, and this should spark management initiative.
>
> The new system is working well in Matanzas. It strengthens centralized planning by forcing the top management to take the employees and the company into account. The Matanzas' company plans were more or less accepted. When they were rejected, the higher levels had to explain their thinking in detail and convince the company and its workers to change their plans.[8]

Continuous planning was unanimously approved by the CTC's 16th Congress in late January, 1990. Martha Cabrisis, a member of the Congress organizing committee said, "for a number of years we have expressed our disagreement with the forms and methods used to discuss economic plans. The company plans are completed and then they talk with workers. It's all purely formal.

"This year, labor decided we would no longer participate in these types of meetings. We said we'll only be there when concrete matters are discussed and real plans made for the work. The national Party and government leadership backed us up. Between June 1st and July 15, 1989, over 40 thousand such meetings were held. The meetings had a new focus," said Cabrisis. "We discussed the fundamental problems in each area where workers could make a difference, like cost savings, quality, efficiency, discipline, the best use of the workday and improved working conditions. Every company's management had to work with the union to prepare a initial report for the meetings. After the meetings, both sides sat down to incorporate what had been said and promised into the 1990 plan."

SHAKING-UP MANAGEMENT

At the Third Party Congress, Cuba's managers or administrative cadres were a burning issue. The quality of management is key under any system. But under socialism, argued Fidel Castro, where workers must be motivated by more than direct economic interest and fear, management—by skill and example—becomes all important. Nothing damages worker morale and socialism more than shoddy or corrupt management, he said, and nothing moves people more to do their best than good honest management.

A comprehensive management policy was approved by the First Party Congress in 1975. The policy called for the careful selection and systematic training of managers. However, little was done to carry out the Congress decision. The 1986 Third Party Congress moved to put policy into practice by creating a special commission to carry out the task. "Our group was created in August, 1986, and from the start given the job of identifying what was holding back management development," explains Division General Senén Casas Regueiro, a Political Bureau member and the man who heads up the national working group on cadre policy. "We came to the conclusion that management development wasn't being prioritized at all levels. We discovered that most directors had little if any understanding of the policy, so how could they carry it out?"[9]

The Coordinating Commission for the Creation of a Single System of State Cadre and Reserve Preparation and Upgrading (SUPSCER) was created in February, 1988, and linked directly to the Council of Ministers. In March SUPSCER opened a national cadre training center. Executive Secretary Silvio Cálvez, explained the Commission was formed because cadres were being trained haphazardly by various ministries and in various socialist countries. "The process was not being directed by the government; there was no cooperation between sectors, no general guidelines or concrete objectives that dovetailed with national interests.

"We have three objectives," said Cálvez. "To upgrade managers on the job . . . To prepare managers and the reserve for future jobs. And to keep management up to date . . . The most important thing we teach is management technique. Methods to improve the use of time, to motivate subordinates, delegate authority, organize, better interpersonal skills and conduct better meetings. Other courses focus on how to organize and analyze data . . . Managers also have to master the technology in their particular sector."[10]

The national working group on cadre policy began yearly company inspections in 1987. The inspections aims were to insure that management had the educational level and general ability to do its job and was providing young people with the systematic training needed to one day take over. After a province's companies were evaluated, management met with local Party, youth, government and union leaders to discuss the results and corrective action.[11]

"When there's intrigue or suspense in a European novel, the author always suggests 'cherchez la femme'(look for the woman). When a company does well or poorly, you have to look at management to find out why." That's how *Trabajadores* reporter Caridad Lafita began a biting opinion piece in the May 13, 1988, edition of the workers' daily. Lafita, who regularly covered cadre policy, described the inspection of Villa Clara Province and detailed how serious Cuba's management problems are. "The Commission visited 75 companies with 4,353 managers," she wrote. "Eighty-two did not have a sixth-grade education, 160 only a sixth-grade level and 1,665 or 38 percent had no more than a ninth-grade education. In other words, more than a third of the managers, 44 percent, have a ninth-grade education or less."

Lafita pointed out that since the 1961 literacy campaign, "27 years have passed, more than a quarter century. Any manager, passing one grade a year, could have risen from no education to the post-graduate level." She noted that tens of thousands of Cubans had done just that. "To be fair," the reporter continued, "it's true that many managers with low educational levels have a great deal of practical experience, and perhaps have worked so hard that they didn't have the time to study." But, she emphasized, some hard questions had to be asked.

"Despite the fact that we are a developing country, is it really possible for someone with a ninth grade education to efficiently direct economic activity? Isn't it logical that this manager will find it difficult to communicate with the specialists and university graduates working under him? There are exceptions, but the vast majority of comrades with low educational levels are a brake on progress. For example, 21 percent of the directors of 14 sugar complexes have a ninth grade level. Given the complexity of their job and the fact that they are in a priority industry, it's really admirable that they have developed the efficiency they have and that the province did well in the last harvest. But how much better could it have done if these managers had a higher education?"

Lafita then pointed out that in Villa Clara's agricultural sector, "seventy-six percent of all company directors the commission evaluated did not have the required education for their job. Yet there is a strong reserve, made up of 98 percent university graduates and specialists." She charged this reserve was not being developed or adequately used.

"There is a human problem," said General Casas, summing up the Commission's work during the first half of 1988. "We still haven't reached the point where everyone understands the need for every manager to be the best. You can't keep a management job for life. Stepping down, which at a certain point was considered reproachable, is now commendable. When a comrade feels he can't handle the job, it should be passed on to someone who can." Casas stated another problem was management evaluation. All managers had to be evaluated on a regular basis but, he said, "the tendency is simply to point out weaknesses when corrective training or other action is needed. We shouldn't be transferring a poor manager to another level because that doesn't resolve the problem. He should be demoted . . ."

Management evaluations were supposed to include the views of the employees and the union. Casas admitted this was rarely done correctly. "Workers are asked to put their views in writing, when they should be interviewed about their opinions and criticisms."

Casas then singled out the training of a management reserve, the group of people in a company with management potential. "Every director and manager must train his substitute so that when someone takes a management job, there is no improvisation . . ." He said the unions should play a key role in forming the reserve by suggesting qualified workers, "especially since we want the majority of our managers to be from the working class and the same company . . . Workers don't like managers brought in from the outside, and are proud when they come from their ranks inside."

As if in answer to Lafita's article, Casas explained: "Rectification is going ahead with the majority of the same people who committed the errors . . . They are being given the chance to change. But, there's a minority who should be doing different jobs. We need skilled management personnel with leadership abilities who are political and moral examples and sensitive to the questions and concerns of their subordinates."[12]

The 1987 inspections of more than 600 companies' management and cadre policy found 65 percent to be "average," 18 percent "bad" and 17 percent "good."[13] The next year, inspections doubled to 1,234 companies. 228 were judged "good," 813 "satisfactory" and 193 or 15.6 percent "bad."[14]

General Casas, summing up 1988 work, stated that the most important problem remained education. "Forty percent of our managers do not have the required education; 34 percent are at the ninth-grade level or below; only 18 percent are university graduates, only 19 percent of all top personnel have the age and education to be considered for promotion. We need to intensify management replacement."

Casas said the exception to the rule were the company directors themselves. For example, "fifty percent of company directors are now university graduates, only 17 percent are over 51 years old, and 30 percent are younger than 40. The majority have two years or less on the job. But we still have over 100 directors with just a ninth-grade education."[15]

The year-end cadre commission report stated:

> Evaluations are much better, in terms of quality. But there is still a lack of an integral approach and supervision. Work with the reserve was not effective. In the majority of companies the cadre reserve was only recently selected, and the number with promotion possibilities is only 28 percent. Its composition indicates a poor use of the potential of specialists and college graduates in the work force . . . Of 40,437 college graduates, only 18,197 or 45 percent are in the reserve. Of 120,838 specialists, only 20,447 or 17 percent are in the reserve. Further, only 47 percent of promotions came from the cadre reserve.

The same held true for the number of young people promoted to positions of responsibility, with just 11 percent of the new managers being under 30 years of age.[16]

Nine months into 1989, Casas' group had inspected 1,415 companies in eight provinces. The commission said development of managers was improving but problems remained with the reserves. In particular, hiring management from the outside, which the commission said "damages worker morale." The education of mangers was still poor. For example, 34 percent of Havana's remained at the ninth grade level or below. In its strongest statement to date, the commission observed: "It's doubtful they can absorb new techniques, economic systems, automatization, new management methods, etc."

The commission also stated there was a clear correlation between higher ages, lower educational level and poor results, especially in terms of shop-level management. "There is excessive job security regardless of performance." For the first time, the commission sharply criticized a paucity of female managers. It stated the problem was glaring, given that more than half of Cuba's economic and management specialists were women. It noted the healthy proportion of women in the reserve ranks, and urged that they be promoted.[17]

INVENTORIES AND COSTS

As rectification got off the ground Cuba came face to face with a disturbing reality. There was virtually no control over the country's shipping and warehouses. This led to artificial shortages and widespread theft at the base, serious corruption at the top and extensive black marketing in general. The situation was so grave that it was impossible to judge a company's efficiency, let alone improve it.

Havana City's finance department inspected 267 of the 410 national companies headquartered in the Cuban capital in 1987. The books of 65 were judged completely unreliable, with the remaining of "little reliability." No one was keeping track of their inventories, internal costs or pay systems.[18]

Cuba's State Finance Committee was assigned the Herculean task of regaining control over state resources and company accounting. A new inventory system was put into practice on a trial basis at 21 companies, including the huge José Martí sugar complex in Pinar del Río Province. The complex's chief accountant, Manuel Salqueiro, explained the new system to *Trabajadores* reporter José Yarnes:

"Before we began to put the system into effect, we carried out a rigorous inventory of all our warehouses and reorganized them to make them orderly and easier to work with. Now, management and workers are responsible for all materials in the warehouse," continued

Salqueiro. "Before, they just received and dispatched materials while someone else did the inventory from behind a desk without ever seeing what was happening. No one was really accountable. Now the employees and management must keep track of everything and pay for whatever comes up short on their shift. Of course, only authorized personnel are now allowed in the warehouses."[19]

In January 1988, Cuba's State Finance Committee announced plans to bring all the country's major warehouses under the new system within a year. It charged hundreds of millions of pesos were being "lost" and that lax control invited theft and corruption. The first targets would be some 19,000 of Cuba's 32,000 warehouses under the ministries, companies and other entities.[20] A year later, on January 13, 1989, *Trabajadores* reported that of the 18,826 warehouses targeted by the Finance Committee, 11,786 or just 63 percent had put the new system into effect. The article broke down by province and ministry the results, highlighting where the work had been poor.

In 1989, the State Finance Committee, with a staff of investigators that mushroomed from 24 to 150, began rigorous nationwide inspections.[21] It's year-end report stated that important progress had been made in bringing resources under control. The Committee had inspected 9,541 warehouses belonging to 3,787 economic entities. Just 13 percent hadn't passed the inspection. The Committee announced it would begin surprise inspections in 1990 to ensure the system was completely implemented and remained in place. In addition, 75 companies had been selected to begin a new program aimed at controlling machinery, tools, office equipment, furniture, air conditioners, cars and other supplies that often found their way out of the factories and offices and into people's homes.[22]

Adequate control of Cuba's resources has no doubt meant the savings of hundreds of millions of dollars and pesos. However, the effort has little long term value if resources are squandered at the point of production. While putting Cuba's new inventory system into place, the Finance Committee also tackled the problem of accounting and costs. A total of 1,156 companies were selected in 1988 to implement a new cost accounting system similar to that in the armed forces companies.[23] A year later all companies and service units were ordered to move in a similar direction.[24]

José Yarnes, writing in the February 14, 1989, issue of *Trabajadores*, reviewed a State Finance Committee booklet issued to guide the switch-over to new cost accounting procedures. The booklet defined the purpose of the change as establishing an accurate picture of real costs in order to improve company planning, efficiency and decision-making, and to increase worker participation in all aspects of production and services.

Since 1977, stated the booklet,

Cost systems have been designed and used mainly to satisfy central planners and the ministries, not the needs of each economic entity. The amount of labor and materials needed to produce a product has not been accurately determined even though that's essential for planning, saving resources, setting prices and analyzing company efficiency. There's been no conscious effort to reduce costs and the problem has been aggravated by poor accounting and resource control . . .

The State Finance Committee called on each entity to take the measures needed to determine actual costs of production and services at the base. They were then ordered to design company-wide cost systems and controls. Those systems would then become the key instrument to judge the use of resources, labor, materials and finance as well as wage the battle to systematically improve efficiency.

By mid-1990 all Cuban companies and service entities were in the process of adopting "budgets by area of responsibility," the basis of the new system. A given company, plant or service unit, for example a hospital or university, is broken down into smaller production or service units. Each area has a budget that details the amount of labor, materials, energy, etc., that will be used to fulfill production plans. Management and workers by area help develop the budget, are responsible for keeping within it and reducing it over time. Current cost is not compared with the previous year's cost, but instead with a detailed study of the optimum cost for producing a product or providing a service.

Trabajadores, in a February 1, 1989 editorial, stated the budgets by area of responsibility goals were to create a solid foundation for company planning and a system which, by giving workers responsibility over shop floor costs, systematically involved them in planning and day-to-day operations. The editorial called on the unions to educate their members to the reality that not just the means of production but all state resources were in the end their's and should be used with care.

Havana Province was one that earned praise from *Trabajadores'* José Yarnes in July 1989 when he reported that production had grown by 1.6 percent or 62 million pesos the previous year despite sharp cuts in supplies. Yarnes credited improved resource control, accounting and worker awareness. He wrote improved efficiency "is one of the revolution's greatest reserves." Yarnes also commended efforts to cut theft. He reported Havana's commercial sector losses had been slashed from 78 to 35 million pesos in 1988.[25]

PRODUCTIVITY AND DISCIPLINE

In 1988, 241 of Cuba's most important companies began to experiment with a series of measures aimed at improving worker discipline, organization and productivity. By 1989, the number of companies and provinces involved had increased; and in 1990, the measures were endorsed by the Cuban Party, government and labor movement and began to be applied throughout the country. The five most important measures involved broadening job descriptions so people worked their eight-hour day; tightening quotas and making wage systems correspond with what a worker produced; cutting excess personnel and shifting them to other jobs; replacing seniority with ability; and bringing systematic attention to working conditions and labor management relations.

Rectification targeted the question of job descriptions, norms (or work quotas) and bonuses from the very start. Under the economic planning and management system copied from socialist Europe, Havana planners designed job descriptions in a particularly narrow fashion. In addition, quotas were often set centrally before a workplace even went into operation. Theoretically, quotas were supposed to be upgraded at the company level; in practice, this hardly ever happened. The result: inflated payrolls, disorganization, wasted work time, unearned income, spreading corruption, a widening gulf between management and workers, and low morale.

From May 30 to June 1, 1988, *Trabajadores* published a three-part round table discussion on what some Cubans call the "norm nightmare." Among those interviewed were national trade union staffers Lázaro Domínguez, Amado Alfonso and Rolando Arias, all of whom worked on questions of labor organization and wages.

Alfonso kicked off the discussion by stating that when rectification began, the labor movement undertook a careful study of every workplace. It discovered that the combination of low norms, large bonuses and even individuals being paid for two jobs within one eight hour shift meant some earned a thousand pesos or more per month while the average wage was less than 200 pesos and the minimum under 100 pesos. One of the first acts of rectification in the economic sphere was to unfold a struggle with workers on the shop floor aimed at convincing them that part of their income was unearned. Simultaneously, Cuba's lowest paid workers received pay hikes. Alfonso said inaccurate quotas were behind inflated salaries. "Some norms were ten years old. They didn't change even after new technology came on line, boosting potential production five or ten times over. So some sectors, and even entire plants, excessively surpassed their quotas and took home huge bonuses. Management kept their mouths shut and often encouraged this."

Trabajadores reporter Magda Martínez asked him to go into more detail on why quotas were so warped. Alfonso blamed a number of factors. First and foremost, paternalism and liberalism on the part of management, the Party and the unions. Secondly, poor training of those who set the norms, along with the fact that most had never worked on the shop floor.

Lázaro Domínguez said the problem went deeper. "There is a fundamental separation between production and quotas. To set the right quotas, you have to study the entire plant and not just isolated work posts. You can't set quotas working from behind a desk with a bunch of statistics. You have to study the process, the flow of supplies to the job, the workers' movements. Sometimes we don't organize the norms around production but production around norms." Martínez pointed out that the country was bursting with those who did just that: "We have 1,500 university-level time and motion experts, 8,000 high school level and 10,000 less skilled quota setters."

Alfonso responded with the charge that many people working on quotas "may have passed some courses but know little about a given workplace or particular sector;" 90 percent of the country's quotas are just common sense," added Domínguez. "Do you know there are three million norms in the country and just a few more workers! We have to simplify all this," Domínguez insisted. "At Havana's Van Troi factory, where all work is regulated by assembly lines, there are over one thousand norms. But you can't do more than what the line dictates. So, in practice, there is only one real norm—not a thousand—the line is the only norm there!"

Untangling the "norm nightmare" and getting a full day's work out of people has proved difficult. However, the national debate did lead to positive changes, especially in new companies. Fidel Castro, speaking in February, 1988, at the annual Ministry of Basic Industry meeting, gave two examples. The Matanzas thermo-electric plant planned to employ 650 people, and in the end began operations with 249. The Felton Thermo-Electric Plant reduced a planned 800-person payroll to

375. Castro stated Cuba's electric companies had employed 146 types of specialists, and that had been reduced to just 10.[26]

Cienfuegos Province scrutinized the payrolls and job descriptions of all its production and service entities. Twelve of the largest companies eliminated a total of 7,000 jobs between 1988 and mid-1990. The process involved extensive discussions with the workers and the election of representatives to carry out the studies. Before a worker could be laid off, a new job, preferably in the same sector, had to be found.[27]

Cuban hospitals provide another positive example. Between 1985 and 1990, 20,000 jobs were trimmed, many administrative, and the employees were shifted to new facilities as they opened up.[28] By 1990, the situation had also radically improved within Cuba's most important economic sector: the sugar industry: 3,517 norms had straightjacketed the 1986–1987 sugar harvest. There were just 559 norms during the 1989–90 harvest and a year later, just 162, with sugar complex directors given new authority to adjust norms to local conditions and the unfolding harvest.[29]

The 1989 year-end report of the National Commission for the Direction of the Economy stated the number of norms was reduced by 17 percent that year and 401,000 norms were updated.[30]

SENIORITY AND ABILITY

In 1987, a handful of Cuban companies did away with using seniority as a criteria to fill new jobs, promote, train and transfer. The decades-old system was replaced with merit. The number of companies using the merit criteria jumped to over 200 in 1988. By 1990, one thousand companies had replaced seniority with ability and, after being endorsed by the 16th CTC Congress, the new criteria became law across the country for hiring, promotions, transfers and layoffs.[31]

The Cubans argue that seniority was a hold-over from capitalism, designed to protect workers from the private owner's "divide and conquer tactics" aimed at increasing his own profits. Under socialism, they believe, seniority undermined efficiency and the common good. The best employee did not always get the job. Some, viewing promotion as automatic, began to think "Work hard? For what?"; and others, especially younger workers, felt they were in dead-end jobs despite their ability and efforts.

The switchover did not come without a storm of controversy and debate. Throughout 1989, the rank and file voted company by company on the issue. What finally assured passage of the controversial change were the new shop-based committees, with elected worker representation, that took over the processes governed by seniority. Francisco Castillo, one of Cuba's best known trade union leaders, argued strongly for the new system in the worker's press. He pointed out that with socialism the working class has every interest in efficient production. Under the old seniority system, he wrote, there was no link between worker's rights and their contribution to society. Seniority, he continued, did not take into account the difference between a worker who put in the minimum and the worker who gave his all.

Castillo argued that more than seniority had to be dumped. "The entire conception and process of evaluation must be transformed," he said. Shop commissions, which included elected workers and those with vast experience on the shop floor, would be in a position to take an integral look at every employee. "Promotion will no longer be based on a one day evaluation or the number of courses a worker has passed," wrote Castillo." The worker's concrete efforts, his potential, and overall approach to work will also be looked at."

Castillo used the example of a machine shop "where the trainees all aspire to become mechanics. Everyone in the place knows . . . who is capable and motivated and who is not. They don't need a test to tell you . . ."

Castillo said the worker-dominated commissions would rid the process of its rigidity, and be responsible for personnel movements within a work center, filling new jobs, awarding training courses, and determining layoffs and transfers. They would base their decisions on the employee's work experience, his or her record of producing efficiently, taking quality into account as well as speed. Seniority would only come into play when two individuals competing for the same job were rated equal.[32]

José Yarnes described the process at Havana's Miguel Fernández Roig Tobacco Company. Director José González Otaño said ten workers were promoted from the fifth to sixth level, jobs demanding "higher quality and real discipline." Comprising the Commission that made the decision were a foreman, the local's union leader, two people from quality control and two of the most skilled workers who were elected from the shop floor. Yarnes questioned whether promotions would go to family and friends of those sitting on the commission. González asserted that the problem had not cropped up. "The commission's decisions have generally been accepted. Workers can also appeal their decision. We had one such case, and the worker won."

Plant Party Secretary Félix Jiménez Pérez told Yarnes: "Before the new system went into effect a good, disciplined worker had to wait till someone died or retired to move up. This often worked against efficiency and quality. People lost interest in the job. They ignored postings of how each person's work performance had been rated. Now they check every day, knowing the results decide advancement."

Mercedes Padrón Escalona, General Secretary of the Union of Young Communists, added that the 101 young people at the factory fully supported the new system and were motivated by it: "Especially young people in the lowest skilled jobs, because they know hard work can quickly pay off."

By the end of 1989, reported the National Commission for the Direction of the Economy, 1,367 such local commissions were operating. They had analyzed 15,150 workers for various jobs with only 136 or .8 percent appealing the decision. Eighty-seven percent of the appeals had been turned down.[33]

PERSONAL ATTENTION TO WORKERS

Fidel Castro revealed his basic belief about developing socialism during the 1986 Third Party Congress. He asserted that you can find good and bad seeds in everyone. The job of the Party, government, management, the unions and other national mass organizations, he said, was to insure that conditions existed to nurture the good seeds and not the bad ones. To the seasoned Cuban observer, this view operates behind the country's free access to health and education, social security, sports and culture. However, by 1986, Cuba's leaders had made the rude discovery that just the opposite was the case in an overwhelming number of Cuban workplaces where individuals spent a good deal of time.

Put simply, working conditions, from the lunch rooms and bathrooms to health and safety, were often abominable. Furthermore, relations on the job—between management and employees, and between the rank and file, Party, UJC and the union were far from optimal. Since 1987, no job-related issue has received more attention from Cuba's leaders and press than working conditions. Statements and articles abound on how drab lunch rooms and meals have been transformed, crash programs implemented to improve the physical plant, and management and factory leaders learning to pay close attention to workers views, needs and problems. Cuba's government and labor leaders appear completely convinced that improving life on the job is both a moral obligation and an important factor to boost overall economic performance.

At the more than a dozen rank-and-file meetings I attended during preparations for the 16th Congress of Cuba's labor federation, workers often debated general working conditions. At a huge steel complex, they were angry that leaking roofs had not been fixed and that there were long delays to get a hot lunch. At the Havana port's main truck depot, there was a long debate over how to improve conditions for women, especially single mothers. At a plumbing fixtures factory, the lack of safety equipment was a big issue. In general there was the sense that management was still not paying enough attention to workers' needs, nor listening to what they had to say; and a feeling that the unions were falling short.

Over the years, I visited countless Cuban workplaces and I have little doubt that the attention paid to working conditions has greatly improved. The easy part is to change the cook at a lunchroom, put potted plants in the passageways of a factory, or assign the safety equipment sitting and collecting dust in a warehouse. Improving management-labor relations is more complex and difficult. A great deal depends on the calibre of who is holding union office, sitting in the director's chair or leading the local Party branch. "The movement for personal attention to the workers is a very positive experience," Pedro Ross told me, explaining his preference for the term "worker" as opposed to "man" which is used almost without exception. After all, stressed Ross, women account for close to 40% of Cuba's work force.

"We now understand the importance of paying careful attention to the workers, the principal actors in the productive process, in building socialism. This does not just mean creating better working and social conditions . . . Most of all, it means building close relations between management, Party, trade union leaders and every worker: showing real concern for any personal or family problems the individual may have and respecting the working person's contribution to society. Not all our companies have accomplished this. What is important, though, is that everyone now knows what's needed—not just in terms of upping production but also what it takes to form the individual worker within our socialist society."

WORKER RIGHTS AND DISCIPLINE

Cuban workers enjoy a series of basic rights and benefits superior to those of workers in the rest of the region, including the United States and Canada. Cubans have won the right to work or an income, the right to organize and participate in company management; equal pay for equal work; and no job discrimination. Cuban labor law makes it just about impossible to suspend or fire anyone; and benefits include a one month paid vacation for all, unlimited sick pay, paid maternity leave, disability, full health coverage and guaranteed social security without paying into a fund. The children of both the blue-collar worker and the highest executive have equal access to quality health care and education.

But with the above mentioned benefits comes the responsibility to work for the higher good of society, something that largely depends on an individual's social consciousness. It's my impression that a solid majority of the Cuban working class is motivated by both an awareness of their obligations to society and their own needs. There are others who are pulled towards doing the right thing by that majority, while a minority actively seeks ways of getting around and personally profiting from the system.

At the heart of all the varied efforts to tackle the problems weighing down the Cuban economy lies the aim of improving worker discipline and motivation. The problem, as can be seen from the joke about the Japanese workers who misinterpreted Cuban work habits as a job action, is no laughing matter. Rectification's persistent message that workers really are the owners of Cuba's means of production and resources has had an important impact on discipline. Also playing an important role has been improved management, increased worker participation in planning and day to day operations, improved working conditions and insuring a full work day.

"There is always a struggle in every workplace," says Pedro Ross. "The contradiction between each worker's immediate interests and needs and society's. Here the role of the Party and union are key to bringing out the best in this internal struggle. For example, there are workers with higher levels of understanding and discipline than others. But when the collective as a whole is on the ball, those with lower levels are pulled along—even if they do not completely understand what's important. The collective is a tremendous force, stronger then the boss who disciplines the worker or, for that matter, a union leader. You get results when people discuss problems among themselves. We've always used this mechanism to one extent or another."

By 1987, the State Committee on Labor and Social Security (CETSS), was ordering management to tighten up discipline, and it began more systematic inspections. Yet, as the following examples show, it was an uphill battle. An April 1989 joint CETSS-CTC inspection of 169 companies in Pinar del Río, with 160,000 workers, reviewed 12,263 disciplinary actions. The inspectors found "a paternalistic attitude on the part of management." Some 70 percent of all infractions (8,609 cases) resulted in just verbal warnings; the same was applied in 400 cases against workers charged with material damages, theft or unexplained losses when the law called for issuing fines at a minimum; no action was taken in 246 cases where the employee missed work or arrived late without a valid reason; and in ten cases, management refused to carry out disciplinary action dictated by a labor court."[34]

A July, 1989 inspection of 43 companies in the same province determined that individuals were apt to:

* appear on the job without having punched a time card (presumably because they came in late);
* disappear during work hours to resolve personal problems or for the entire afternoon without punching out;
* have a friend punch their time card when absent for the day;
* leave for lunch without punching out;
* take too much time at lunch break;[35]

As rectification took hold in Cuba and production became more organized, discipline problems became more visible. And no one appeared angrier than the average worker who was trying his best, while the guy at his side did nothing and got away with it. Before the CTC held its 1990 Congress, it was workers and their unions who raised their voices loudest to demand that the labor law they themselves designed in the early 1980s be scrapped. It wasn't just management that was slack, they argued, but the entire process of judicial review of disciplinary cases. The workers said that the higher up the labor court, the less it understood about a case. They advocated adopting worker control of discipline at the shop level.

In June 1990, the Cuban government began to implement the idea, picking Villa Clara Province to conduct a one year experiment. After lengthy discussions with management and workers, some 1,500 Labor Justice Committees were established and in full operation by the end of the year. As a rule, each committee consists of five members and two alternates. Three full members and two alternates are elected by the rank and file of a given factory or workplace; one full member is appointed by the union and the remaining full member by management. The Committee elects its own president and secretary, and the president must be one of the three members elected by the rank-and-file. Any member can be recalled for cause after a general assembly is held, and no member can be a top executive or hold union office.

When management disciplines a worker for any reason, he or she has seven working days to appeal to the Labor Justice Committee. The Committee must hold a public hearing on the case within five days and then issue its ruling within three days. Management is obligated to open its files for the Committee. A disciplined worker can either represent himself, be represented by the union or get a lawyer. Except in cases where a worker has been fired or suspended for more than six months, neither the worker, union nor management can appeal the Committee ruling. In the case of a firing or lengthy suspension, the ruling may be appealed outside the company to a municipal labor court. That ruling is then binding. By 1992, Labor Justice Committees were forming in all Cuban workplaces.[36]

Tighter discipline policies have gone into effect in a number of economic and service sectors where, due to the special nature of the job, Cuba's leaders felt discipline could not wait: in 1988, the public health sector and education came under new regulations; in late 1989, transportation, in particular the railways; and in 1990 international tourism. While the regulations differ according to the peculiarities of each sector, they all have moved to reorganize work, employ rank-and-file participation in evaluating personnel, evolve more rapid disciplinary procedures and give management more power to transfer or fire workers.

For example, the Cuban government passed Law #122 governing labor organization at international tourist facilities in August, 1990. The move followed two years of study and discussion with the employees working in the sector. As stipulated by the law, each facility established a commission comprised of a representative from management, the Party, UJC, union and one worker elected by the rank-and-file. The commissions were empowered to evaluate all personnel currently employed in international tourism, using three broad categories: competent in his/her current position; suitable for tourism work but lacking the basic skills needed for the job; not suitable for working in tourism. Those falling in the first category were in line for future promotion; those in the second were given the choice of upgrading their skills, opting for a lower skilled job, or finding work elsewhere; those who fell in the third category, including individuals with past criminal records or unusually bad labor histories, were given two months pay and referred to their municipality to find new employment. Workers could appeal only to similar commissions set up at the provincial and national levels. The commissions are also in charge of promotions and hiring.

Law #122 established new work rules. Labor organization was carefully studied with the goal of broadening job descriptions to insure a full day's work; and when that wasn't possible, workers were expected to do more than one job. At the same time, workers in the sector are now paid ten percent more than their counterparts in national tourism or other sectors. Finally, the law set up a special bonus system, geared to productivity and quality, equally applicable to all staff, from administrators to cleaning personnel.[37]

On December 8, 1990, *Trabajadores* reported that by December 1st, Law #122 had been applied to 20 tourist centers with 180 still to go. The paper stated more than 2,000 workers had been evaluated and, of that number, 103 had been found unsuitable and 275 reclassified and given the option to upgrade their skills. In addition, payrolls at the 20 centers had been reduced by 14 percent from 2,204 employees to 1,953.

At the October, 1991, Fourth Party Congress, tourism was a major focus of discussion. Reports from various officials praised the new system. More than half of Cuba's 36,000 tourism employees had been evaluated, 981 employees had been let go and close to 3,000 reclassified and given the option to upgrade their skills . . .[38]

Chapter Four:

RECTIFICATION IN THE CITIES

The Revolution's Urban Policy

The Cuban revolution brought new national priorities. For the first time rural needs were stressed over urban needs and the entire country's over the capital's. There were moral, practical and theoretical reasons for the new policy. Capitalism, colonialism and neocolonialism created two Cubas: urban centers, particularly Havana, where wealth and services were concentrated; and rural Cuba, particularly the mountainous zones, where there were literally no services and abysmal poverty and suffering reigned. If the revolution was to make good on its promise of an equal right to life, liberty and the pursuit of happiness, Cuba's limited resources had to flow first to rural areas and provincial urban centers. Practically speaking, Cuba's leaders wanted to avoid massive migration to Havana, with the demands on urban services, the social problems and rural labor shortages that would follow. Theoretically, Cuba's leaders hoped to bridge the cultural gap between town and country.

When I first arrived in Cuba, many people told me to visit the countryside as often as possible. "There are two Cubas," they would say, "Havana and the rest of the island." They were not referring to the traditional contrast between town and country, but just the opposite. "Havana isn't nearly as revolutionary," they said. "It's in the provinces that Cuba has really developed." Later, I discovered there was a great deal of truth to this: countless times I found myself refreshed and energized after trips to the provinces.

Cuba's decentralized development policy spared the country many of the catastrophic problems faced today in major Latin American cities. Havana is the Latin American and Caribbean capital that has shown the slowest population growth over the last thirty years. Between 1970 and 1981, Havana's population increased by just .7 percent and between 1981 and 1988 by about 6 percent.[1] The 1981 census registered 3,711,600 people living in Havana and Cuba's 13 provincial capitals. In 1988 the figure was 4,166,700, an increase of about 12 percent. By that same year, 2,100,000 people lived in the capital, close to 20 percent of Cuba's population; 397,000 in Cuba's second city,

Santiago; 279,000 in Camagüey; 227,000 in Holguin; and less than 200,000 in each of the other provincial capitals.[2]

Cuba classifies over 70 percent of its population as "urban," but only those living in the major cities should really be classified as such. The remaining three million plus "urban" dwellers actually live in rural towns, some with as few as 100 residents. They are considered urban zones by Third World standards because they boast electricity, running water, education, health, cultural and other facilities.

HAVANA

Havana in particular, but also Santiago and Cuba's other provincial capitals, are contradictory places that have left dozens of reporters and visitors scratching their heads. On the one hand they boast excellent health care, education and cultural facilities, are relatively crime-free and adorned with historic buildings and beautiful parks. But on the other hand, they are no-frills affairs that, despite their garbage-free streets, desperately need a face lift, suffer from serious infrastructure deterioration, shortages and exasperating services. There is not a hungry or illiterate kid to be found, not one! Yet supermarket shelves stock only the essentials, and some of these, like vegetables and fruits, appear only in season. The cities team with vibrant, healthy people who one minute bitterly denounce bureaucracy, shortages and poor services and the next minute rally in support of the government.

Rectification once more adjusted Cuba's development policy with the decision to seriously tackle Cuba's urban ills. Havana, the city with the most serious problems, but also the seat of the revolution's leadership, became the model for Cuban-style urban renewal. It was in Havana, with a population density of 2,845 residents per square kilometer, almost 30 times the national average, that Cuba's urban problems were first analyzed and plans developed to solve them.

Seven of Cuba's top architects, one engineer and a sociologist were brought together into the Special Advisory Group for the Integral Development of the Capital. The group toured various cities around the world, then set to work advising what was already a burgeoning movement to transform the city.

"There was an almost complete paralysis when it came to solving Havana's problems," Fidel Castro told a special meeting of provincial Party leaders on December 13, 1989, portions of which were televised and which dealt extensively with work in Havana and how to spread it to other urban areas. "The technocrats," he said, referring to planners who never stuck their noses out of the office, rarely taking people into account when they made their calculations, "complained there were no resources, no labor force for the job." Now, using mainly Havana's own resources, said Castro, "by relying on better organization and the people, we are solving Havana's problems, and in an integral way."[3]

Havana was indeed on the move by 1987, with construction under way on just about every block. Forty programs aimed at improving everything from housing, transport, child care, education and health facilities, to road construction, potholes, aqueducts and sewers, services and garbage collection. Castro and the provincial Party leaders discussed to what extent similar programs were taking root in Cuba's other urban centers, the need for the Party to take the initiative, and where work was slow, what could be done to speed it up.

THE MICROBRIGADES

Cuba's plans to tackle urban problems rely on important government resources combined with people's own efforts, especially through microbrigades and voluntary work. The microbrigades first appeared in 1971, but had died out by 1978. That was a grave error, proclaimed the Cuban Communist Party during its 1986 Third Congress.

The microbrigades rely on public participation to solve social problems, particularly housing. Brigades are formed in a ministry, a group of companies or a single workplace. Labor unions are in charge of recruitment, and workers, especially those in need of housing, volunteer to take leaves of one, two or more years to work in the brigades. Brigade members' workplaces continue to pay their salaries, and their fellow workers cover their absence by either working harder or overtime without increased pay.

The microbrigades build facilities for the community, and housing for themselves and those picking up the slack in the shop. Through 1990, half of brigade-built housing units were distributed by labor union locals, based on need and merit; and the other half distributed by government to people who could not join the brigades. The ratio shifted in 1991, with 80 percent of brigade-built housing distributed through the unions, and 20 percent through the state.

Workers and community volunteers build the housing, and government pays for materials. Families who move into new homes receive a government mortgage that runs between 8,000 and 10,000 pesos with a 2 to 4 percent interest rate, payable over 20 to 30 years. The new homeowner pays off the mortgage at a rate of no more than 10 percent of the chief breadwinner's income.

Over the years, I stopped to talk to microbrigade workers dozens of times and a number of my Cuban friends joined the brigades. Whenever friends or colleagues from the United States came to town, I would make a point of steering them to the nearest construction sight.

Francisco Calderón Flores, 43 years old, is not an exception, but the rule. It was a Sunday morning in November 1990 when I approached him. He was working on the final touches of an apartment building on the corner of 17th and 10th streets in Havana's Vedado section. "We've finished three buildings in three years, two with eight apartments and this one with ten," Calderón told me. He pointed to a tall structure going up across the street: "but that's the big one, with 48 apartments. We'll have it done by next year."

Calderón said he used to run special effects for a TV studio, had volunteered for the brigade in 1989, and was now head of its 33-member crew. "We don't just build housing," he explained. "We have 33 people in the brigade, 19 here and 14 working on child care centers, schools, and family doctor offices. Hundreds of people from the union and community have done voluntary work with us as well."

The buildings appeared sound and were very attractive, but the brigade was made up of people from Cuba's Radio and Television Institute, far from a seasoned construction crew. Calderón explained they managed with professional assistance from architects, engineers, master plumbers, electricians and other advisers assigned to the brigades. He said the microbrigade movement also had three night schools to train its members. Calderón's brigade was just one of 1,122, with 37,932 members, hard at work in Havana by 1990. Another 700 engineers, architects, foremen, inspectors and other professionals oversaw the construction boom. And these figures did not include close to 200 social microbrigades rebuilding and renovating entire neighborhoods, and other brigades formed to refurbish Havana factories.[4]

The microbrigades worked on everything from housing to hospitals. The heaviest work, building new highways around the capital, bridges, hotels, facilities for the 1991 Pan American Games, dredging rivers, etc., was in the hands of five construction contingents, made up of an additional 10,000 volunteer workers. Between the various types of brigades and contingents, this added up to 60,000 people working ten-to-14 hour days, six or seven days a week, building and rebuilding Havana.

Gerardo Rios Nazco, deputy director of Havana's microbrigades, told me: "This rebirth of the microbrigade movement came with rectification in 1986. It's fundamental to the rectification process and one of its main achievements." He logged two reasons. "The first is ideological and political. The movement is much more than the micros, the social brigades and contingents," he said. "The whole city is working to develop Havana. Just about everyone is putting in volunteer work at the construction sites. The brigades have become a rallying point." He said that while the brigades of the 1970s concentrated on housing, today's operate at a higher level of consciousness, building community facilities and involving the neighborhood in their efforts. In 1989, Havana's Central Labor Council reported that the city's 700,000 workers had put in 19,466,430 volunteer hours in 1986; 31,765,484 in 1987; 48,174,322 in 1988 and 17,267,779 during the first half of 1989.[5] Cuba's trade unions also donated tens of millions of pesos from their social funds to the movement.[6]

"The second achievement, of course," said Rios, "is what we are building." At the Havana brigades' third anniversary, September 30, 1989, director Máximo Andión listed some of their accomplishments: 16,515 apartments completed and 28,000 under construction; 111 child care centers built, each with a capacity for 210 children; 1,657 three-story combination home-offices for family doctors and nurses, with another 350 under construction. Andión reported the brigades had teamed up with regular construction crews to help build three new hospitals and expand or renovate others. By the end of 1989, they had also built 24 special schools and 20 community health clinics. Then there were the 22 bakeries, a primary school, 6 new construction materials plants, a construction equipment plant, video theaters, markets, seniors homes and social clubs.[7]

As the year drew to a close, the microbrigade movement nationally had helped erect 9 new hospitals and expand 24 others. The movement had under its belt 27 community health clinics, 6,500 home-offices for family doctors and nurses, 324 child care centers, 56 special schools for children with serious physical or behavioral problems, 49 primary schools, 49 junior and senior high schools, tens of thousands of apartments and various other projects.[8] In Havana, Gerardo Rios told me: "We are rebuilding OUR city, transforming it, making it more humane, beautiful and practical. In other countries making money motivates people. But here, we have broader interests at heart."

THE SOCIAL BRIGADES

"When Fidel first came here and saw what this huge group of ordinary people were doing, even Fidel himself, with his great faith in people, was astonished. He said we should rename La Güinera, 'La Maravillas' (the Marvels)."

Josefina Bocour Díaz, 51, used to be a telex repair woman. By 1989, she was the leader of the La Güinera social brigades in Havana's Arroyo Naranjo Municipality. Cuban President Fidel Castro dropped by when he could. That same year he brought Mikhail Gorbachev and his wife with him. The former Mayor of Burlington, Vermont and current U.S. Congressman, Bernie Sanders, also visited. So did trade unionists from around the world, including the United States, who were in Cuba for International Workers Day activities in May.

Josefina Bocour Díaz is known to everyone as Fifi. Apartment buildings, some still under construction, were the backdrop for our series of 1989 interviews. She talked about what her people had accomplished with the same energy that transformed her into the undisputed leader, without portfolio, of the 20,000 resident La Güinera community.[9]

The social microbrigades had completed three buildings with a total of 49 apartments, built a children's center, cafeterias, bakeries and 22 three-story home-offices for family doctor-nurse teams, all in just 11 months. "We are building a special school for kids with behavioral problems and the three apartment buildings over there will be completed by the end of the year," said Bocour Díaz. "We have ten microbrigades," she explained, "each made up of 33 people, all neighborhood residents." Eighteen people from each brigade worked on the apartments, 14 on community projects and one on roads. There were more than 200 people on a waiting list to join the brigades, "but there are not enough materials," Bocour Díaz lamented.

Social brigades like those in La Güinera were formed throughout Cuba by 1988, wherever conditions remotely resembled a shanty town. Unlike the microbrigades, they are largely made up of community residents, housewives and young people unemployed between school and a job, some with criminal records. By 1990, this meant another 10,000 people at work in Havana alone. The social brigades in some Havana neighborhoods repair run-down housing. However, in 62 others, with 50,000 residents, entire new communities are being built. In these communities, the housing and services were completely substandard. The communities resembled shanty towns, with some differences. They are tiny compared to those surrounding Latin America's urban centers, there are no drugs, far less violence, and everyone enjoys free health care and education and has enough to eat.

Jorge Lezcano, First Secretary of the Party in Havana, told me: "We came to rely on a series of planning and other economic mechanisms that were more and more devoid of the political and organizational work needed to mobilize people to make a new world for themselves." He was explaining the essence of rectification. Lezcano, a Political Bureau member, emphasized that "the struggle to develop socialism is not solely a question of economic development, but most importantly of human and social development." Among the errors to be rectified, Lezcano mentioned the death of the microbrigades in the late 1970s. "If we had kept them up," he said, "Havana would have 50,000 more apartments today." He also referred to the 111 childcare centers built by Havana residents in 1987 and 1988. "Between 1981 and 1986, they were going up at a rate of just one per year." On government neglect of the 62 rundown communities, like La Güinera, Lezcano noted: "There is no excuse. Rebuilding them has top priority."

Bocour Díaz said the work moves ahead quickly in La Güinera "because of the government's material and organizational support and people's natural desire to transform their own neighborhood and lives." People who are not working and take a job with the brigade get paid 10 hours a day by the state. Those who are released from other workplaces continue to collect their salary based on a 44 hour work week. Once a building is finished, 60 percent of the apartments go to brigade members and 40 percent to the state for distribution to people unable to work on construction, but who live in the community. Each apartment costs 8,500 pesos but, if you helped build yours, you receive a ten percent discount. Families own their own apartments and pay about 10 percent of their salary each month to the state on a government-held mortgage, at 2 percent interest.

Bocour Díaz noted that "most of us work 14 to 16 hours a day, Saturdays and Sundays, too. Whole families come and work, people from the community organizations, the women's federation, the old people, school kids, everyone is pitching in." She said she had no idea how many people volunteered each week, "at least 500. That's why we can do everything we are doing."

Fifi called over Pedro Acosta Ramos, known as Pedrito. Sixty-two years old, he moved to La Güinera in 1946 "when there were no more than 20 families living in this area." Pedrito said he didn't want an apartment, and didn't get paid. "I've put in thousands of hours, I really have no idea exactly how many," he told me. The retired dock worker collected his pension and had been on the job day and what he called "communist nights" since ground was broken in February of 1988. "You should have seen this place before," he exclaimed. "It was all mud, weeds, shacks. Now look what we've begun! I'm doing this because it's my neighborhood. These are my people, Cuba is my country and La Güinera has to change."

The most important thing happening in La Güinera and in other places like it isn't the new apartment buildings, but the complete social transformation under way. Alcides Hernández, head of political work for Arroyo Narranjo's Communist Party, arrived at the construction site during one of my visits. "The brigades are sparking a new community spirit," he said. "They are solving far more than the housing problem. They are building commercial services, schools, medical posts, recreation centers, things that benefit everybody." Change does run deep, and needs to, at La Güinera. "There are 140 young people working here," said Maria Pérez, General Secretary of the Union of Young Communists (UJC). Among them, 40 young single mothers and 45 people who had done time in prison, some more than once. Many of the young people had finished or dropped out of school, and were not working. Now they were learning a trade and soon would be getting their own homes.

Pérez said that just about all the "delinquents" had been turned around. "They work with us just like anyone else." Bocour Díaz interjected with the example of 26-year-old José Manuel, who spent seven years in prison. "He is now head of his local block association, has won various prizes for his masonry skill and has applied for membership in the Union of Young Communists." Maria Pérez added, "José says he feels like a human being for the first time in his life."

And she pointed to Fidel Vitón, also under 30 and with a long prison record. "He's head of the union committee at one of the construction sites now." Bocour Díaz, with obvious admiration, said that Vitón's local was the best. "He lays bricks like no one else." Pérez said the UJC did extensive political work here. "We recently had an event on Nicaragua, big events for International Women's Day and International Children's Day. We all went to the May Day march together." The social brigade sponsored a chess club and baseball team; some women were doing gymnastics. There were also art, dance and singing groups. And, Maria Pérez said, "we all participate in defense preparations, so if something happens (a phrase Cubans use to refer to the possibility of a U.S. invasion), we can defend what we have built."

Vilma Espín, leader of the Federation of Cuban Women (FMC), came to La Güinera in 1989 to announce the FMC's upcoming 5th Congress. "What's happening here in La Güinera," said Espín, "is what our struggle as women is all about." The women demanded to know why only men had been sent to Nicaragua to help rebuild housing destroyed by Hurricane Joan, and whether women were going to be included in the construction crew being organized to help the people of Armenia rebuild after the 1988 earthquake. (They won their case.)

One reason for the national and international interest in La Güinera and its social brigades comes from the fact that its leadership and 70 percent of the workers are women, many former housewives. Fidel Castro says, "These social brigades are the most efficient, the best organized; their work as good as anyone's." Forty-year-old Pastora Rincher told me that until she began working, she lived with her five children on Cuban social welfare assistance. "Just imagine the change in our lives," she exclaimed. "Now I earn my own living. I just got a new apartment, my older children pitch in here when they can, and my entire family is proud of me. I want to work on construction the rest of my life."

Pastora had become a qualified mason. She had recently come in second in a provincial masonry competition. She was leaving in a week for an all-expenses-paid vacation she won and was taking her 15-year-old daughter with her. Pastora's kids were all in school or childcare; thus she had time for the social brigade. During summer vacations, her younger children would attend a day camp organized by the La Güinera brigades, staffed by brigade members with education and recreation experience.

"This neighborhood has always been very machista (sexist)," said Bocour Díaz, "and we decided that breaking that down was key to the entire area's social development." From the start, women were put in charge of the La Güinera Social Microbrigades. Bocour Díaz believed she and other women were "remaking relations between men and women here." She cited her own husband. Married 32 years, the couple had four children, one under 15. "He never washed a dish or a piece of clothing in his life," she said. "Now when I get home he has often cooked and always has the washing machine loaded. The only thing I haven't been able to do is convince him to let the neighbors know what he's up to."

EDUCATION

My interview with Rogelio Caballero Jiménez, Havana's deputy education director, was just about over when director, Zoila Benítez Mendoza, flew into the room. Out of breath, yet still an obvious bundle of energy, she said: "I'm sorry I'm late. I don't know if I'm the director of the microbrigades, the contingents or education any more." In fact, just three months after our November 1989 meeting, she would be elected Vice President of Cuba's National Assembly of People's Power and Caballero Jiménez would take over the director's job.

Benítez was just back from Quivicán, a farm area outside the capital where six of 20 new boarding schools for Havana's high school students were being built. "It's at the high school level where we have some serious over-crowding," she explained, "but within three years, almost all the high school students will be studying and working in the countryside." She then listed the childcare centers, special schools and other education-related projects built by the microbrigade movement. "Next year, we start renovating our primary and secondary schools, and building some new ones," she said. "So you can imagine, I'm running around like crazy."

I was talking with Caballero about the role Cuban education plays in fighting racism when Benítez sat down. She jumped right into the conversation. "The first thing you have to do to eliminate racism is have a revolution," she said. "You can have 20, 30 or 100 programs and you won't resolve the problem. Socialism allows you to do away with the unequal social structures that promote and maintain racism. Then education plays an important role in this fight. You can only get rid of racism when everyone, black and white, has a free and equal education, and equal opportunity right through university level. Every child, black and white, has to be well fed, cared for and go to the same quality school from preschool on up."

The future Vice President of Cuba's parliament agreed vestiges of racism and prejudice still exist in Cuban society. "The family can pass it on, parents may not want their child to have an interracial marriage," she reflected. "But the structure of a socialist society and its education system work against, not in favor of, racism. If the kids, from their first day in school, have the same uniforms, sit together, have the same rights, life itself works to break down racism."

No one doubts that socialist Cuba boasts the best education system in Latin America. All education is free, and there is no illiteracy. In 1959, the average educational level in Havana was the 4th grade, and 30 percent of the population was illiterate. The pre-revolutionary government spent a mere 11 pesos per capita per year on education.[10] Today, Cuba with 37 teachers per 100 students, boasts more teachers per student than any nation in the world.[11]

Havana's government allocated 115 pesos per inhabitant for education in 1990, and just about everyone had attained a ninth grade education. While governments throughout the region slashed their education budgets by 25 percent or more, Cuba's continued to go up. Havana's education budget, not including construction, higher education and trade schools, stood at 209 million pesos in 1985. By 1989, the education budget was 223 million, up about 11 percent. Half the city's population of two million were enrolled in some kind of study program. There was literally a school or childcare center on every block.[12]

Deputy Director Caballero told me one of Havana education's biggest gains is that it can now offer pre-school services to the majority of working mothers. In 1990, Havana boasted 456 childcare centers for 56,200 youngsters (from 45 days to 6 years old). My daughter, Dhara, was one of them, and I can recommend her center highly. The city also had 503 community based primary schools (kindergarten to 6th grade) with 168,600 students. There were 163 junior highs for 77,200 students. Over 10,000 other students were in country boarding schools outside the capital.[13]

Caballero said: "If you compare the census and enrollment, you can see that 100 percent of our kids get an education through ninth grade. We even have teachers in the hospitals and visiting teachers for kids who for one reason or another are at home. After ninth grade it drops off a bit, but it's still above 95 percent." He also credited the community for such a remarkable achievement. "If a kid doesn't show up at school, the neighbors are as anxious as the school to know why."

At the end of ninth grade, students are tracked. They can opt for high school, technical school, trade or teacher training schools. Selection is based on grades, tests, extra-curricular activities and interviews. In 1989, Havana had 20 urban high schools, 36 high school-level technical schools, 17 trade schools, 2 teacher-training schools, plus 10,000 students boarding in the countryside. The city also had 67 adult education centers with 25,600 students, and another 250,000 studying at home and attending classes one evening a week.[14]

The next year, Cuba became the first country in the region, and one of a handful in the world, to cover 100 percent of its special education needs. There were 110 such schools in the capital alone, 24 built between 1988 and 1990. Many doubled as specialized clinics. Students with visual, hearing, retardation and other serious physical problems attended, often boarding during the week.[15]

There are no drugs or weapons in Havana's schools. Behavior problems do exist, but are relatively few by U.S. standards. Part of the reason can be traced to community and parent participation. Cuba's various national mass organizations and parents sit on every school's board of directors. Another reason is that each of Havana's municipalities has a special diagnostic center to evaluate kids with learning or behavioral problems. The centers work with the family and teachers to keep kids within the regular school system, but also to give them special attention when needed. I pointed out to Caballero that in the United States going to a special school can mark a kid for life.

"The efficiency of our special schools is judged by how quickly the kids are re-integrated into the normal system and how well they do once back," he replied. "They only take very serious cases. For example, slow learners or behavior cases that originate from social or family problems. We have a lot of experience in this area and so far more than half the kids spend just a year in special school and then return to the regular system."

Cuba's rectification process brought to the fore the question of what makes for quality education. "The biggest problem we have is the educational level of our teachers," said Caballero. "There are still teachers without a high school diploma, let alone university. We know this is a big problem, and for the first time, Cuba is in a position to solve it. Over the coming years, a high school diploma will become the rule even as more and more teachers earn a university degree. By the year 2,000, we hope all teachers will have a degree before starting in the classroom."

Caballero said that the Education Ministry at the national level and in Havana had drastically changed its style of work. "We were resting on our laurels. We used to evaluate and improve our program every five years or so," he said. "Now it's become a continuous and more democratic process. Our problems are constantly being worked on, and from the bottom up, not the top down. We have hundreds of our best, most experienced teachers evaluating and improving our programs and giving monthly seminars to all our personnel."

Caballero also said with rectification, more weight is being given to "Martí's idea that study and work go hand in hand." He pointed to the plans already mentioned for all high school students to study and work in the countryside then said all Havana's technical and professional schools were being directly linked to state-run companies or services. "The students study and work; the professors and workers share experiences and often switch roles; the boards of the schools and companies overlap."

PUBLIC HEALTH

Cuba's capital is a sprawling city and like just about all urban areas, it has many problems. From my own experience living in Havana and having a child there, I can attest to the fact that health care is not one of them. It's free, from the most complex transplant operation to the local family doctor visit, dental and mental health care. The city's

1986 health budget, not including construction and major equipment purchases, was 200.7 million pesos. The budget had grown almost 25 percent by 1989, to 249.7 million.[16]

Infant mortality in Washington D.C., stood at 21 per 1,000 live births in 1986, and for African American babies at 24. It's gone up since then.[17] Havana's infant mortality in 1986 was 12.4 and, because everyone was guaranteed equal access to health care, race and income were not dividing lines for healthy babies. Havana's 1987 infant mortality rate dropped to 11.2, then 10.6 in 1988, 10.1 in 1989 and by the end of 1990 it had dipped below 10 deaths per 1,000 live births, less than half that of Washington's. Infant mortality in Havana's most rundown section, La Güinera, stood at 8.5 in 1990; and in Washington D.C.'s poorest area it was over 30.[18]

The United States continues to let its urban health systems deteriorate. Cuba is doing just the opposite. Health, like education and enough to eat, and now housing are considered the most basic and important human rights in socialist Cuba. And they are included as such in the Cuban Constitution. Longevity now stands at 75.6 years, comparable to the developed countries, and well above life expectancy in U.S. minority communities.[19]

Surprisingly then, when Cuba's rectification movement took shape, Havana's health care system was number one on the priority list, and Cuba's President took personal charge. "During 1985 public complaints were on the rise," Antonio González Fernández, Havana's deputy health director, told me in early 1990. "They were especially upset with hospital services and long waits at the community clinics. There was some crowding and the quality of care was not always the best."

Dr. González said Fidel Castro met on a monthly basis with all the health officials and hospital directors in the city. "At the time Fidel thought the problem was a human one—poor organization or that people were not dedicated enough to their work," he explained. "But when the directors began to explain the problems, it became clear that in part it was also a question of resources." Health care in the rest of the country had been prioritized, and as a result, there was some serious deterioration in the capital.

Fidel Castro, national and Havana health officials, hospital directors and others worked out a comprehensive plan to tackle the situation. The plan included increasing available hospital beds, building new community clinics and improving hospitals and clinics already in service. It also called for putting the family doctor program in place as quickly as possible.

Since 1985, said Dr. González, "we've completed 1,019 projects related to hospitals and other major health institutions." They included three new hospitals, a medical school, plus numerous expansions and reparations. In all, there were 5,000 more hospital beds as 1989 came to a close and services, such as emergency and intensive care, had also been improved and expanded. Hours for many minor services and consultations had been stretched into the evening; 3,603 major pieces of medical equipment had been installed and 22 new community clinics built for a total of 81 in Havana. As 1990 opened, 2,897 family doctor-nurse teams were working and living in the Havana neighborhoods they served.

Havana's deputy health director said an intensive effort was under way with health staff to improve services and cut costs. There was a new emulation between units and departments within medical facilities and between the facilities as well. It emphasized quality, costs and patient feed-back; the goal to earn being called a "model unit." The rewards ranged from the material to public recognition. Just as importantly, workers now took part in disciplinary procedures, planned and controlled costs. Worker committees decided promotions, and where possible, job descriptions had been expanded to ensure an 8-hour work day. The number of workers per patient had fallen from 2.65 to 2.08. Excess staff was shifted to new facilities, not put out on the street. In many hospitals, costs had been cut 20 percent or more.

Dr. González lit up when talk turned to the family doctor program. "The big change is from a passive to an active approach," he said. "Before the health system waited for people to come to it; now it goes to where people are. And the practical emphasis has shifted from curing illnesses to preventing them. Finally, the family doctor guarantees personalized medical attention to each patient."

Plans, said the doctor, called for a family doctor-nurse team for every 120 Havana families or 600 residents. And other teams are at work in the schools, child care centers and workplaces. The family doctor-nurse teams live in the same neighborhood their patients do, and a good many of their patients have pitched in to build their combination home-offices. "The idea is to have all the people involved in their own health care," explained Dr. González. "The family doctor-nurse teams have to meet regularly with families and the whole community to find out what the people want and need and then to organize a collective health effort."

VIOLENCE, DRUGS AND CRIME

"In 1988, we conducted a survey asking people what their major concerns were in Havana," said architect Mario Coyula Cowley, vice president of Cuba's Advisory Commission For the Capital's Integral Development. "Their number one concern turned out to be Havana's cleanliness and hygiene." That might surprise the average U.S. urban dweller. What about violence, drugs and crime? Coyula told me that no one mentioned drugs or violence, though crime in general was a concern.

Cuba's Attorney General gave a summery of crime rates to Cuba's Parliament in July of 1990. In 1989, he said, there were a total of 186,688 crimes reported. Of these, 70 percent were robberies, 57 percent of which were against property and the vast majority petty thefts of under 100 pesos. Only 8 percent of the robberies involved more than 500 pesos. Violence was used in only 2,385 robberies, and force (breaking and entering) in 21,058 cases. There were 401 murders and 368 manslaughter cases in all of Cuba during 1989. Ninety-five percent involved personal feuds and only 5 percent financial gain; most were committed under the influence of alcohol; 3,606 people were seriously hurt when assaulted and 1,530 rapes were reported. In all of Cuba there were only 948 drug cases, almost all involving marijuana or abuse of prescription drugs.[20]

According to the United Nations, developing countries had an annual rate of 1,600 robberies per 100,000 citizens and 10.7 murders in the 1980s.[21] The figures for Cuba were 857.12 robberies, and 3.28 murders.[22]

During my seven years in Cuba, I never found any evidence of intravenous drug use; and violent crime, by U.S. standards, is low indeed. You are able to walk Havana's streets day or night (though purse snatchings and pickpocketting are a possibility in any of the world's capitals).

My sister, Michele Frank, at the time finishing medical school in Havana, told me that in her many conversations with visiting U.S. doctors, nurses and other health workers, they were always struck by the differences between Havana's emergency rooms and those in U.S. cities.

On Friday night, November 24, 1989, I planted myself in the emergency rooms of Havana's Miguel Enriquez Hospital. It serves the eastern part of the city, including some of Havana's most run down areas. I didn't leave the place till 4:00 AM Saturday morning. No one suffering from drug abuse passed through its doors. I saw one knife wound, a minor one, in the left shoulder of a 17 year old who had gotten into a fight over a girl. And there were two suicide attempts, both involving prescription drugs.

On an average day, director Francisco Caballero Casanova told me, some 1,000 people pass through the hospital's emergency room, the largest and most modern in the city. Some 600 come in for minor clinical reasons; 400 suffer from more serious problems, like heart attacks, broken bones, burns and wounds. Dr. Caballero, 37, showed up at the hospital around two in the morning. A general surgeon, he dropped by after operating at a nearby children's hospital. I asked him about drugs and violence.

Caballero told me he had begun working in emergency rooms as a student back in 1971. Since then, he said he had worked in all the major Havana hospitals that handle large numbers of trauma cases. "In all these years I've seen many accidents and other types of trauma cases. I've treated many alcoholics and suicide attempts," he recalled, "but I can't remember ever treating an intravenous drug abuser."

The hospital director said wounds did come in, "but they are almost always the result of spontaneous actions, not organized or premeditated violence." Caballero noted there had been a recent drop in such cases, which he attributed to stepped-up crime prevention activities in local communities. "But we still see some wounds, usually knife wounds," he said. "Gunshot wounds are very rare."

I got a chance to ask the same question to Dr. Julio Luis Barrionuevo, in charge of emergency that Friday evening. "I've been working in emergency rooms for over 25 years and there just isn't any drug addiction here. I have never seen a drug addict in a Cuban emergency room," he said. I walked through the intensive and intermediate care wards of the hospital and asked half a dozen doctors about drugs and violence. I got the same report: no hard drug addiction cases, few bullet wounds and some knife wounds.

Pedro Chávez is President of Havana's provincial government, the equivalent of a big city mayor. He told me in January, 1990, that three factors have helped the city win the battle against drugs and keep an upper hand over violent crime. First, the vast social changes that have come with Cuban socialism. Second, strict control of drugs and weapons. Third, public participation in the fight against crime. Chávez pointed to Havana's health system, its education system, the right of every citizen to a job or income, the fact that there was full and equal opportunity for all Havana's citizens.

"I think the control we exercise over the circulation of drugs is also fundamental," he continued. "Real, effective, systematic drug prevention not just by the police, but by all the various institutions and community organizations. Everyone is on the lookout for the first sign of drugs, for the entry or cultivation here of any drug, or the circulation of any chemical or paraphernalia related to drugs. I'm not an idealist," he continued, "and I have no doubt that if we gave a chance to drugs, there would always be some people who would fall into the trap. That's why our efforts are aimed at preventing drugs from being introduced in the first place." Chávez said the same basics apply to the relative lack of violent crime in the city. Since 1964, personal ownership or carrying of handguns has been prohibited in Cuba and hunting rifles are strictly licensed. Nor can you sell or buy weapons. People are forbidden to carry knives or any other type of weapon on the street.

CRIME PREVENTION

Many Cuban Ministries and national community based organizations once had their own crime prevention program. But with the rectification movement, the country adopted a more integral approach. The Ministries of Education, Health, Interior, Justice, Culture and Labor along with the Trade Union Federation, Women's Federation, Committees to Defend the Revolution, the Party, youth and student organizations all joined the effort under the umbrella of the National Commission on Crime Prevention and Social Problems.

"Our basic line of work is prevention," emphasized Mirta Caridad Cardona, President of the Commission's Havana branch. "Especially with young people. For example, we sit down with the education ministry to look at the dropouts in every school. We have between 2,000 or 3,000 dropouts through the ninth grade in the city," noted Carmen Rivera, City Commission vice president. "That represents about .5 percent of the class. It's insignificant in a thousand other cities—no one worries about it. But here in Cuba, it's a big, big problem because we start from the position that 100 percent of our kids must get an education."

Sometimes it's not easy: early pregnancy and teen marriages take their toll. "Last year there were 230 of these cases," said Carmen. And when a youngster has been out on the street for a year or more it's hard to get them back to school. On the other hand, Cuban labor law prevents teenagers from going to work until they are at least 17—special parent consent and Ministry of Labor approval may exceptionally reduce the limit to 16, especially for apprenticeship cases. The goal, say Commission leaders, is to encourage youngsters along a productive path, even if they don't like school.

Single mothers, especially adolescents, are a Commission priority. "These are young women who get pregnant between 13 and 16 years old," said Carmen. "They drop out of school, and neither the girl nor the boy is prepared for marriage. Even if they marry, they often break up. And the tragic result is a 17 or 18 year old single mother who has dropped out of school and has no job and no skills." She said the commission approaches these young women, first of all to see that they have good medical attention; then to make sure they know their rights to special social security payments. And second, to encourage them to enroll their child in a childcare center, and to go back to school or to work. "And we also prioritize the father, to see that he takes responsibility for his child. Sometimes, this means helping to find him, and ensure that he at least pay child support," said Carmen.

The Western press reports an increase in juvenile delinquency and crime in Cuba. Yet, the country isn't building any new prisons, and in 1988 parliament reformed the penal code, decriminalizing 60 offenses. "Crime in our country has its high points and low points, like everywhere," said Mirta. "But when there is an increase, it's not large nor are we talking about serious offenses, which have steadily declined. Other types, like robbery, have dropped over the long term, but can also peak at times. If this month, there are 200 robberies in Havana, next month there may be 210. For us, that's an increase; but in the long range picture, we see slight ups-and-downs, not a steady trend up."

And if a young person commits crimes and eventually goes to reform school or prison, what happens when he/she gets out? Carmen responded: "We work with everyone. Not just with young people. There is good rehabilitation in our prisons, and our work is not really separate from that. But if you release someone and leave them alone or outcast, if you don't help in the transition to get a job, make sure they are accepted in the community and at work, then they will commit a crime again. That's where we come in."

Mirta reported that in Havana, 99.6 percent of people released in 1988 were given jobs; and 95 percent of those released in 1989. I found the figure hard to believe, but both women insisted. In a later interview, Teresita Soto Cardenas, the commission president in San Miguel del Padrón municipality, backed them up. "Last year, with the penal code reform, we received 374 former prisoners and 54 minors from reform schools. To date 12 have returned to prison and all the rest are working."

San Miguel del Padrón is one of the Cuban capital's 15 municipalities. In 1989, 38-year-old Teresita Soto Cardenas was secretary of the local government and president of its crime prevention commission. "This is a people problem," she told me. "And so it takes people—working through community organizations and the commission—to help." Sometimes, said the biologist, now turned political leader, "a person will find they are caught in a vicious circle, with no apparent way out, and so they commit a crime. The first job of the commission is to help them out of that circle before they get even more desperate."

San Miguel del Padrón municipality is broken up into 86 districts, part of the 1,439 that make up Havana. Each has 1,000 to 1,500 residents. They elect delegates to local government every 2½ years, and have the right to recall them at any time. Each district also has a prevention commission.

Mario Luisa is the name of the neighborhood covered by district 39. On November 9, 1989, the leaders of the communities prevention group were waiting for me at the home of primary school teacher and 39th district delegate, Jesús Galvez Labarca, who also leads the group. He had invited electrician José Manuel González, delegate from a neighboring district. Also present: Local CDR leader, Vicente Carbojal, Women's Federation head Carmen Ojeda, and senior citizen leader Claribel Castro Ferrea, all members of the group. The captain of the local police precinct, also a member, was off working.

"We meet the first Tuesday of the month," explained Jesús, "and review progress on each case before deciding how to follow up." What kind of problems do the young people have? I asked. Do they do drugs? I got an emphatic no. Are you talking about kids carrying guns or forming gangs? Another no. Are you talking about one out of every two kids dropping out of school? Wrong again. "When we talk about problems," ventured Claribel, "we mean kids who need more activity than others. Kids who face social or family problems and need extra support. For example, a kid who does not show up at school because of their situation at home. Maybe the mother works and the kid needs more supervision. More activities after school. This is where we can help."

Jesús added that in his area the most serious problem is fights breaking out at teen parties, especially where liquor is served. He pulled out a notebook when I asked for more details on the groups everyday work, and peered at its contents. "This year, we helped a teenage single mother place her child in a center. We also found a senior citizen's home for an older woman who couldn't cope any longer on her own. We found a job-training course for two young people who weren't in school or working. They've both graduated, and we now have two more in the course, one 17 and the other 19. We had two older people who didn't know how to get their social security pension; and we helped one resident in the area recently released from prison to get a job and feel welcome in the community. We got jobs for two unemployed young people. We had three young people, between 14 and 16, who simply refused to go back to school. We got them job training and made sure they stuck with it. We have begun various activities aimed at young people between 14 and 29 years old. Our first initiative was to form a local baseball team; Juan Antonio heads that up and can tell you about it."

"The problem is that we have kids on the street after school or outside work hours and they get into trouble," said Juan Antonio, a retired university worker. "It's just mischief, but it irritates people. So, last year I organized our baseball team, and now we have 19 kids playing. Right now I'm putting together a women's softball team."

Jesús said the group was about to start a "sports Saturday," and also sponsors a dance once a month. "The kids have a good time, and we also try to get a plug in for other important efforts—like AIDS prevention. It's very important that the entire community support the dances," he continued. "It's our way of thanking the young people for everything they do for the community. The CDR is involved, the women's Federation, the Grandmothers decorate the place."

Delegate José Manuel González is an electrician, but his real love is music. "So I got this group of 12 kids together. They are not music students, they play by ear and are great. They call themselves the Hot Grains Of Sand. They'll make their debut at next month's dance night.

"We also have a movie night at the community culture center," continued José Manuel. "And it's not all activities—sometimes its just hanging out with them. When we ask for help on community projects, these kids are among the first to volunteer. That's how both our districts built outdoor cement dance floors."

Vicente Carbojal headed up the area's senior club, which, like thousands across the country, began in 1987. "We have 53 active members and support everything going on in our community. We give ideas, work with this group, support the childcare center and school." Grandparents are at the heart of the Cuban family, and seniors in general are deeply respected. "We are here all the time and know who's who and if a kid is not going to school or not working," said Vicente. "So we try to talk with them and their families. It's our problem, not just theirs. And sometimes people listen more to us."

Claribel added, "Our local primary school is trying to become a model school and thanks to the grandparents attendance and punctuality have improved. One of them comes to the school almost every morning and asks the director what kids haven't shown up. Then they hit the streets."

Vicente concluded our meeting with: "I'll knock on the parents' door in the evening, and I talk straight: 'Listen! Did you know your child missed school today? Why? It's very important for your child's sake, to be in class.' Just like that, and it works. Because they know I really care. Community is the best way to help people change."

Chapter Five:

FROM LAND REFORM TO MODERNIZATION

Rural Cuba

When Cuba's revolution came to power, .6 percent of Cuba's land owners controlled 35.2 percent of the land; 1.5 percent of the landholders more than half, including all the best quality soil. And 28 sugar companies, the largest belonging to U.S. firms, controlled 83 percent of the land producing sugarcane.[1]

Central Camagüey Province provides a good example. At the time of the revolution, one percent of the Province's landholders, 35 people, owned 42 percent of its land; 452 landowners, domestic and foreign, owned 72 percent.[2]

Back in 1959, most of Cuba's 157,000 small farmers were tenants and share-croppers. Half a million agricultural workers roamed the island alternating between back-breaking work on sugar and coffee plantations and unemployment without benefits or services of any kind.[3]

On May 17, 1959, Cuba's first agrarian reform limited holdings to 1,000 acres, expropriating the lands of the large sugar companies and 12,000 of the biggest private owners. A total of 110,000 sharecroppers and farm tenants were given title to land and joined the existing 45,000 small farmers in the countryside. A minimum amount of land for a family of five was set at 67 acres with the right to buy 100 more. And 44 percent of Cuba's farm lands passed into state hands.[4]

Cuba's second land reform went into effect in October 1963, limiting total holdings to 167 acres and expropriating 10,000 large farms. Another 20 percent of the land came under state control.[5] Almost all the expropriated landowners and their families went to Miami and formed the backbone of the Cuban opposition in exile. Their past victims, Cuba's rural poor, for the first time enjoyed their own land, year-round work, enough to eat, health care and education for their children. They became the backbone of support for the revolution in the countryside.

Agrarian reform in some socialist countries meant the simple redistribution of land among small and medium sized private farmers and cooperatives who then sold at least part of their produce on the open market. The Cuban state, however, maintained control of most of the land and began to develop sugar, rice, citrus and livestock on an industrial scale. Private farmers received credits and general government support in exchange for selling what they produced to the state for distribution to the public.

Through 1975, two forms of property predominated in the countryside: huge state farms and small private farms loosely organized into credit and service cooperatives or associations. The main theme in Cuba's countryside began to change from land reform to the modernization of agriculture. Massive investments were plowed into sugar, citrus and other agricultural sectors; a new cooperative movement began, along with stepped up efforts to train a skilled agricultural labor force. Before the revolution, Cuba perhaps had 1,000 university graduates in agricultural fields. By 1986, their numbers had mushroomed to 45,000, plus 80,000 agricultural technicians and over 1,000 scientists.[6]

STAGNATION AND RECTIFICATION

By 1986, rural Cuba had developed into a patchwork of over 180 agro-industrial complexes (CAIs), 156 of which were surrounded by huge sugarcane plantations and the remainder by citrus, rice and tobacco. There were also hundreds of state farms and ranches, 1,332 farm cooperatives and 78,000 individual farms. Sixty-four percent of the Cuban land mass, or 17 million acres, was considered arable. The state sector worked 82 percent, the cooperatives ten percent and individual farmers eight.[7]

Thousands of communities dotted the landscape—all boasting essential Cuban political, health, education, service and cultural facilities. The towns were organized into rural municipalities, the political hub of everyday life for one million agro-industrial workers and their families, 140,000 cooperative and individual farmers and their families, and over 270,000 students studying and working in country boarding schools; plus of course all the service workers and public employees in each municipality.[8]

Yet, Cuba's sugar industry and agriculture in general were not performing well. By the mid-1980s, a serious drought, the country's inability to overcome decades-old production and distribution problems to meet rising public expectations, unmet international sugar contracts and a changing socialist market created a crisis in Cuban agriculture.

The main problem was poor yields. Aldolfo Díaz, Vice President of the Executive Committee of the Council of Ministers, told the National Assembly of People's Power on December 26, 1990, that sugar yields rose from 43 to 57 tons per hectare (2.5 acres) between 1960 and 1988; citrus from 5.9 to 8.9 t/h; rice 1.8 to 3.2; potatoes from 10 to 18.2; banana from 6.2 to 7.6; tobacco and vegetable yields stagnated; while corn, bean, yucca, sweet potato, coffee and cacao yields declined. Cuban yields in general, said Díaz, remained well below those of developed countries.[9]

Deputy Agriculture Minister, Eduardo Chao Trujillo, told me the problems were popping up like weeds: burgeoning administrative payrolls, phoney production statistics to gain bonuses, a growing split between what was sown and what actually made it to market, production of the most profitable crops for export and neglecting those the population needed, salaries without a productive foundation, poor work habits and a general lack of control despite ever-mounting paper work. "We got down to work," the Deputy Minister said, "with the aim of cutting bureaucracy and paper work, producing year round and producing everything, improving yields, increasing control, and making sure people are on the job and are paid accurately for their work."

The Third Party Congress concluded that Cuba's agricultural problems could be solved through a four-pronged approach: stable water supply and up-to-date irrigation systems; the introduction of scientific advances; improved planning and management-labor relations to attract and keep an adequate labor force; and better collection, storage and distribution of agricultural products.[10]

SUN, SOIL, WATER AND SCIENCE

The basis of Cuban agriculture is of course sun (which there is plenty of), soil (of varied quality), and water (which there is not plenty of). The soils of 34 percent of Cuba's arable lands are rated excellent to good, and the remainder average to poor. It rains hard four or five months a year and hardly at all the other seven or eight. Worse still, 75 to 80 percent of the rains fall between May and November, Cuba's hottest months when conditions are the poorest for most agricultural work. The dry season, from November through May, coincides with optimal growing conditions except for the lack of rain. Cuba also suffers from the fact that it is a small country, has few rivers and climatic conditions are relatively uniform. Thus, the periodic hurricanes that slam into the island do damage that can't be compensated for by unaffected parts of the country; the rainy season and tropical heat impact agriculture across the board as do droughts, like the one that gripped the island from 1984 through the end of the decade.

THE SOIL

Dr. Miguel Pérez Valdivia, Deputy Agriculture Minister in charge of Research and Development, told me in early 1990 that Cuba has an agriculture development strategy through the year 2000, "based first and foremost on the study of our soils. What we can sow, where and how much we can expect to produce. It all starts with the soil, and then you add irrigation, science, attention to crops, labor power . . ."

I began looking into the technical aspects of Cuban agriculture by searching out engineer Humberto Vasquez, second in command of the National Research Center on Soils and Fertilizer. "You need a little history first if you want to understand what we are doing," he told me. "Before the revolution there were some soil studies done in Cuba, fundamentally for the U.S. sugar companies." It wasn't until 1972 that Cuba began its first national study of all soils. In 1980 we started our most sophisticated study," continued Vasquez, "linked to a computerized system that takes dozens of factors into account. We are using our own classification system that includes soil, climate, precipitation, the heat, and soil humidity. The system allows us to predict yields of different crops on the same stretch of land anywhere in the country. It tells us what inputs are needed for each variety." The study, said Vasquez, is aimed in part at opening up the possibility for intensive land exploitation. At discovering what mix of crops can be grown year round and what combination improves instead of exhausts the soil.

I pointed out that in today's world, soil problems are mounting due to poor use of fertilizers, to contamination, indiscriminate exploitation of forests, poor water use . . . Vasquez admitted Cuba has similar problems—mainly contamination, erosion and salinization. "Our job is to stop the process and repair the damage already done. Our efforts to stop contamination are based on waste treatment, so it can be re-used as fertilizer and animal feed. We have a program to reverse salinization, and we are working on halting erosion through reforestation." Vasquez said the need to cut imports and protect against future damage has also led to more reliance on organic fertilizers and pesticides. Worms, he explained, are being used to enrich animal feed and top soil; sugar industry waste is now treated and recycled as nutrients in the cane fields; tons of pesticides have been replaced by biological agents. "Between 1971 and 1975 we used 100,000 tons of organics and in 1989 we used 2.5 million tons," he noted. "Environmental studies are now built into new agricultural plans and in fact all development plans across the board."

IRRIGATION

"The answer to Cuba's water problem lies in reservoirs, canals, more efficient and effective irrigation and drainage," argued Pablo Hernández Santana, who heads up irrigation for the Agriculture Ministry. In 1961 and 1962, a serious drought hit the island followed by Hurricane Flora in 1963 which caused grave flooding in eastern Cuba. The government responded by beginning a crash waterworks program aimed at harnessing the rains for the dry season and controlling periodic flooding in the rainy season.

"We literally had to start from scratch," explained Hernández. In 1958, only 400,000 acres of agricultural lands had any kind of irrigation at all, and stored water capacity stood at just 48 million cubic meters, all under the control of the U.S. sugar companies. By 1975, stored water capacity had jumped to 4.127 billion cubic meters and by 1980 to 6.245 billion, with some two million acres under irrigation. But in the late seventies and early eighties, Cuba's water works program all but ground to a halt. "Only 18 new reservoirs were built, adding a mere 389 million cubic meters to stored water capacity," noted Hernández.

One of the most important results of the rectification movement has been to prioritize waterworks and introduce modern irrigation and drainage systems, using contingents as the driving development force. "The power of the contingents is impressive," said Hernández. Between 1986 and 1991, 53 reservoirs were built with over two billion cubic meters capacity. Plans through 1995 call for the construction of another 104 reservoirs with a total capacity of 4.78 billion cubic meters. In 1986, Cuba had 230 miles of central canals that diverted water from Cuba's few rivers and many reservoirs to its agricultural lands. One hundred and twenty more have been built since 1986, and another 250 miles were nearing completion in 1992.[11]

Cuba's water goes first and foremost to grow sugar—32 percent at the close of 1990. Since 1986, and at an accelerated rate since 1989, construction workers have been leveling Cuba's cane fields and building new irrigation and drainage systems that raise yields an average of 30 to 50 percent with half the water. By 1990, close to a million of Cuba's over five million acres of sugar lands were under modern irrigation, still a mere 20 percent of the total. Forty-five brigades, 40 of which were formed in 1990, were working on installing irrigation systems and meeting plans which called for over two million acres of cane to be under irrigation by 1995 and close to three million by the year 2,000. In addition, by 1990, 201 brigades were leveling and installing drainage systems in the 40 percent of Cuban cane fields suffering from serious drainage problems. 1990 began with 134,000 acres under the new drainage system and closed with 260,000. Plans called for 200,000 acres to be added each year until the job was done.[12]

Cuba's rice plantations, which use 26 percent of stored water capacity, are undergoing a similar transformation and with even better results. In 1986, 95 percent of Cuba's 355,100 acres of rice lands benefited from irrigation, but it was an outdated system that wasted precious water, nutrients and labor. A new system that doubles yields, cuts water use by 40 percent, allows for increased mechanization and humanizes the work began to be introduced in the late 1980s. By the end of 1990, 15 construction brigades had brought 50,000 acres under the new system.[13]

Nineteen percent of Cuba's stored waters go to vegetable production on 737,000 acres. In 1987, about half the area benefited from some form of irrigation: but 80 percent of that amounted to outdated systems. By December 1990, ten percent more of the lands were under modern irrigation, mainly using Cuban made frigate systems and to a lesser extent super efficient localized systems. Irrigation work will be accelerated through the year 2,000. The more modern systems double and even triple yields while conserving water, fertilizers and pesticides. Similar irrigation development programs were under way in citrus, tobacco and Cuba's pasture lands.[14]

RESEARCH AND DEVELOPMENT

Since rectification began, Cuban science and education have moved to the center of Cuba's agricultural efforts. Seven agriculture schools and universities have been moved to the countryside and linked directly with state farms and ranches, as have 32 research centers and top scientists, forming what's now called production-education-research units.

"There are 1,100 Ph.D.s, 144 Ph.D. candidates, 383 university-level investigators and thousands of researchers working with the Agriculture Ministry—29 percent of all scientific personnel in the country," beamed Dr. Miguel Pérez Valdivia in January 1990." Dr. Pérez, in charge of agriculture research and development, said progress has been made in selecting better personnel and guiding research so that it dovetails with Cuba's national priorities and resources. "Research is aimed at solving concrete problems—to improve our food supply, substitute imports and increase exports," stressed Dr. Pérez. The Academy of Sciences also checks on the work, keeping track of projects and making sure they mesh with the nation's efforts as a whole.

"With the rectification movement, we have stopped thinking of top scientists as advisers, hovering over new researchers; now we see them as pioneers who have to get their hands dirty. In fact, the higher a person's scientific level, the tougher the problem they should be able to tackle—and the more effective results we should expect from them," insisted Dr. Pérez.

Scientific efforts are also taking an "integral" approach, looking to solve production problems by tackling a cluster of issues at once. For example, in sugar, along with new irrigation and drainage systems, scientists are developing higher yield and plague-resistant seed varieties; organic fertilizers and treated wastes to substitute for chemical fertilizers; biological agents in place of pesticides; studies to improve the timing and methods of sowing, cultivation and harvest; and new forms of management-labor relations.

In other crops: twenty new seed varieties were developed between 1986 and 1991, and higher yield and plague-resistant potato, banana, yucca, dasheen and tomato seeds began to be produced in Cuban labs using genetic engineering. Science chief, Rose Elena Simeón, predicts this program, accelerated in the coming years, will "revolutionize Cuban agriculture and save tens of millions of dollars on imported seeds." Ten biological agents were developed to fight disease and plagues between 1986 and 1991, and hundreds of local stations set up to put them into action.[15]

Livestock efforts have proceeded in an integral way, too: genetic cross-breeding to improve stock, then embryo transplants and artificial insemination to develop the herds and flocks. Research concentrates on sugar-based animal feeds, better animal care and rapid diagnosis of illness, the use of animal waste as feed and fertilizer, and new organizational systems for more efficient development of herds and flocks.[16]

THE NATIONAL FOOD PROGRAM[17]

Soil study, the crash waterworks projects, new irrigation and drainage systems, research and development, improved planning and management-labor relations have all been brought together under the National Food Program. Actually, it consists of 36 different agricultural programs aimed at improving the Cuban diet, substituting imports, diversifying agricultural exports, and attracting workers back to farming. Since the collapse of European socialism, it has moved center stage in Cuba's fight for survival.

SUGAR

Cuba divides agriculture into two sectors: sugar and everything else. The sugar industry is by far the most important in the country, accounting for some 80 percent of export earnings through 1990, 20 percent of the Gross National Product and providing raw materials for many other sectors of the Cuban economy.

Despite large investments, Cuban sugar production remained more or less stagnant in the '80s, picking up a bit the last two years, signaling rectification's impact on the sector. With the single exception of the 1983–84 harvest, when sugar production topped eight million tons, production during the decade hovered at 7–7.5 million tons annually, until the 1988–89 and 1989–90 harvests once again hit the eight million mark. The 1990–1991 harvest came in at 7.6 million tons of sugar and the 1991–1992 harvest at 7.1 million tons, an extraordinary accomplishment given the economic situation Cuba faced.[18]

Many people question Cuba's decision in the early sixties to base industrial development on sugar, and its increasing dependence on sugar exports, albeit at preferential prices, to socialist markets. They point out that in the eighties sugar's world market price averaged just half of production costs. However, the Cubans argue that sugarcane remains by far the best crop for the country because it has the potential to produce ten times more energy than is needed to grow it, and serves as the basis for Cuba's vast derivatives industry.

Sugar Minister Juan Ramón Herrera Machado points to the 1989–90 harvest. He says it brought in 75 million tons of cane which Cuba turned into 44 million tons of products, just eight million of which was sugar. The rest went to derivatives, the most important being fuel for the industry itself which saved Cuba four million tons of oil. Second in importance were the various animal feeds produced from cane, replacing imports valued at hundreds of millions of dollars. Third was a host of byproducts ranging from rum, particle board and paper to dozens of chemical substances used in everything from fertilizers and paints to cosmetics, pharmaceuticals and food processing.

The Food Program calls for Cuba to increase its sugar production to 10 to 12 million tons and over-all cane production to 120 million tons by the year 2000.

CITRUS

Cuba produced 85,900 tons of citrus in 1958, exporting 18,700. By 1990, citrus production topped one million tons, some 800,000 tons exported and 200,000 put on the domestic market, for a per capita consumption of 40 lbs. Cuba's citrus plantations cover 350,000 acres and plans call for another 75,000 acres to be brought into production. More plantations combined with modern irrigation, improved methods to fight plagues and disease, new seed varieties and other measures are expected to bring production up to two million tons before the year 2000. There are similar detailed plans to double three other key export products: tobacco, coffee and cacao.

RICE

Rice is a staple of the Cuban diet. In 1958, the island produced 253 metric tons; in 1989, 536 metric tons, still only about half of what Cubans consumed. Under the Food Program, Cuba wants to become self sufficient by 1995. Rice lands will increase from their current 440,000 acres to 550,000, and they'll boast new irrigation systems, seed varieties and methods to control plagues and disease. For the first time, two harvests a year will be reaped from some 100,000 acres.

VEGETABLES

Starchy fruits and vegetables, in particular potato, plantain, sweet potato, yucca and dasheen make up an important part of the Cuban diet, along with tomatoes, onions, garlic, cucumbers and beans. The country produced 492.2 thousand tons of these vegetables in 1969; 1.2 million tons in 1979; and 1.6 million tons in 1989. Most vegetables disappeared during the off-season; some remained scarce all year round.

Plans are to expand vegetable lands from the current 740,000 acres to at least 850,000. Where good soil is scarce, as in Santiago, and to put a dent in off-season shortages, super-productive hydroponic farms are being introduced—400 acres worth by 1991. The rotation of crops, in particular tomato and beans on rice, sugar and tobacco plantations has also begun, as well as the introduction of genetically engineered seed, more productive irrigation and various incentives to attract a stable labor force.

LIVESTOCK, DAIRY PRODUCTS AND EGGS

Cuba's production of meat, milk and eggs is impressive. Yet, the country continues to import a portion of these proteins, and even before the current crisis, the availability of meats and cheese paled by middle-class U.S. standards. The main problem is feed. Cuba imported some 200,000 tons of corn and grains valued at about 14 million dollars in 1958. Thirty years later, in 1988, Cuba imported some 1.8 million tons of corn and grains valued at 172 million dollars.[19] Cuba experimented with many sugar-based animal feeds over the years, but it was not until 1987 that Saccharina was developed—capable of substituting 50 to 70 percent of feed imports. The discovery was considered Cuba's most important scientific advance during the 1986–1990 period. Cuba's ambitious plans to increase meat, milk and egg production are based largely on Saccharina, and in turn on improved yields in the cane fields.

The Island's favorite food is pork, and production has steadily increased over the years. State pork production averaged an annual 10,000 tons during the 1966–1970 period; 28,000 tons the following five years; 57,500 tons during the 1976–1980 period; 76,000 tons the following five years and in 1990 it topped 100,000 tons.

On July 30, 1989, Cuba's first Integral Pork Production Center opened in Santiago. Fifty similar centers, 27 new and 23 based on the expansion of existing pig farms, will go into production in the 1990s. The centers, each capable of producing 2,500 tons of meat per year, are called "integral" because the pigs are raised from artificial insemination through their slaughter, feed is produced on site and all waste products are recycled. Cuba estimates the state sector will be producing some 187,000 tons of pork by 1994, and a contingent-style management-labor system is being put in place at the centers.

In Cuba, every child through seven years of age is guaranteed a liter of milk a day at the subsidized price of 25 cents. Until the current crisis, so were the elderly. Whole milk, cheese, yogurt and butter were also freely sold. Now, what there is, is tightly rationed. By 1986, well before Cuba's current economic woes, the climate, feed problems and poor work combined to make cattle raising and milk production a real bone of contention in the country. By 1988 the situation had been aggravated by continued drought and more acute feed shortages. Cuba had an average 361,600 head of cattle producing milk between 1966 and 1970; and just 378,100 between 1986 and 1989. Yet, milk production rose from 368 million liters to 900 million, thanks to an advanced genetic breeding system that tripled milk yields.

Cuba's food program includes a crash plan to double dairy herds by 1993. The most ambitious project is in Camagüey Province where 6,000 square kilometers are being developed into 18 state dairies, employing 24,000 workers. Smaller projects are unfolding in seven other provinces. Saccharina is the key to expanding herds, plus contingent-style management-labor relations to insure their care. However, beef consumption is not expected to improve in the short term as 100,000 to 200,000 head are shifted to agricultural work to cope with Cuba's energy crisis.

Chicken, and especially eggs, account for a good share of the extra protein in Cubans' diets since the revolution. The country produced 1.36 billion eggs and 22,600 tons of chicken annually from 1966 through 1970; and 2.5 billion eggs and 113,600 tons of fryers annually from 1986 through 1989. The Food Program calls for 2,127 new chicken farms to be in operation by 1993, plus a more modern incubation system. Plans call for increasing egg production to 3.25 billion per year and meat to 172,000 tons, eliminating the need to import chickens and making up for the decline in beef.

Cuba is also developing non-traditional sources of protein. They range from algae to rabbits, "jutia" (a large edible rodent), and even buffalo and their milk products. Flocks of geese, ducks and turkeys now dot the countryside. The number of these animals is still too small for industrial use, but they do complement local consumption in some areas. The one exception is sheep. There were 125,100 head in state hands in 1985, and by 1990 there were 740,000 head, with an additional 865,000 being raised by the cooperatives and private farmers. Plans call for raising sheep wherever the land won't support other livestock.

FISH

The islanders once turned their noses up to fish. Today, fins are as important as feathers domestically, and more important when it comes to exports. In 1958, Cuba's fishing fleet netted 21,900 tons of fish; by 1988 the catch had multiplied ten-fold to 230,000. Cuba's salt water catch is expected to remain stable or decline, due to fuel shortfalls, and the expense of maintaining and replacing the fleet. Planners say the slack will be taken up by fresh water varieties and the development of fish farming on the island's shelf.

With rectification, Cuba moved into fresh water fish and shrimp breeding. The Food Program aims to accelerate the process, cultivating fish in every Cuban reservoir. 8,700 tons of fresh water fish were sent to the domestic market in 1981. By 1985 the figure stood at 15,400 tons; and in 1990 over 21,000 tons. Cuba hopes to produce 50,000 tons of mainly bass, carp and catfish by 1993; and 100,000 tons by the year 2,000. Fishling production skyrocketed from 5.4 million in 1981, and 18.8 million in 1985, to 49 million in 1990.

Cuban shrimp breeding, begun in 1986, has also taken off: in 1986 Cuba produced 103 million shrimp larvae, 500 million in 1990, and plans are to reach over a billion by 1993. Cuba captured a few hundred tons of shrimp in 1986, largely for export. The figure for 1990 was 1,200 tons and its expected to double by 1993.

THE FARMERS' MARKET

In the early summer of 1986, Cuba closed down its farmers' markets, the only area of the economy that remotely resembled classic capitalist economic relations. Supplied by small farmers, the produce, which, according to Cuban officials, represented just two percent of Cuba's agricultural production, was sold to the urban population at prices determined solely by supply and demand.

The shutdown brought howls from Washington, contrasting it with Eastern Europe's love affair with the "free" market. To this date the closing of these produce markets is often referred to outside Cuba as the one and only act of the rectification movement. The farmers' markets, often open only on weekends, did fill an important need to supplement, in terms of variety and regularity, the fare offered by state-run "agros." I shopped at both regularly. The farmers' prices were high by Cuban standards, but usually one could find the ingredients to make a decent salad. The markets' closing was combined with a pledge that the cooperatives and state farms would pick up the slack. There was little visible opposition to the move in Cuba; more, I would say, ambivalence and to be sure a skepticism that the state and coops could make good on their promise. Four years later, they hadn't, at least in Havana. But the situation was improving, thanks to the Food Program and the reorganization of distribution, linking many farms and cooperatives directly to the "agro" markets.

Adolfo Martín Barrios, a leader of the National Association of Private Farmers (ANAP) since 1959, told me the farmers' market, which opened at the end of 1979, was aimed at getting more produce to the cities, and in essence was successful. But, he continued, "the markets began to undermine our cooperative movement and the morale of workers on the state farms. The market created a whole sector of middlemen speculating off farmers' labor and urban workers' wages."

Here, said Martín, Cuba's leaders made three mistakes. The market was started before the cooperatives were consolidated; there was no limit set on prices; and government proved completely ineffective in controlling the situation or preventing middlemen from taking over. The original idea became distorted. And finally, the cooperatives, which were always against the market because they saw it as undercutting their organizing efforts, demanded it be closed down.

Güira de Melena, about an hour's drive south of Havana, is farm country and boasts some of the best soil in Cuba. It was cooperative farmers like Orlando Gómez Martín, President of the Niceto Pérez cooperative, who became angry as the farmers market got out of hand.

"I grew up right here," Gómez told me in late 1989. "Me, my two brothers and father farmed some 100 acres of land. In the fifties, you couldn't study agricultural sciences, so I went to school and learned accounting. I graduated in 1956, and my father told me to go work in an office. I said no way. There was repression; we didn't own the land; we had no secure market. But I wanted to farm."

With the revolution and agrarian reform, Gómez's family was given title to the land, and he joined the Association of Private Farmers. "I was named production chief in this municipality," he told me, "and from then on, I was active in the association. Today I'm a member of Municipal Bureau, Provincial Board, and National Committee."

The First Party Congress called on Cuba's small farmers to develop the cooperatives—joining their lands in common ownership, to take advantage of modern farming methods. Gómez and his father wanted to join the movement, but his two brothers didn't. "We finally convinced one of them, and we helped form the first cooperative in Güira de Melena back in 1979. We didn't have any material need to join the cooperative: ours were some of the richest farms around. In the seventies, a good tobacco crop sometimes brought us 40 or 50,000 pesos. Now, I average 10,000 pesos a year. So you see, I had no economic motive. My incentive was Cuba, agriculture and production. I knew the only way to technically and scientifically develop agriculture here was by forming cooperatives. But it hasn't been easy. The farmers here are very powerful and know with a guaranteed market and credits, fair prices and good land, they are rich, so why join a cooperative. We took the lead here and formed the first cooperative with just 22 members and eight pieces of land, 350 acres in all. Today we have 252 members and thousands of acres, and there are two other cooperatives in this area. We are one of the top vegetable producers in the country." Gómez told me he was always opposed to the farmers' market because it ran counter to his efforts to form cooperatives and improve agriculture. He charged the market amounted to "a state incentive not to join a cooperative, even as the Party urged us to convince farmers to join." Then later, it got completely out of hand, he said, "with the middlemen, speculation, the private exploitation of farm labor."

Not half a mile from the entrance to the Niceto Pérez Coop sits the farm of Juan Martínez, President of Güira de Melena's small farmers credit and service association, the post held by Gómez before he went coop. "Before the revolution," said Martínez, "this farm belonged to someone else. We paid an annual rent of more than 500 pesos for about 70 acres of land. My father, grandfather and brother had to work outside the farm to get up the rent. I was nine at the time of the revolution and already working with my father. I've worked on this land all my life." Martínez has three children. His son is in the armed forces, and his two daughters are studying to be teachers. He grows vegetables on his farm and supplied the farmers' market before it closed down.

"The market proved to be a mistake," Martínez told me. "I made more than ever, but it became corrupt. The big problem was the middlemen." I asked how he could call the market a mistake when he was making money hand over fist. "There wasn't a big difference really: without the market we make up to 20,000 pesos a year," he said. "The middlemen made us look bad, gave us a reputation we didn't deserve, and they were the ones that made the real cash."

Coop president Gómez's opposition to the market and Martínez's take-it-or-leave-it attitude are typical of Cuba's cooperative members and small farmers. Most state farm workers opposed the market, while many urban residents still feel the market should return if their needs can't be met.

THE SMALL FARMER AND THE STATE

Juan Martínez's service and credit association is made up of 21 farms and 52 members who together own close to 4,000 acres of land. Juan said that as president he met regularly with the government, which "gives me a yearly plan of what they want us to grow. The association then meets to discuss the plan and adjust it if need be," he explained. "I then go back to negotiate." The state provides the farmers with credit every six months and a guaranteed market. In addition, the farmers buy supplies and equipment from the same store as the cooperatives, and at the same low price.

"The credits—at eight percent interest—depend on the crop and growing time," Martínez continued. "Our association also has a credit fund and we charge two percent interest. In addition, we pay into an insurance fund, for protection against bad weather and natural disasters."

Martínez says he thinks of himself as "a revolutionary"; and I asked him why, then, hadn't he joined a cooperative? "I think its a matter of tradition, the love I have for this land. There is a long tradition of private farming in this area. To tell you the truth, I never thought there would be cooperatives here, but now there are three, and two of them are among the best in the country."

I asked Martínez if there was pressure on the small farmers to join the cooperatives. "Yes, yes," he responded immediately, "their members even visit us to talk about joining. But our relations with the cooperatives are good; we help each other. More than pressure, I would say that there is debate among old friends. Its natural, we have all known each other for years. The cooperative members say they are better for the country, so we should join. I tell them no, I feel fine right here. I'm in the revolution too. All of us help. We produce six tons of produce every year."

THE COOPERATIVES AND THE STATE

Quivicán is a Havana Province farming community located about an hour's drive southwest of the capital. As you wind through the rolling hills and valleys leading to Havana's green belt, traffic thins out, replaced by trucks, tractors, buses, bicycles and even horse-drawn carts and carriages. To get to the May 17th Cooperative, I had to pass through Quivicán itself. Typical of rural Cuban towns, it had a supermarket, corner coffee shop, butcher, vegetable market, cultural center, church, health clinic, schools, sugar mill, and movie theater; the offices of the local government, Communist Party, various national mass organizations, including the National Association of Private Farmers (ANAP); and of course, the ubiquitous ice cream parlor.

It was nine in the morning. People criss-crossed the streets on errands; a tractor belched along leaving chunks of red earth in its path;

and a microbrigade was putting up a family doctor home-office. Everybody seemed to know where the May 17th cooperative was: its President, Manuel López, is a local and national legend. In his day, López single-handedly cut more sugar cane with a machete than just about anyone else in the country.

"We began the coop in September 1977," said López, who in 1989 was also a member of the Communist Party's Central Committee. "At the time there were only 12 of us, seven men and five women. Together we had just 200 acres of land and just a couple tractors. Today, there are close to 200 families in the coop and we have over 5,000 acres."

Production manager Abilio Jarez ticked off the coop's precious assets: 36 tractors, three earth movers, five sugar combines, 11 trucks, an agricultural engineer, a veterinarian, a mechanical engineer and a planner. "We have our own repair shop," he went on, "plus a kitchen, baseball team, fishing club and bus for recreational trips. With the help of government housing loans at three percent interest, we have built 150 new homes for our members. All have electricity, fans, refrigerators, TV's. We live as well as anyone in Cuba."

"Our main product is sugar, but we also produce rice, beans, vegetables, grains, pork and fruit—mainly for our own consumption but some for sale to the state," López told me. "We organized our cooperative through lengthy discussions with local farmers who were also our friends," he explained, "and by proving in practice that the cooperative provided a better way of life."

The Coop holds monthly membership meetings where decisions are made democratically, including the annual election of officers by secret ballot. López said the formula for success was simple: "No single farmer working alone can produce what he can in a coop fully backed by the government. Take sugar cane. Not every farmer can have a combine or the most modern irrigation system. A combine produces as much in a day as 40 men, and a modern irrigation system can double yields." López also cited advantages the coop provided for the farming family. "It is difficult for the government to electrify tens of thousands of scattered farms; it is hard to shop and go to school living miles away from these services. When we put our homes closer together, these problems can be solved. The coops are also keeping some young people on the land. Children of private farmers go off to study and rarely return. Our children and grandchildren study too—but many are now coming back, as skilled laborers, engineers, vets, mechanics and qualified machine operators. The coops are also a necessity for the country," López continued, as if he wanted me to join. "We have to modernize and mechanize agriculture to provide for Cuba's growing population and needs."

Yorida Sánchez Cabezas, the coop's financial wizard, answered my questions about planning and relations with the state: "We work out our plan each year—how much we will produce and on how much land. Everybody participates. Then the state approves the plan, and agrees to purchase our produce. The government gives us a credit, at four percent interest, that covers up to 80 percent of production costs. We can also buy machinery and whatever else we need at the same prices offered the state farms.

"Last year, with a loan of 600,000 pesos, we produced 1,800,000 pesos worth of sugar. After paying back the state, we netted about 1,100,000 pesos. We all received bonuses, which boosted our members' monthly incomes to about 500 pesos. After all production costs, we had 500,000 pesos left over." Half that amount, said Cabezas, went into a special fund to purchase lands and assets of new members and to pay for recreation, the vacation cottages the coop has for its members and other benefits. Another portion went to future purchases of new equipment and the rest into an account that in a few years will make the coop self-financed, eliminating the need for state loans.

But not all the cooperatives are or were as successful as Quivicán's May 17th. In 1986, at the second national meeting of the cooperative movement, in 1987 at the National Association of Private Farmers' Seventh Congress and again in 1988, at the third national meeting of the cooperative movement, the leaders of Cuba's cooperatives, Fidel Castro and many other Cuban officials poured over the movement's weaknesses and laid out plans to improve performance.

When rectification began, perhaps 40 percent of the cooperatives were doing well; another 20 percent were getting by; and 40 percent had heavy debts and were on the verge of folding. The problems, as in Cuba as a whole, ranged from poor planning and administration to poor work habits and lack of modern techniques. The solutions ranged from creating special departments in the Agriculture and Sugar Ministries to attend to cooperative needs, to making dozens of changes to boost economic performance and get the coops to accept agricultural engineers and scientists into their ranks.

"A number of factors led to the coop's problems," Aldolfo Martín Barrios told me. "There was a lot of pressure to make the cooperatives bigger and bigger without the administrative experience and leadership needed to run them well, nor a proper infrastructure."

Many farmers moved from running a small farm to coops with thousands of acres. They often had no knowledge of planning, accounting or modern technique. Many cooperatives also had and still have a lack of qualified technical personnel (Havana and Ciego de Avila provinces being the two big exceptions). They often invested in modern machinery, but did not know how to use and maintain it properly. They could not achieve the yields needed to make the modern equipment profitable.

"Many coops made investment plans without the proper analysis," said Martín. "They said they needed ten tractors when they only needed one. A dairy cooperative might have only a hundred head of cattle, but purchase equipment used in operations with herds in the thousands."

Martín said small farmers' healthy work habits also degenerated in some coops. Some became top heavy with paper pushers and leaders; in others, people worked by the hour, their pay not linked to what they actually produced. "There was a certain idealism that opposed imposing norms on farmers who had never worked by pre-set standards," he said. "When norms were applied, it wasn't always clear how: Someone would complete the norm in the morning and take every afternoon off."

I asked Gómez of the Güira de Melena Necito Pérez Cooperative why his outfit was one of the best in the country, and hundreds of others didn't turn a profit or meet their production goals. "In part, it's the land," he replied. "The soil here is some of the best in the country and that makes a big difference. But good leadership, organization and use of modern science are also fundamental. We have coops on good land with poor results. What's key are economic indicators and demanding leadership when it comes to work and quality control. Election to leadership of a coop can't be seen as a way to enter the office and leave the fields behind, just the opposite. A coop leader must be constantly checking the work and solving problems on the spot."

I put the list of 194 reforms adopted by the seventh ANAP Congress on Martín's desk and asked him what were the most important. He said the government was making more of an effort to meet the private sector's needs, freeing up ANAP to do political work and organize instead of pulling bureaucrats teeth. With rectification, the Agriculture Ministry created a deputy minister post and new department to attend to the cooperatives and small farmers (with the exception of those who grow sugar cane). The structure includes a new level of attention at the provincial and municipal levels as well. In addition, the ministry set up a new service company to supply only the cooperatives and private farmers, so they no longer have to make the rounds of ministries and companies to get what they need. The Sugar Ministry also created a new deputy minister slot and department at the national and provincial levels to attend to the 410 cooperatives in the sector and to the private farmers growing cane.

Martín said leadership and technical training are also prioritized now. At first ANAP gave 30 day courses to administrators and coop members, then 45 day courses. Some moved to three months and now many are six months long. Martín confirmed the push for cooperatives to accept young engineers and technicians, and said ANAP was also urging new graduates to work in the cooperatives. "There are now 300 engineers in the movement and 1,000 middle-level technicians," he told me. Young people are also coming up in the ranks of the cooperatives. There were maybe 20 young people leading cooperatives in 1986, and over 100 by 1989. "We are also cutting unproductive staffs and leadership not linked directly to production," he continued. "Everyone works and everyone's pay should be linked to production. In some cooperatives, the officers were earning more and doing less. That's been stopped."

With rectification, all cooperatives' investment and credits plans were reviewed by a commission of experts to make sure they were realistic. The National Bank tightened control over credit. "Some cooperatives used to say they needed credit for one thing and actually used it for another. Everyone, ANAP, the ministries, the bank, everyone is demanding more in terms of accounting and economic control now," stressed Martín.

The movement also decided to insist on a minimum work schedule of 24 days a month and 8 hours a day, with a month's vacation. It's also urging members to organize work by brigade, with norms and monthly pay and year-end earnings based on the amount, quality and cost of each brigade's work.

Martín explained that the cooperatives in the most trouble have been given special attention. A national commission made up of representatives from ANAP, the Agriculture and Sugar Ministries, the National Bank, People's Power and Party was formed in 1986 to work with them. The Commission sat down with each cooperative to look at its situation and adopt measures to get the coop out of the red. "Too much land, sell some off," said Martín. "Too many tractors, get rid of some. You have two sugar combines and can get by with one and a 20-man brigade, saving 50,000 pesos in fuel alone. In many of these coops, people worked only six hours or less a day and only 15 or 20 days a month. To make a profit, you have to work at least eight hours. When people worked their own farm, they worked more than 8 hours and every day.

Our aim is to save these cooperatives, not break them up. Because we know it's a higher form of production, socially and economically. The National Bank gave them a grace period to get themselves in order, and debt payments are based on a percent of profits so they don't loose their incentive."

A GREAT DEBATE

The debate continues in the Cuban countryside over what is the best form of production—state farms, cooperatives or private farms. "I have been to Germany, Bulgaria and some other countries," said Gómez of the Necito Pérez Cooperative. "I think cooperatives are a good form, combined with a policy of supporting, not pressuring, individual private farmers. State farms have good possibilities because they can apply science and the most modern techniques, but the experience to date hasn't been positive with all crops. State farms are best for rice, citrus, meat, milk and eggs. But with vegetable production, there are problems. I'm not sure why. I think a farmer or worker has to be linked in another way to production. My own view is that it should be more like the cooperatives, not exactly, but there has to be more of an incentive and salaries tied more closely to results. The same people are in the cooperatives and state farms, and one does better than the other. Why? Because in the cooperative, you are paid according to your work; in the state sector, they apply a norm, and that's it—and it's usually not much of a norm either. It doesn't motivate them to make an extra effort, to sacrifice. With all the science, qualified personnel and modern machinery at its disposal the state should be doing a better job."

Manuel Hernández, a member of the municipal Party Committee in Güira de Melena agreed with Gómez. "The state farms are simply too big and the directors can't cover them. A medium sized farm is best. When it's too big, one man can't keep track. We have to restructure our farms."

"What's the best form of agriculture production, the most productive?" mused small farmer Juan Martínez. "The cooperatives, without question, and life has proven it. The state farms have many problems. There is no love for the earth, and their administrators are often not from the land. The cooperatives and their members are from the land. Together they produce even more than private farmers. Of course I'm talking about mechanized crops. When it comes to other types of crops that can't be mechanized, the small farmer is the best."

Chapter Six:

DEVELOPING THE MOUNTAINS

The Turquino Plan

"Within 20 years the mountains will be the paradise of Cuba. First, because of their natural beauty and clean air. Second, because the mountains, with a modern life secured—with housing, electricity, roads, medical care, recreation, sports and all the services—will develop the highest quality of life in the country."

I had asked Deputy Agriculture Minister, Osvaldo Acosta Martínez, what Cuba's mountains would look like in the year 2000. Acosta, who in 1990 was the Ministry's man in charge of what's known as the "Turquino Plan for Integral Mountain Development" preferred to talk in terms of the year 2010.

Turquino Peak in Santiago's Sierra Maestra range is Cuba's highest point, at 1,974 meters above sea level. But its symbolism goes much further. The area provided cover for Fidel's Rebel Army, and climbing "el Turquino" has been a challenge to generations of young Cuban revolutionaries.

Acosta, nearing 50 at the time of our 1990 interview, told me he worked for the U.S.-owned Guantánamo Sugar Company before the revolution. So did his three brothers and his father. Despite five men working, he said, "we were poor, very poor," and he joined the July 26th Movement that swept the U.S.-backed Batista dictatorship from power. Later, Acosta worked his way through junior high and high school in his spare time, then through the university. He has been a Party cadre for years, and says it's his lifelong association with the mountains that prepared him for his current job.

Cuba is a long, thin island with mountain ranges forming the backbone of the emerald-green alligator it resembles. In the west, Pinar del Río's Sierra del Rosario and Organos cover 160 kilometers, followed by a series of ranges including the central Escambrays. In the east, Cuba's most formidable range, the Sierra Maestra, stretches 250 kilometers in length and is 30 kilometers wide. Cuba's mountains are a spectacular site from above, but even more breathtaking are the sudden glimpses of peaks and sub-tropical valleys that only a climber can appreciate—or the dizzying view straight down into the turquoise Caribbean from a mountain cliff.[1]

Mountains comprise 20 percent of Cuba's national territory and are home to about 700,000 people.[2] Cuba's century-long struggle for independence ebbed and flowed from the mountains, and the "campesinos" living there have been among the staunchest supporters of the revolution, since the Rebel Army set up not only camp, but also medical posts on the hillsides in the 1950s.

With the revolution's triumph, the mountains—Cuba's least developed zones—received priority attention. "We had a moral debt to the people who provided our first grassroots base," Acosta told me. "All our programs started in the mountains: the literacy campaign, the first hospitals and schools." But the development program did not have the force it needed to keep people from moving to the cities, where even more opportunities were opening up.

Migration from the mountains to the planes, cities and towns was common during the first 28 years of the revolution. Some 100,000 people, mainly young, moved out and with their departure came a dramatic deterioration of the mountain economy, ecology and main crops—coffee, cacao and tropical fruits.[3] The 1961–62 coffee harvest came in at 60,300 tons and cacao at 3,000 tons. By 1978, the coffee harvest had plummeted to 16,100 tons and cacao to 1,500 tons. The 1976–80 and 1981–85 five-year plans called for revitalizing these crops, and this was partially successful. Investments in equipment and other inputs resulted in an average annual 1981–85 coffee crop of 23.8 thousand tons and 1,780 tons of cacao.[4]

As the rectification movement got off the ground, Cuba's mountains once more captured the attention of its leaders. There were three reasons for their concern. First, the development of Cuba's defense strategy—mobilizing every able-bodied person—depended on the mountains for cover and the basics of survival. Second, both coffee and cacao had the potential of earning much-needed hard currency. And third, Cuba was facing its shortcomings, and the failure to develop the mountains and stop migration was a glaring one.

"The Turquino plan is aimed at bringing more people and keeping more people in the mountains," said Deputy Minister Acosta. "Past efforts simply aimed at increasing a given crop or improving a certain aspect of mountain life. To reverse migration, you need a far more complex approach designed to end the substantial differences in the quality of life between the mountains and the rest of the country. Thus, economic goals and programs are accompanied by social and cultural goals and programs."

The Turquino Plan is jointly led by the Party and government, and it gets an added boost from Raúl Castro, Party Second Secretary and

Defense Minister. Acosta told me attention to people's needs is key to the Plan; coupled with an economic program that includes food self-sufficiency, and the development of secondary industries, coffee, cacao, reforestation and tourism. "People are decisive," said Acosta, "especially in the mountains where it's difficult to mechanize production. And to attract people, you have to create conditions that appeal to the cultured people we are today. Remember, Cuba's young people now have much more education and higher expectations. So, we have to offer them mountains that no one dreamed of 30 years ago." Working in Cuba's favor, said Acosta, is the narrowness of the island itself: Theoretically, you can live in the mountains and never be more than an hour's drive from a provincial capital, or more than 24 hours from Havana.

The Turquino Plan is blanketing Cuba's mountains, a number of layers going down simultaneously. The most important is infrastructure—roads, electricity, communications, water and sewers through extremely difficult terrain that would challenge even a developed country. Around this infrastructure a series of small towns are springing up with many of the amenities of city life. Each community is linked to local economic projects aimed at ensuring full-time employment for men and women, and the towns are brought together under the umbrella of municipal government.

By 1990, construction brigades, contingents and members of the Armed Forced had carved out central road-ways through the mountains. In Pinar del Río, they completed a 100-kilometer road, planned for decades, and 300 kilometers of secondary roads. In the eastern provinces, a series of major roadways such as the 230 kilometer Via Mulata, the 50 kilometer Baconao and 80 kilometer Granma highway neared completion, along with over 1,000 kilometers of secondary roads, many involving complex bridge and tunnel construction. During the same period, 5,508 kilometers of power lines were strung, bringing electricity to 849 towns, 112,000 homes, 139 work camps and half a million people. The family doctor program was first put in place in the mountains; and phone and other communications brought in. Special relay stations were built to ensure Cuban TV reached mountain homes. Half a dozen major reservoirs and many smaller ones were built or are under construction to control flooding and harness waters for agriculture, local industry and domestic use.[5]

The clusters of small towns are expanding, bringing together nearby families and the trickle of people returning to the mountains or deciding to remain after completing a job—-about 25,000 as of 1989.[6] During the first three years of the plan, over 6,000 new apartments were built.[7]

As a rule, each town has 30 to 100 families, electricity, water and a sewer system, phone and telegraph, a general store, video sala, cultural center, beauty and barber shop, a primary school and family doctor. Many are the centers of farming cooperatives, and others of state farms.

Moving to town or joining a cooperative or farm is voluntary, said Acosta, though efforts are made to persuade people. "We explain to them the Plan's importance for the country and their lives," he continued, "and also that Cuba does not have the resources to run roads and power lines to thousands of scattered mountain homes." Cooperatives usually take shape if the townspeople are mainly private farmers who have come together to share their resources and benefit from the Turquino Plan. A state farm, where private farming is not dominant and the state has put in most of the work to develop the local economy. A mixture is also possible.

There is a strong emphasis in the mountains on food self-sufficiency. Here, farmers produced some 135,000 tons of roots and vegetables in 1989, 24,000 tons more than in 1987.[8] Sheep, hogs, cattle, dairy herds and chickens are also being raised in greater numbers—between 1986 and 1990, 55,000 sheep were added to mountain flocks.[9]

COFFEE AND CACAO

Israel Rodríguez Castro, national director of Cuba's Coffee and Cacao Program, told me that for the first time he felt confident that coffee and cacao were coming back to stay. "The problem is developing a stable labor force," he said. "For the most part, you can't mechanize coffee and cacao production. Preparing the soil can be semi-mechanized to humanize the work a bit, but that's about it."

Historically, Cuba's coffee and cacao were completely in the hands of private farmers. Today, 48 percent of coffee and 30 percent of cacao is in state hands, the remainder harvested on private lands—about half by cooperatives and half by individual farmers. State lands are being tended by the Young Workers Army (YWA), recruits and volunteers who do their army stint in the fields, backed up by scientists and engineers.[10]

Historically, the YWA has been a highly productive labor force. As part of the Turquino Plan, thousands of its members have taken to the mountains where they build base camps and begin developing coffee plantations. The camps are the heart of future permanent communities, and eventually boast all the services. To date, over 33,500 acres of coffee plantations have been developed this way and many more revitalized.[11]

"In 1986," said Rodríguez, "we had only two professionals working in coffee. Today we have 380 agricultural engineers and 2,000 technicians. Our first mountain university has been opened, and along side it a technical school." Located in Guantánamo's Sabaneta municipality, the university has 700 students. It caters mainly to young people already living in the mountains, and specializes in forestry, coffee, cacoa and the "mountain sciences."

Science is expected to play a critical role in boosting Cuba's coffee and cacao production. A specialized team is at work in the mountains, and there are 20 experimental stations. Rodríguez told me nurturing a quality harvest is a complex job—and special attention is paid to soil quality, seed varieties, the proper moment to plant and harvest, regulation of sun light, and techniques for preventing erosion or other types of damage. He said scientific advice is provided free of charge, not just to the state sector but to private cooperatives and farmers as well.

Average Cuban coffee yields range between 100 and 200 pounds per acre. The experimental stations have achieved yields up to 800 pounds. Plans call for Cuba to produce 50,000 tons of coffee annually, and 3,000 tons of cacao—more than double their 1985 levels.[12]

REFORESTATION

In the year 1500, Spanish Friar Bartolomé de Las Casas wrote: "you can go from one end of the island to the other, forever shaded by the trees."[13] In 1959, it was possible to go from one end of Cuba to the other with no shade at all. In 1500, 80 percent of Cuba's territory was covered by forests, including precious woods and tropical fruits. By 1900, the forested area had been reduced to 53 percent; and by 1959, a meager 14 percent. What the Spanish colonizers hadn't destroyed and pillaged, U.S. corporations did. Thus, between 1900 and the 1959 revolution, 11 million acres of Cuban forests disappeared. The loss went much further than the dollar value of the lumber and fruits. It caused serious erosion and environmental damage, led to the extinction of many animal and plant species and hurt Cuba's defense capabilities.[14]

On June 3, 1990, a group of young people made it to the top of the Turquino Peak and planted the billionth tree of what is called the Manatí Plan.[15] The plan actually began in 1982 with the aim of reforesting the island, and it picked up steam with rectification. Plans call for planting another 1.5 billion saplings by 1995.[16] Thanks to the Manatí Plan, Cuba is one of the few countries in the world that has reversed deforestation; and today, the total area covered by forests has expanded to over 20 percent.

"At the start of the revolution we talked about reforestation," said Agriculture Deputy Minister Acosta. "There was a push in that direction but at the same time agricultural development—in rice, citrus and cattle, cut into the forests. We also didn't completely understand the problem, and in general used the land irrationally."

Las Tunas's Manatí municipality became the first to experiment with the popularly based reforestation plan back in 1982. "Manatí was picked because of the minimal rainfall in the area and its less-than-ideal soil," said Acosta. "If we could reforest Manatí, we could reforest the country." The experiment was also linked to Cuba's new defense strategy and need to develop tree cover. Like that strategy, it was a precursor to rectification, as it sought out the people to tackle the problem with the help of better organization and Cuba's scientists and technicians.

Supported by a special team from the Academy of Sciences, Manatí's population set about growing saplings and planting them literally everywhere. The elderly, housewives and children found containers and grew seedlings at home; everyone, from factory workers to primary school students, was assigned an area to plant. What to plant where was determined by the Academy of Sciences. For example, certain varieties for coastal zones, others to protect reservoirs from salinization, others where forests could be developed, and of course in every yard and park fruit trees for the juicy pleasure of eating.

By the end of 1985, Manatí had planted twice as many trees as the Cuban State Forest Company. The effort was declared a remarkable success, and with rectification, the Manatí Plan went nationwide. Today, every municipality, electoral district, most Committees for the Defense of the Revolution, schools, factories, and cooperatives are taking part, with the guidance of a nation-wide study of soil conditions, a special scientific group and dozens of technicians.

"This effort is directly linked to rectification because people play the key role. The work is well organized and the motivation comes from our political work. Before people will voluntarily participate, they have to fully grasp the trees' importance for the environment, economy and defense," said 46-year-old Ramón Beltrán Oliviera, in charge of the Agriculture Ministry's forestry program. "Once they do understand the importance, they do the job. We have many people who have produced 20,000 saplings in their back yards!"

Beltrán said Cuba is the most advanced in the region when it comes to the study of its forests and reforestation. And since the island boasts some 400 species, it's a complicated enterprise. The Manatí Plan also promotes environmental education. "Every local municipality has a group studying and leading the reforestation effort," Beltrán explained. "That's led people to understand the difficulty and time needed to grow trees and why deforestation has to be reversed."

Beltrán emphasized that the Manatí Plan is directly linked to the Turquino Plan. "It's fundamental to the mountains and their crops. On the one hand, development is proceeding in a manner that protects existing forests. On the other hand, vast areas are being reforested and trees used to protect new coffee and cacao plantations from erosion and to regulate the sunlight." Practically smacking his lips, Beltrán concluded with "we are also planting tens of millions of fruit trees in the mountains."

PHOTO CAPTIONS FOR PART ONE: pp. 3 TO 125.

1) Fidel Castro congratulates newly-weds: The grooms, and a few of the brides, helped remodel and expand Havana's Miguel Enríquez hospital. They decided to postpone their weddings until the work was completed; celebrate with a collective wedding; and make Castro the guest of honor. (AIN-1989)

2) Fidel Castro at a Blas Roca Contingent collective birthday party. The Contingent holds the parties for its members and their families. (AIN-8/13/89)

3) Fidel Castro on a tour of Ciego de Avila province. Castro tours various parts of the country every year, as do other top Cuban leaders. They spend most of their time in encounters like this one. (AIN-5/9/89)

4) Fidel Castro and Blas Roca Contingent leader Cándido Palmero celebrate the second anniversary of the contingent, an experimental model of new management-labor relations now being generalized in Cuba. (AIN-10/1/89)

5) Young people dancing in Havana's streets. Such scenes are common place throughout Cuba. (AIN-3/8/90)

6) Pedro Ross, First Secretary of the National Organization of Cuban Trade Unions (CTC), inaugurates the Cuban labor movement's 16th Congress. (AIN-1990)

7) Workers at Havana's Antillana de Acero steelworks debate the economy, rectification and plant conditions in preparation for the CTC's 16th Congress. The banner reads, "The Unions in the Process of Rectification." (Len Kaminsky-1989)

8) Angry construction workers at the Pan American Games site voice their complaints and demand action as they meet in preparation for the CTC's 16th Congress. (Len Kaminsky-1989)

9) A family doctor and nurse in Granma Province's mountains. I'll never forget a visit to the area by a group of activists from Peru, Bolivia and Colombia. Many broke down in tears at the difference between life in Cuba's mountains and that in their own countries. (PL)

10) One of thousands of family doctor-nurse combination home offices built by microbrigades and community volunteers. This one was built by religious activists and was completed in June, 1990. (AIN)

11) Opening the "los Abelitos" childcare center in Havana's Boyeros Municipality. Havana's microbrigades and community volunteers built 111 of these centers in 1987 and 1988. (PL)

12) Playing ball at one of Havana's many special school-clinics. By 1990, Cuba had become the first country in the Third World to adequately meet the special education needs of its children. (PL-1990)

13) Josefina Bocour Díaz or "Fifi." The telex operator turned construction chief is leading a community effort to transform one of Cuba's worst shanty towns, La Güinera, into a modern community and strong hold of the revolution. (Author)

14–15) La Güinera before "Fifi" and her social microbrigades took over (14). And the same spot a year later as local residents celebrate the opening of the first apartments. (PL)

16) Cuba's first mountain university opened in Guantánamo's Sabaneta municipality in 1988. (AIN) **17)** The "Turquino Plan for Integral Mountain Development" has resulted in new communities like this one in Sancti Spiritus's Escambray mountains. (AIN-1988)

PHOTO CAPTIONS FOR PART TWO: PP 131–209.

a) Havana women debate the future of their city, nation and gender in preparation for the Fifth Congress of the Cuban Women's Federation. (Author-1989)

b–e) The fall of the socialist camp and U.S. blockade left Cuba in 1992 with a little over a third of the oil it consumed in 1989. The country's leaders responded by looking for alternatives. 200,000 oxen have been pressed into service and over two million bicycles imported from China. The use of solar energy has become common place and windmills have gone up on farms across the island. (b) Oxen haul banana's to market in Pinar del Río. (AIN-2/12/92) (c) Delegates to the 6th Congress of the Union of Young Communists bike through Havana in support of Special Period policies. (AIN-1992) (d) Solar power being used in Pinar del Río to heat water and run a small machine.(AIN-1992) (e) Building a windmill in Las Tunas Province. (AIN-1992)

f–g) Since 1981 Cubans have been preparing for "The War of the Entire People" with the United States. Today most Cubans wear two hats, one civilian and the other military. The average citizen puts aside one Sunday a month for defense training and many spend a month or more each year on maneuvers. (f) Preparing for the worst in Havana. (AIN-1988) (g) And to fight to the end in the countryside. (AIN-1988)

h–i) Fidel Castro and Young Communist leader Roberto Robaina at the "Cuba VA" rally 12/28/1989. The rally, like many before and after, combined political speeches with concerts featuring Cuba's most popular bands and singers, for example (i) Silvio Rodríguez shown below at the same rally. (AIN-12/28/89)

j–m) The United State's Christmas invasion of Panama set off massive youth demonstrations in Cuba. They marked the start of an ongoing mobilization of young people in defense of their country and socialism. (j) Young people march through Havana protesting the Panama invasion. (AIN-1989) (k) And rally in front of the U.S. Interests Section in Havana. (AIN-1990) (l) Havana rally to reaffirm the socialist character of the Revolution and celebrate the choice of the Capital to host 1990s July 26th celebrations. (AIN-4/16/90) (m) Just days before I left the island I stood amongst these young people in Revolution Square as they roared their determination to carry on the fight for independence and socialism. (AIN-4/3/91).

n–o) Three Cuban American terrorists caught in Matanzas Province December 29, 1991. (o) The three planned to use these arms and explosives on civilian targets in hopes of creating chaos and convincing the world that Cubans had taken up arms against their government. (AIN-1992)

p) Esteban Lazo Hernández, Party First Secretary of Santiago Province and a Political Bureau member, opens the Fourth Congress of the Cuban Communist Party. Banner reads "Our Most Sacred Duty is to Save the Nation, the Revolution and Socialism. (PL-10/10/1992)

5

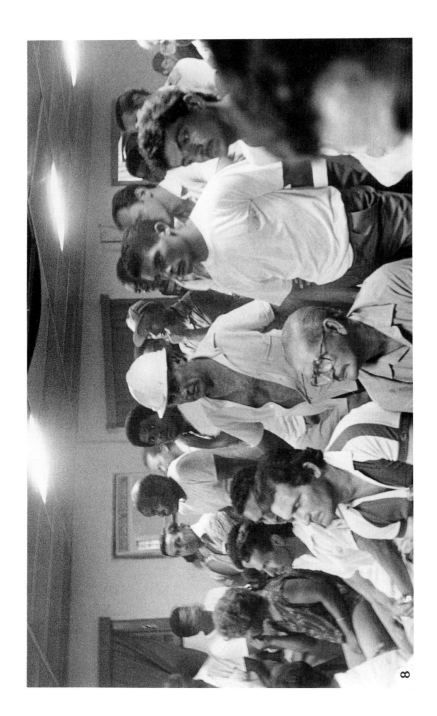

8

10

"CON METODOS DE MASAS, METODOS DE PUEBLO" FIDEL

12

13

14

15

b

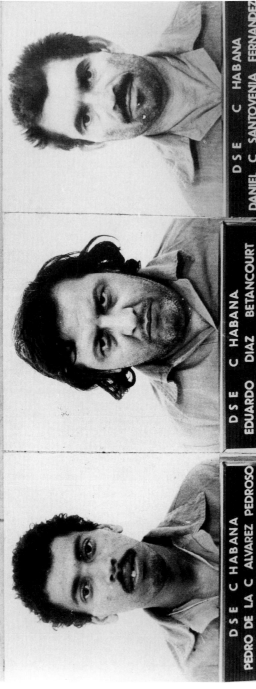

D S E C HABANA
DANIEL C SANTOVENIA FERNANDEZ

D S E C HABANA
EDUARDO DIAZ BETANCOURT

D S E C HABANA
PEDRO DE LA C ALVAREZ PEDROSO

nuestro deber mas sagrado
SALVAR LA PATRIA,
LA REVOLUCION
Y EL SOCIALISMO

PART II:

Chapter Seven:

THE END OF AN ERA

On December 7, 1989, Cuba laid to rest the remains of 2,289 of its sons and daughters who had died since 1959 on internationalist missions in Africa, Asia and Latin America. The Cubans had been brought home from the far away lands where they perished and were originally buried. The dead included 2,085 service men and women and 204 doctors, nurses, teachers, technicians and ordinary workers. (A U.S. equivalent would be about 60,000.) During Cuba's 13-year mission in Angola, 2,016 had died; 160 in Ethiopia and 113 in other countries. Combat casualties were 863; 597 succumbed to illness and 829 died in accidents.[1]

Cuba's decision to bring these dead home for a final tribute marked the end of an era. To be sure, Cuba would continue to send more doctors to poor countries than any other nation or international organization in the world; Cuban teachers and specialists would continue to fan out year after year on humanitarian missions abroad. At home, Cuban hospitals and schools would still hold out help and hope for thousands of Third World people. Yet it was the end of an era. The changes in Eastern Europe, the Soviet Union and East-West relations meant no large Cuban military missions would be deployed abroad in the future, not even to defend a country like Angola from U.S.-backed South African aggression. For better or worse, a new world order was in the making.

December 6 and 7, 1989, were declared days of official mourning. Millions of Cubans paid their respects to the fallen and their families. The funerals took on a life of their own as people poured into the streets to reaffirm their support for what their martyrs had died for, the Third World's struggle against foreign domination and a profoundly unjust international economic order. Their support of the right of every nation to independence, self determination, economic and social development. Their empathy with those who had not achieved the minimum family security and peace they themselves had won.

Cubans waited 6 hours and more to file past the coffins laid out across the island. Faced with one endless line after the other, I gave up and returned home at 10:00 pm on the 6th. The following day, funeral processions and services were held in every municipality and province. The national service took place on Havana's outskirts, at the "El Cacahual" monument where Antonio Maceo and other Cuban heroes are buried. President Fidel Castro, flanked by Angolan President, Jose Eduardo Dos Santos, presided over the ceremony as a light rain fell on the crowd.

Cuba's history is an extraordinarily rich one, filled with epic battles for independence against Spanish and then U.S. domination and dotted with great men and women who rose to the challenges of their day to forge the country's independence, national identity and culture. A much overlooked reason for Fidel Castro's success, that of the July 26th movement which brought him to power in 1959, and the Cuban Communist Party today, is their profound knowledge and identification with Cuban history, and the inspiration they draw from this exceptional past. Theirs is a knowledge, identification and inspiration they seek tirelessly to pass on to the Cuban people. Picking December 7, 1989, to bury Cuba's internationalists was no exception.

On October 10, 1868, a cross-class alliance of Cubans launched the country's 30-year war for independence from Spain. The alliance included businessmen, plantation and slave owners, small farmers, artisans, agricultural workers and slaves. It was a war against great odds. Yet, the outnumbered Cuban fighters known as Mambises—often barefoot and with only machetes in hand—defeated the Spaniards time after time on the battlefield. Then, Spain changed its tactics and began to woo Cuba's businessmen, land- and slave-owners. As a result, Cuba's colonial masters successfully divided the independence forces, and on February 11, 1978, the wealthiest insurgents and Spain cut a deal in the Cuban village, of Zanjón. The Cuban elite would get a bigger slice of the pie and some reforms in exchange for dropping their demands for total independence and the abolition of slavery.

No sooner had the Zanjón pact been signed than the man Cubans call the "Bronze Titan" and their greatest general, Antonio Maceo, rallied 1500 officers and men to the town of Baraguá. Maceo denounced the pact as a terrible betrayal, and declared the war for Cuba's independence would continue. On March 15, 1878, Maceo met with the Commander of the Spanish troops at Baraguá. Terence Cannon, in his book *Revolutionary Cuba*, records the dialogue:

"Then we are not in agreement?" the startled Spanish general asked.

"No," said Maceo, "we are not in agreement."

"Then hostilities will break out again?"

"Right now is all right with me," replied Maceo. Their meeting came to be known as the "Baraguá Protest."[2]

But the Zanjón pact set back Cuba's independence struggle. It was not until 1898 that Cuba, with a population of just one million, finally drove 200,000 Spanish troops into the sea. Antonio Maceo did not live to see their triumph. On December 7, 1896, he was killed in combat, taking to his grave 26 scars, marking the wounds he suffered in battle after battle for Cuba's nationhood. On December 7, 1989, Cuban President Fidel Castro honored a new generation of heroes, and delivered a modern day Baraguá protest against what Cuba's leaders saw as another Zanjón pact in the making—this time on an international scale. "Cuba is forever Baraguá" became the revolutions's rallying cry, as it girded against the capitulation of its closest allies to imperialism and the hostility of a U.S. administration seemingly drunk over its "victory" and new-found power.

Fidel Castro for the first time delivered an exhaustive critique of the rapidly unfolding events in socialist Europe and the new world order in the making. The Cuban President read from a prepared text, a rarity which indicated that the address was important enough to require the prior approval of Cuba's Communist Party and government leadership.

"Capitalism," declared Castro, "its market economy, its values, categories and methods can never pull socialism out of its present difficulties or rectify whatever mistakes have been made . . . It has been said that socialism needs improving. No one can deny this principle, which is inherent and always applicable to every human endeavor. But can socialism be improved by forsaking Marxism-Leninism's most basic principles? Why must the so-called reforms be along capitalist lines? If those ideas are truly revolutionary, as some claim, why do they receive the imperialist leaders' unanimous and enthusiastic support?"

The Cuban leader defined capitalism quite differently from the notion circulating in parts of Europe:

> Capitalism means unequal terms of trade with the people of the third world, the exacerbation of individual selfishness and national chauvinism, the reign of irrationality and chaos in investment and production, people's bitter sacrifice on behalf of blind economic laws, the survival of the fittest, the exploitation of man by man, a situation of everybody for himself. In the social sphere, capitalism implies many more things: prostitution; drugs; gambling; begging; unemployment; abysmal inequalities among citizens; the depletion of natural resources; the poisoning of the air, seas, rivers and forests. Most of all capitalism means the plundering of developing nations by industrialized capitalist countries. In the past, it meant colonialism; now it means neocolonialism for billions of people, using the most sophisticated and cheapest, most effective and most ruthless economic and political methods.

Fidel Castro expressed deep concern that the threat of monopoly capitalism or "imperialism" was being ignored by reformists and pro-Western forces in then socialist Eastern Europe. In fact, he warned, emerging political forces in some East European countries and even the USSR appeared ready to join in the plunder of the Third World.

"It's a matter of grave concern," he argued, "that the concepts of anti-imperialism and the principles of internationalism have all but disappeared from the media and have virtually been stricken from the political dictionary. In their place, capitalist values are gaining unusual force."

Castro charged that many people in socialist Europe held false and idealistic views about capitalism, ignoring the fact that the system not only eroded society's moral fabric but also inevitably developed into monopoly capitalism and imperialism—the domination of the big banks and corporations over world affairs. He criticized the growing tendency to buy into the illusion that capitalism worked when history revealed that what had "worked" was imperialism. Capitalism, he said, had created a handful of wasteful consumer societies—built on a long history of slavery, colonialism, neocolonialism and domestic exploitation. This had resulted in unacceptable poverty levels, even within the wealthy industrialized nations, and complete marginalization for Third World peoples. Castro pointed out that a small handful of industrialized capitalist countries were consuming the lion's share of the world's resources. What would happen if China or India followed suit? How long would resources last, and how fierce would the competition become for those resources? He reasoned it would be impossible for Eastern Europe, the Soviet Union or the rest of the world to follow the U.S. or Japanese development model.

"Now," Castro warned,

imperialism is inviting the European socialist countries to join it in this colossal plunder—an invitation that seems to please the theoreticians of capitalist reforms. Thus in many of those countries, no one speaks about the tragedy of the Third World, and their discontented multitudes are guided toward capitalism and anti-communism . . . The prize promised by imperialism is a share of the plunder wrested from our peoples, the only way of building capitalist consumer societies.

On improved East-West relations and the "new world order" in the making, Castro warned:

They speak to us of peace, but what kind of peace? Of peace between the major powers while imperialism reserves the right to intervene in and attack the Third World countries . . . The consecration of the principle of universal intervention by a major power spells an end to independence and sovereignty in the world.

The Cuban president praised efforts to eliminate nuclear weapons, stating "it would be of unquestionable benefit and would increase world security—but only for a part of humanity." He pointed out it would not bring peace, security or hope to Third World countries. "Imperialism doesn't need nuclear weapons to attack our people," charged Fidel Castro. "Its powerful fleets, which are stationed all over the world; its military bases everywhere; and its ever more sophisticated and lethal conventional weapons are enough to insure its role as the world's master and gendarme."

Fidel Castro then struck a familiar theme for Cubans.

Forty thousand children who could be saved die every day in our world because of underdevelopment and poverty. It's as if every three days a bomb similar to the ones dropped on Hiroshima or Nagasaki were dropped on the poor children of the world . . . If these developments continue on their present course and the United States isn't forced to renounce these concepts, what new way of thinking can we speak of? Following this course, the bi-polar world which emerged in the postwar period will inexorably become a unipolar world under the hegemony of the United States.[3]

As Castro spoke and Cubans mourned, U.S. soldiers at the occupied Guantánamo Naval Base in eastern Cuba fired not once but twice on Cuban guard posts, narrowly missing their occupants. Within two weeks, 30,000 U.S. troops invaded Panama. A few months later the Sandinistas fell, victims of a decade of U.S. low intensity conflict. One East European Communist Party after another succumbed under the unbearable weight of external pressure, internal problems and the illusions of "free" market economics. A year later, under the guise of a UN mandate and with the help of its new squadron of allies, the United States bombed Iraq back to the Stone Age, killing 200,000 people in less than a month, and leaving at least an equal number of civilians, mainly the very young and old, to die slow deaths from hunger and disease.

Cuba, a member of the UN Security Council at the time, condemned Iraq's invasion of Kuwait. But just as heatedly, and often alone, it also condemned the U.S.-led rush into war—charging that this will go down in history as perhaps the most one-sided, barbaric and cruel war ever fought. A triumphant President George Bush proclaimed a "new world order" and "Pax Americana." Cuba dug in for an eternal Baraguá, and declared that its people's main internationalist mission was now right at home, to stand up to imperialism, defend the country, maintain Cuba's solidarity with the poor nations, and continue to build an independent model of Third World development with social justice. The stakes were high on both sides.

Chapter Eight:

CRISIS—THE SPECIAL PERIOD IN PEACETIME

Time Runs Out

Jorge Lezcano, First Secretary of the Havana branch of the Cuban Communist Party, stood before 1,000 women gathered at the Máximo Gómez Military Academy some ten miles outside the Cuban capital on December 9, 1989, two days after President Castro delivered his modern day Baraguá Protest. Lezcano reviewed efforts underway to improve life in the capital. He then urged "Time! Time! That's what we need, just a little more time!"

The Havana women had debated for ten hours the status of their city, country and gender in preparation for the upcoming fifth Congress of the Cuban Women's Federation. The Havana meeting, like 13 other provincial gatherings around the country and thousands of municipal and block-level meetings that preceded the Congress, was a family affair. I was the only foreign journalist present.

"What are the material problems we face?" asked Lezcano. "Eighty-five percent of our economy is integrated with the socialist countries. What's happening in Europe is going to affect us; we may even have to declare a special period in peacetime (a Cuban euphemism for an economic state of emergency). We have to prepare the public. More than ever we have to promote the moral, political, ideological and patriotic values of the Revolution. The spirit of sacrifice and resistance shown by the Cuban people throughout our history. We have to prepare for the worst. We have to bring our families together . . . We have to work harder than ever for the unity of all our people around the Party and government. We have to explain why U.S. imperialism is bound to be more aggressive, and the struggle between the two systems harsher than ever."

Less than a year later time ran out and Cuba declared the Special Period was on. An inkling of what was in store came just a month after Fidel Castro and Jorge Lezcano spoke. On January 22, 1990, the Government announced that grains, wheat and other raw materials used to feed livestock and bake bread were late arriving.

For 20 years, the Soviet shipments for the following year's plan arrived in November and December to guarantee the flow of Cuba's food supplies. This year the docks sat empty. To cushion some of the shortages, Cuba had bought feed, wheat and raw materials from Canada, but clearly not enough, for hard currency was also in short supply. The official notice warned that with no immediate relief in sight, the country's precious livestock would certainly suffer.

Throughout Cuba, the bread ration was reduced to 20 grams a day. In Havana, where bread was not rationed, the price rose five cents a pound. The price of an egg jumped from 10 to 15 cents across the Island.

The Western press played up the story as if Cubans ate only bread and now even that was being taken away! Actually, bread is a small part of the Cuban diet and even two years into the economic crisis the nation's nutritional level remained the highest in Latin America. The Western media also buried the government's simultaneous announcement that as Polish, GDR and Soviet ships failed to pick up citrus exports, tens of thousands of tons of grapefruit and oranges would be diverted to the Cuban market. There was less bread than normal on Cuba's streets but more fresh fruit and juice.[1]

These first trade problems with Eastern Europe and the Soviet Union were minor compared to what loomed on the horizon. By the summer of 1990 more shortages appeared in Cuba, though again no one went hungry. The Food Program became the country's top priority, and Cuba's national leadership seemed to be closeted in permanent emergency session. Something akin to an economic tidal wave, set off by events in socialist Europe, was headed straight for the island. It hit Cuba dead center in 1991 then rolled back over the island again in 1992, cutting foreign trade by as much as fifty percent and the GNP by perhaps half that much; shutting down factories and other workplaces; forcing the adoption of the strictest rationing in socialist Cuba's history and a crash program to restructure trade, the economy and daily life.

IMPERIALISM, THE SOCIALIST CAMP AND CUBA

Cuba, like all developing countries, is saddled with a foreign debt owed largely to the industrialized capitalist countries and their banks. The big creditor exception, of course, is the United States. Cuba's national bank reported that by the third quarter of 1990 the country owed $6.1 billion, with interest running at about $500 million a year.

Like the combined Third World's $1.3 trillion foreign debt and $100 billion a year interest payments, Cuba's debt and interest had become unpayable by the late 1980s, due to international economic conditions. This restricted Cuba's access to all but short-term, high-interest loans from the capitalist world.[2]

To understand the economic bind Cuba and all developing nations are in, look at international currencies, prices, exchange and interest rates. Like all Socialist and Third World countries' currencies, the Cuban peso is not recognized by the Western world, its banks and corporations, nor accepted as legal tender on the world market. Put more simply: it is not freely convertible. Cuba buys Western medicines not with its peso, but with U.S. dollars. Japanese tractors are purchased with yens, Western computers with marks or francs or other "hard" currencies. To obtain those hard currencies Cuba, like all developing nations, must sell its products on the world market or borrow from Western governments and banks.

Transnational corporations monopolize international trade. They fix the prices of many Third World exports and imports, notoriously low for the former and high for the latter. That bind forces the developing world into exporting more, importing less and borrowing what it can to make up the difference. By the mid 1980s that became little more than desperately trying to meet foreign debt interest payments.

The UN Center for Transnational Studies reported that in the 1980s transnational corporations (TNCs) controlled one-third of the world's industrial production, more than half of all foreign trade and 80 percent of new patents and technologies. TNCs dominated over 90 percent of the metals-related mineral trade. The world's 15 largest agriculture-related TNCs monopolized 80 to 90 percent of the world trade in wheat, coffee, corn, tobacco, cotton, jute, pineapple, cocoa, etc. Three transnationals—United Brands, Castle and Cook, and Del Monte—controlled over 50 percent of the banana trade; and ten transnationals, the sugar trade. Monopoly control of international trade funneled the lion's share of wealth produced by Third World workers into the coffers of the transnationals, thus out of the hands of Third World nationals for those of the elite of the world's handful of developed capitalist countries.[3]

In 1990, the Latin American Economic System reported that between 1980 and 1988 the region increased its export volume by 56 percent, but the average price received per unit dropped 25 percent. Hence, gross export earnings increased by just 15 percent for a net loss of $70 billion.[4]

The Third World's foreign debt became another mechanism for Western pillage, facilitating the takeover of Third World industries, services, and resources, and serving as yet another lever for political control. In the 1960s, interest rates averaged three percent; and in the early '70s up to six percent. Third World governments and businesses took out loans, often with floating interest rates. Those interest rates soared by 1979 to 12 percent; and up to 16 percent by 1981. Interest rates averaged over 10 percent in the 1980s. Unable to meet debt or even interest payments, Third World governments were forced to renegotiate their debts and take out new loans, often just to meet interest payments. Western banks and governments, working through the International Monetary Fund, forced Third World governments to "modernize" to qualify for loans. They imposed crash programs that drastically cut social spending on already poor countries, geared economies increasingly to exports and led to the selling off of industries and resources at fire-sale prices. The alternative was a Western trade and credit cutoff and total collapse.[5]

Many Third World countries have actually paid back their total original foreign debts in interest and service charges. However, their registered debts remained higher than ever due to these governments' need to borrow to meet payments on a debt and interest that continue to compound. For example, Latin America's foreign debt stood at $222.5 billion in 1980. The region paid out in principal and interest some $350 billion over the next ten years, only to still owe $423 billion as the new decade opened![6]

Venezuela provides a good case of the foreign debt trap. The oil rich country owed $21 billion in 1982. By 1990, the government had paid its creditors, mainly U.S. banks, $25 billion, yet Venezuela's debt had risen to $31 billion.[7]

Through 1990, Cuba escaped the brunt of the Third World's economic crisis, actually a one-two punch of unfair trade terms and high debt interest and service charges. A number of factors contributed to Cuba's relative economic and social stability, the most important being that the bulk of Cuba's financial and trade relations were with Eastern Europe and the Soviet Union.

Cuba's financial and trade relations with the then socialist camp were based not on monopoly-fixed prices, wildly fluctuating interest rates and the controlled hard currencies of the "free world market" and "international economic system." Cuba's relations with the European socialist countries were the inverse—a model, the Cubans insist, of what economic relations between developed and developing nations should look like; of the "New International Economic Order" which the Third World has been demanding for decades: fair prices and development aid aimed at compensating for the massive damage caused by slavery, colonialism and neocolonialism and summed up in the term underdevelopment. Cuba joined the Soviet-led Council for Mutual Economic Assistance (CMEA) in 1972. The CMEA sought the economic integration of the world's socialist countries. Cuba's economy was structured in close coordination with Eastern Europe and in particular with the Soviet Union. Development plans were carried out as part of the "international socialist division of labor," and with a conscious understanding that the more developed socialist countries would aid the less developed.

Cuba's entire economy rested on the following assumptions: stable and expanding markets for Cuban sugar and other exports; stable and expanding supplies of oil and other strategic materials; trade through barter and rubles, not hard currency; preferential trade terms and development credits to help Cuba overcome the legacy of Spanish colonialism and U.S. neocolonialism; and five-year agreements that allowed Cuba to make long-term development plans.

Cuban economist Dr. José Luis Rodríguez writes that between 1959 and 1988, 63 percent of all Cuba's trade was with the Soviet Union and about 80 percent with the European socialist community. Credits, at four percent interest, essentially covered Cuba's trade deficit with the Soviets, the equivalent of about $11.5 billion. In addition, terms of trade between Cuba and the USSR steadily improved to Cuba's benefit. The Soviet Union had also loaned Cuba 3.8 billion in development funds at a two percent interest rate.

The Cuban economist says that between 1960 and 1986, 360 industrial and other projects were completed with Soviet assistance and 289 more were under construction. An additional 174 projects were planned for the 1986–1991 period. The Soviets also provided Cuba with extensive technical assistance in all fields. Bulgarian development assistance focused mainly on agriculture; Czechoslovakia on energy and machine building; Hungary on transport and communications; Poland on shipbuilding; Romania on oil production; and the German Democratic Republic on machine building and the construction materials industry.

Rodríguez estimates Cuba's debt to the Soviets at some $20 billion. But contrary to Western claims, Rodríguez points out there were some real advantages for the Soviets. For example, while they bought Cuban sugar at three times the world market price, the investment was still below what domestic beat sugar production would have cost. And the Soviets also purchased other key products from Cuba, such as nickel, at well below international market prices.[8]

Cuba's National Bank reported that in 1989 $11.2 of Cuba's $13.5 billion in trade was with the Soviet Union, Eastern Europe and to a lesser degree other socialist countries. Cuban exports to the socialist community totaled $4.3 billion and imports from the area $6.9 billion, resulting in a $2.6 billion trade deficit.[9] Some $9.5 billion of Cuba's trade was with the Soviet Union and most of its deficit. Trade with the GDR, Cuba's second trading partner, amounted to about $600 million, Czechoslovakia $570 million, with the other East European countries between $100 million and $300 million each. Cuba also received half a billion dollars in development aid and credits from the Soviet Union and some 150 million from Eastern Europe—in particular from the German Democratic Republic.[10]

WORST CASE SCENARIO

Cuban and East European diplomatic sources reported by the summer of 1990 that trade with the GDR had slowed to a trickle. West German Foreign Trade Minister, Juergen Warnke, told an August 29th news conference that a united Germany would scrap all agreements with Cuba, provide aid only through the churches and review all trade, citing Havana's refusal to adopt a market economy and Western-style democracy.[11]

Cuba fared no better with Czechoslovakia, Poland and Bulgaria.[12] In a unilateral decision announced August 1, 1990, Budapest put trade with the island on a dollar basis at world market prices.[13] Cuban workers and students returned to the island from all the East European countries by year's end, as East European experts and students in Cuba packed their bags and left for home as well.

1991 and 1992 trade negotiations between Cuba and Eastern Europe stalemated. The problems were both political and economic. Some of Eastern Europe's new governments—such as Poland's and Czechoslovakia's—were profoundly anti-socialist with a big ideological and political stake in seeing every socialist model fail. Further, faced with grave domestic crises, the governments of Eastern Europe were reduced to begging for aid from the United States and other capitalist powers, aid no doubt conditioned on cutting off even "normal" trade relations with Cuba. Thus they became de facto partners in the U.S.

strategy of strangling the island. But politics aside, the economic disaster befalling Eastern Europe in the early 1990s was of itself enough to mean the end of aid to Cuba, a drastic reduction in trade and growing demands for Havana to repay its debts—in hard currency.

Moscow at first bucked the trend, signing a record $12.2 billion trade agreement on April 17, 1990—boosting trade 8.7 percent above the 1989 level. The deal included some $7 billion worth of Soviet exports to Cuba and a little over $5.5 billion in Cuban exports to the USSR. The two countries also established a joint ministerial commission to study a new five-year plan—a difficult task, admitted both sides, given Moscow's plans to move towards increased private property, a market economy, and trade in hard currency at world market prices.[14]

The Cuban and Soviet governments said they were optimistic that bilateral trade would continue to expand. But, by the end of the year, trade had actually declined, the result of a 25 percent shortfall in Soviet deliveries—in particular 3.3 million tons of oil. Soviet developmental and military aid continued, though in amounts never disclosed. Cuban exports to the USSR broadened to include a number of new pharmaceuticals and advanced medical equipment. In a humanitarian gesture Cuba also began providing free medical care for thousands of children poisoned by the 1986 Chernobyl nuclear accident and for Soviet soldiers wounded in Afghanistan.[15]

Negotiations over a 1991 Cuban-Soviet economic agreement went down to the wire. On December 30, 1990, the two countries announced that their traditional five-year economic agreement was being scrapped in favor of a one-year deal. For the first time all transactions would be pegged to U.S. dollars and world market prices, the one exception being Cuban sugar, the price of which dropped from $800.00 per ton to $500.00, a price still above that set on the world market. Moscow also promised to export some $5 billion worth of goods to Cuba, including ten of the traditional thirteen million tons of oil; and Havana pledged to ship the Soviet's way a similar $5 billion worth of goods and services. The deal for the first time included no new development assistance, though close to $1 billion in unspent Soviet aid was to be carried over from previous agreements.[16]

Speaking on October 10, 1991, at the opening of the Fourth Party Congress, Fidel Castro reported that as of September 30, the Soviet Union had delivered just $1.3 billion worth of goods to Cuba. Critical oil deliveries, although reduced by agreement, were more or less on schedule, but just 45 percent of the contracted animal feed, grains and flour had arrived, and little if any of the food and basic household products like detergent and soap. Only 16 percent of the fertilizers

Cuba counted on for its agriculture had arrived, but no sulphur, caustic soda, sodium carbonate or other vital raw materials for industry. The same held true for contracted supplies of cotton and other textile materials. The devastating list went on: 1.9 percent of the laminated steel, 15 percent of the tin, 1.6 percent of car and truck tires, 11 percent of the synthetic rubber, 54 percent of the ammonium, and 26 percent of the nonferrous laminates and metals. Deliveries of already greatly reduced quantities of construction, agriculture, transport and factory equipment stood at 40 percent or less, and vital spare parts at just 10 percent. A mere 1.1 percent of the spare parts ordered for durable consumer items, like Soviet-made refrigerators and washing machines, had been delivered. Castro said supplies for 84 Cuban-Soviet economic cooperation projects, including such strategic ones as Cuba's first nuclear power plant, were hostage to the crisis gripping the USSR and that Cuba had also been forced to assume hundreds of millions of dollars in unplanned shipping costs. He added the obvious: no one could venture a guess on how much worse the situation might become.[17]

The end of 1991 was marked by the demise of the Soviet Union, the resignation of Mikhail Gorbachev and the emergence of the Russian Commonwealth led by Boris Yeltzin. The Cuban government reported that trade with its former ally had plunged further. Two years earlier Cuba was conducting some 75 percent of its trade with a few dozen Soviet ministries. The job now was like trying to pick up the pieces of a shattered windowpane: the few ministries had become over 25,000 separate companies and bodies operating in 11 separate republics. Two years earlier Cuba had consumed some 13 million tons of oil. By 1992, the country's leaders predicted they would have to get by with five million tons. Two years earlier Cuba had sold over four million tons of sugar to the USSR. Now Cuba would be lucky if it could sell half that to its former allies—and at a third of the previous price.

Such a dramatic drop of close to 100 percent of Cuba's foreign aid and well over 50 percent of its traditional trade, plus the loss of membership in a large market that is a must for a small country like Cuba, would be enough to devastate any nation. But there was more: virtually all of Cuba's industry and machinery came from the former European socialist countries. Most of Cuba's plants were built to their specifications, relying on materials and spare parts available only in a socialist Europe that had disappeared, and often from companies that had closed up shop. Finally, Cuba faced increasing U.S. efforts to block any attempt to secure aid, trade, markets, materials and parts from new sources.

A friend who repairs mainframe computers told me in January 1991 that many of Cuba's GDR-made computers were in danger of shutting down because there were no more spare parts. Another friend reported that the search was on for a new source for parts for Cuba's most efficient thermo-electric plants, boasting Czech equipment. The situation was also deteriorating at sugar mills, dependent on the former socialist European countries for parts, and at rice plantations where one combine harvester after another sputtered to a halt.

BATTENING DOWN THE HATCHES

Perhaps the biggest mistake people make in relation to Cuba is to assume that the island's people sit on their hands as international events rock their world. Quite the contrary. As early as 1987, when some Cubans hoped Perestroika, Glasnost and better Soviet—U.S. relations might improve socialism and lead to a thaw in Washington's Caribbean cold war with Cuba, the island's leaders cautioned Gorbachev's policies could lead to just the opposite.

On the eve of the 20th anniversary of Che Guevara's death—on October 8, 1987—Fidel Castro told the nation that the idea that socialism could be reformed through privatization and classic market economics was highly questionable. Warning that such measures bred self-interest and competition rather than cooperation on an individual, national and global scale, he charged that they undermined socialism's moral footing.[18]

On July 26, 1989, before the fall of East-European socialism, and more than two years before the demise of the Soviet Union, Castro also warned: "We can't say with certainty that the supplies from the socialist camp—which have been arriving here like clockwork for 30 years—will continue to arrive on schedule." The Cuban President reviewed the deepening crisis of European socialism as he assailed those gleefully predicting in Washington that Cuba's days were numbered. He forecast that Cuba would survive "even if there is a debacle in the socialist community . . . if tomorrow or any other day we receive news of a great civil war in the Soviet Union, or even that the Soviet Union has fallen apart . . . ."[19]

Months later, on March 8, 1990, Castro stated:

When news of destabilization in the Soviet Union reaches us, we are logically deeply concerned . . . We clearly see the danger that nationalist movements of all kinds could be unleashed, which would put the existence of the Soviet Union at great risk . . . There's another phenomenon: currents

. . . opposed to the type of economic relations currently existing between the Soviet Union and Cuba, . . . currents unquestionably associated with reaction and imperialism, openly advocating an end to this type of relations. . . . We see in certain sectors examples of widespread demagogy. Were these events to negatively evolve, it would have very damaging repercussions for the supplies our country receives and our country's economy.

Castro then urged the nation "to study what to do if economic relations with those former socialist countries continue to deteriorate and if one day there are serious problems in the U.S.S.R . . ."[20]

Cuba's leaders were doing just that. As socialism crumbled, they came forward with a plan to survive, pick up the pieces and resume development. Cuba's strategy, dubbed the "Special Period in Peacetime," has three stages, geared to a 30, 50 and 70 percent cut in oil supplies. The first phase took effect in late 1990, as Cuba scrambled to shift its trade from East to West and South, and restructure its economy; the second during the third quarter of 1991 and the last phase, in 1992. Each phase combined an orderly reduction of traditional consumption with alternatives where possible and sacrifice where not. The best known example; before the crisis 71 percent of Havana's bus riders were under 30 years old, the majority students going to and from school. A drastic reduction of public transportation has gone hand-in-hand with bicycle sales to students and young workers, cushioning the impact of urban transit cuts.

In March, 1990, Cuba's key workplaces, from ports to steel plants, staged a one-day dress rehearsal to cut energy use within the Special Period. The rehearsals would be staged throughout the year, both to prepare people for the hard times ahead and to test new energy-saving ideas as they emerged from workers and management. Hand-pulled carts replaced fork lifts; workers loaded ships by hand; office workers opened the blinds and windows as they turned off lights and air conditioners; cafeterias used wood and charcoal to fire stoves; and workers mapped out ways to keep the assembly lines rolling with one less blast furnace.

On August 29, 1990, the Cuban government announced the first of a series of emergency measures to cope with the economic impact of socialist Europe's fall. They included an unspecified cut in gas and diesel fuel to all state enterprises, as well as a 50 percent cut in the gasoline ration for government vehicles. Gasoline for private car owners, already rationed, was cut by 30 percent, and all households were ordered to reduce electricity consumption by 10 percent or face a 3-day cutoff. Community volunteers, working with the power company and local government, fanned out to every home, helping residents draw up energy-saving plans and determining on a case-by-case basis the households that needed a little extra.

Most Cubans worked a rotating 5-day 40-hour, then 6-day 48-hour, workweek. The government announced that wherever possible the Saturday workday would be phased out with no loss in pay. Investments would also be cut with ever-diminishing resources going only to "the most important economic and social development programs." Many secondary projects had to be scrapped, and cement and other building materials production reduced.[21]

Each economic and service unit, every household, city block, municipality and province began adopting energy-saving measures. Long distance shipping was transferred from trucks to trains and barges; work shifts were reorganized to cut demand at peak hours when less fuel-efficient generators went into use; public transit was cut and reorganized and finally a number of factories were shut down.[22]

The second emergency decree descended on September 25, 1990. Shipments of Soviet newsprint and materials for the national printing industry were delayed, paralyzing Cuba's two paper plants. The government took action before remaining supplies dried up. Within a week, only one of Cuba's three national dailies, the Party's *Granma*, and 14 regional newspapers, remained in circulation. Two national dailies, the trade union's *Trabajadores* and *Juventud Rebelde*, geared to young people, switched to weekly editions. *Granma's* price was raised from 10 cents to 20 cents, *Trabajadores* from 10 to 15 cents and *Juventud Rebelde* from 10 to 20, while the cost of provincial papers rose from 5 to 10 cents. Cuba's most popular weekly magazine, *Bohemia*, would still appear on the stands, but slimmed down. Dozens of other magazines, journals and specialized publications—like the Armed Forces *Bastion* newspaper—went out of circulation.[23]

The Cuban government issued its third emergency decree on September 27, 1990, to deal with increasing shortages of consumer goods and to prepare for 1991, when Cuba would have to purchase such goods from Eastern Europe, the USSR, or elsewhere with hard currency and at world market prices.

The basic family basket, made up of 36 food and household products, would remain on the ration and be sold at subsidized prices. Almost all other light consumer goods and processed food products, previously sold off-ration in state-run stores, would be put back on ration for equitable distribution when available. Two months later, all state-run off-ration food stores closed down as Cuba instituted rationing for all foods, with the exception of fruits and vegetables.

The government also announced that most home appliances, all imported from the USSR and Eastern Europe, or built with parts and materials from those countries, would completely disappear from the shelves in 1991. All refrigerators, washing machines, fans, air conditioners, and televisions currently in stock would go to health care facilities, childcare centers, senior citizen homes and other collective services.[24]

On November 24, 1990, plans were announced to cope with rising unemployment as factory shifts were cut and the first of many plants and offices were closed. The measures guaranteed laid-off workers full pay for one month and 60 percent thereafter until rehired. Workers and their families would continue to be cushioned by Cuba's free social services and remain fully covered by social security.

The new law stated that if efforts to find an employee a job in the same company or job category failed, she or he could be offered any other work available in the same province but with no cut in pay. Provided that there were no health, personal, or transport problems, the worker had to accept the job or lose the unemployment benefits. In either case, the worker kept re-call rights at the original workplace.[25]

The government also established a series of guarantees for recent graduates facing rising national unemployment. Every municipality would keep lists of recent graduates in various fields. While waiting for their first job, graduates would be paid a monthly 75-peso stipend. The government would encourage unemployed college graduates to work for advanced degrees, pursue other studies, or take what work was available. When a graduate accepted employment outside his/her field, he/she would be guaranteed a salary equal to that in his/her chosen career.[26]

By early 1991 authorities had reorganized the island's huge pharmacy network. Imported medications were now sold only through hospitals to those who absolutely had to have them, while tight controls were placed on the sale of all other medications to stop hoarding and black marketing.

The continued deterioration of Cuban-Soviet trade during 1991 and the final breakup of the USSR prompted even more drastic measures in 1992. On December 16, 1991, the government announced that oil shipments from the former USSR had dropped dramatically since September and that the country was running on less than half the fuel consumed just two years earlier. The statement applauded the public efforts in 1991, reporting state energy consumption dropped 19 percent and that household consumption, which had risen at an annual rate of six percent, had dropped by 3.5 percent despite the addition of tens of thousands of units to the energy grid. Yet, faced with the prospect of even worse trade relations with Cuba's former allies, it cautioned that more cuts were on the way.

The government announced new unspecified shutdowns and layoffs, especially in light and secondary industries, transportation, construction and the central ministries and agencies. The number of state-run stores were reduced and the national distribution system streamlined. TV broadcasts were diminished to five hours on weekdays, nine on Saturdays and fourteen on Sundays. A number of movie theaters closed, air conditioning was turned off except where absolutely necessary; evening sports events cancelled and street lighting reduced; and everyone was urged to use natural light whenever possible. Each province and municipality, assigned a daily electricity quota, received a stern warning that any excess one day would be met with power outages the next. Consumers using over 150 kilowatt hours per month were instructed to reduce the excess by 50 percent, effective immediately.

Dramatic new cuts in gasoline consumption also went into effect. Public transportation—reorganized again—was cut in half; all state owned taxis were pulled off the streets except those servicing hospitals, funeral homes, airports, train stations and bus depots; state contracting of private trucks and other vehicles was halted; extra gas rations to private truck and taxi owners dried up; the gas ration for private car owners and government vehicles was reduced another 30 percent and the extra ration for professionals by 70 percent.[27]

CREATIVE CONSERVATION

Pinar del Río's San Cristobal municipality borders Havana province. Its 550 square miles stretch from sugarcane-covered flatlands to family doctor-covered mountains where infant mortality stood at an astonishing 0 per 1,000 live births from 1988 through 1990.

San Cristobal's 63,000 residents were asked in the early 1980s to develop plans to withstand a naval blockade of the Island and war with the United States. Among their goals: to become as self-sufficient as possible in everything from food and energy to medicine. With the deepening crisis of European socialism, the pilot project's framework changed—to learning how to survive and develop if trade with the socialist camp collapsed.

By 1989, San Cristobal had become a model for the entire country. In an interview, Juan Carlos Santos, head of San Cristobal's local government, explained that as early as 1982, the government asked local residents to brainstorm on how to save resources and substitute imports. A systematic study began of the resources on hand—from labor power, land, wind power and food to machines and health care.

"In the end, we came up with 500 measures that have systematically been put into practice," Mayor Santos told me.

"Our first priority is to make sure we have enough food and a reserve to share with others. Today, every workplace, town and even home tends a garden and, wherever possible, raises poultry and livestock. We've even learned to bake bread and pizza using flour from yuka and sweet potato.

"Our second priority, really on par with our first, is developing alternative energy sources. Right now, we can cover 60 percent of our energy needs in an emergency. We are replacing gas and diesel fuel with charcoal, windmills, solar energy and hydraulic power. We know how to put our entire labor force to work under virtually any circumstance."

At San Cristobal's November 30th Sugar Complex, energy is no problem. The complex was the first built by Cuba alone, and is actually a huge, fully automated cluster of factories that transform cane into sugar and its numerous derivatives and by-products.

Like the rest of Cuba's 156 sugar complexes, the operation runs on cane refuse. But unlike Cuba's other mills, during the 1989–1990 harvest, many of its trucks and tractors operated with a homemade system that turned charcoal made from wood, cane and other plant life into a gas that replaced fossil fuel in combustion engines.

Until 1988, the complex fed its 5,000 workers by drawing on the state and provincial food supply. Now workers feed themselves and contribute to San Cristobal's food supply. For the last three years the complex has developed its own agricultural resources side-by-side with the sugarcane. Meat and fish production are based on a natural, home-grown feeding chain, beginning with animal feed based on cane. For example, the pigs (it now produces 40 tons of pork a year) eat the sugar-based feed. Their waste is processed into gas, and into pellets fed to ducks and fish being raised on and in a man-made lake. The ducks' waste also helps nourish the schools of catfish, carp and bass. The sugar complex's herd of cattle provides ample milk for the workers, while fields of vegetables, fruits and spices add variety and nutritional value that their hot lunches lacked before. In 1990, the complex supplied produce to the nearby town of Tico-Taco, and in 1991, meat and fish.

Pinar del Río's Comandante Piñares Teaching Hospital is also located in San Cristobal. The hospital's Director, Dr. José Almeida Corrente, explained how his staff went to work to find alternatives for the Special Period or war. The dozens of innovations added up to a 10 percent budget savings for the 500-bed hospital. These included sutures that Almeida insisted were as good as imported ones; hospital-grown herbal medicines that had replaced 39 regular medications; and acupuncture, with needles made at the hospital. As of May 1990, over 800 patients had been successfully treated with the method taught to the Cubans by Chinese and Vietnamese specialists. Acupuncture had been used as an anesthetic in 220 minor operations and 16 major ones. Hospital staff had also designed and built a complete set of physical therapy equipment, a hand-run generator employing a bicycle wheel that also separated plasma from blood, as well as manual and solar-powered sterilizers. Dr. Almeida gave me a tour of the staff-tended vegetable garden, and plots of rice and beans.

The José Martí farm cooperative's main crop is sugar, but by 1990, its 59 members and their families were harvesting enough food to feed themselves and ship extra beans, rice, meat and fish to market. Engineer David Morales said the coop, since its founding in 1982, always worked towards food self-sufficiency. However, in 1989, the pace accelerated and new scientific techniques were introduced. Livestock are fed on a combination of animal waste, cane and vegetable refuse. Rabbits are raised in industrial quantities and their waste helps nourish worms which in turn help feed the rabbits and produce all the top soil the cooperative can use.

Thirty-year-old Juan Carlos, director of San Cristobal's Humberto Nuñez State Farm, explained how the management council and its 400-strong labor force met in 1988 to plan for the coming crisis. "The radical ideas introduced raised more than a few skeptical eyebrows," he said, "but today everyone is a believer." The farm's irrigation pumps once accounted for 40 percent of all energy consumption; they now run on charcoal from the farm's own plant that produces 15,000 sacks a year. The tractors run on a mixture of fuel, water and chemicals that cuts gas consumption by over 80 percent. The ten trucks that once brought snacks, ice water and lunch to workers in the fields have been replaced by horse-drawn canteens. Oxen have replaced the 21 tractors that transported produce to the state collection center. Five windmills are in operation. The farm also uses worms to produce 10,000 tons of top soil annually. A farm laboratory, developing organic substitutes for pesticides, already had replaced 30 tons of imported chemicals. The farm branched out to raise livestock. Pigs are fed with waste materials and cane grown on the farm; their waste helps fuel a generator that produces 67 kilowatts of electricity a day. Fish from a nearby reservoir are processed on the farm, and the remains are turned into flour for animal feed. The farm is raising everything from ducks, geese and turkeys to sheep, hogs and deer with the aim of developing good breeders to send to Pinar Del Río's 110 defense zones.

STRATEGY FOR SURVIVAL

In 1991, and 1992, the people of San Cristobal and all of Cuba drastically tightened their belts, while scrambling to develop local alternatives for vanishing resources. World events left them no choice. However, far from rebelling, they rose to the challenge. There are many reasons why Los Angeles, California, *not* Havana or Santiago, exploded in 1992. First, Cubans know the hard times are equally shouldered—if anything, they cut deeper for those who are better off. Despite the sacrifices, every Cuban, and most importantly the children and the elderly, continue to have enough to eat, guaranteed health care, a decent and equal education. And people hold on to the hope for a better future, joining in the brain-storming and government programs to brave the crisis.

The Special Period prioritizes food, education and medical care, while the country radically retools its trade, development plans and labor force. By 1992, Cuban trade had already shifted dramatically from East to West and South. In 1988, Cuba's trade with the West totaled 1.7 billion dollars, some 953 million dollars of that in imports, and about 800 million in exports. By 1992, Cuba's trade with the West had jumped over 300 percent to 6.5 billion dollars. Western imports accounted for four billion of that sum, and Cuban exports for some 2.5 billion. At the same time Cuba strove to replace Soviet aid and investment with Western investment in the form of Joint Ventures. Over 60 joint ventures were in operation on the island by 1992, and another 200 under study.[28]

The bulk of Cuba's resources and foreign investments are being directed into three crash development programs: agriculture, biotechnology products (in particular, pharmaceuticals), and tourism. These programs, based on Cuba's natural resources and its highly educated work force, profess two goals: (1) to restructure Cuba's trade, economy and labor force so that the country can resume development in a completely changed international environment; (2) to rapidly generate the hard currency needed to survive in the meantime.

AGRICULTURE

As detailed in Chapter 5, soil study, crash waterworks projects, new irrigation and drainage systems, research and development, improved planning and management-labor relations all converged by 1989 into the National Food Program. However, chronic labor shortages remained as the economic crisis hit. Many crops demand huge amounts of labor and tend to respond best to regular care by farmers who know the land and climate and are flexible in their work habits. Vegetables and root crops perish quickly if not harvested, carefully stored or brought quickly to market. Cuban experts state that as much as half the island's vegetable and root crop was lost each year due to the lack of labor power to tend them and insure timely harvests. The loss was compounded by poor handling and distribution.

The capital and Havana Province—burdened by growing numbers of consumers and shrinking numbers of field hands—provides the clearest example of the problem and what is being done to solve it. In Havana province, 100,000 acres were dedicated to vegetable production in 1990, with eight state farms responsible for 70,000 acres and private cooperatives and individual farms the rest. Manual labor on the state farms had dwindled to just 1,900 people! The slack was somewhat picked up through periodic mobilizations and by high school students, who put in a few hours work a day, but were absent from June through August when heat and rain turned the fields into steamy havens for weeds and pests, cutting yields by as much as 75 percent.[29]

As a temporary solution to the problem, in 1990 Havana's microbrigades shifted most of their efforts from urban construction to building 50 campsites on Havana Province's eight state vegetable farms. Starting in July, Havana residents began putting in two-week volunteer stints in the fields, living in wood-frame campsite dorms. By 1991 some 20,000 people were in the fields at any given moment, collecting their regular salaries while working to insure there was food on every table during the Special Period. The effort quickly took on a life and spirit similar to the microbrigade movement it largely replaced, directly involving city dwellers in the struggle to feed themselves, their families and friends.[30]

There was no shortage of Havana residents willing to wear the "campesino's" straw hat at two week intervals. Just about every Havana resident I knew volunteered at least once that first year. They returned with sore muscles, but somehow invigorated, more appreciative of what it takes to get food on the table, and ready to go back for more. Many boasted they out-performed regular farm workers. Its important to note that volunteers ranged from ordinary people to Cuba's top stars and political figures. Television anchors, Party leaders, salsa musicians and parliamentarians seeded and weeded with the best of them. One friend's father, a deputy foreign minister, had gone not once but twice into the fields and was preparing yet another stint when I left the island. After the 1991 Pan American Games, Cuba's many medal winners had their turn in the fields before taking well-deserved vacations.

Havana's emergency agriculture program calls for building 40 communities on Havana province's eight state vegetable farms, which will then be broken down into smaller more manageable enterprises. 32 contingent brigades with 10,000 volunteers went to work building the towns and developing key crops, in particular bananas. The communities will have all the trappings which, when combined with improved working conditions and higher wages, are expected to attract a permanent agricultural labor force.[31]

In 1989 Havana Province produced three million tons of vegetables. The 1990–1991 crop came in at close to four million, and the 1991–1992 crop looked like it would top five million tons. The goal is to reach 7.5 million tons, satisfying demand in the Capital and surrounding Havana Province.[32] Similar programs are underway throughout Cuba involving as many as two million people. For example, Camagüey Province reported that an additional 200,000 residents had been mobilized in 1991 for agricultural work. They ranged from people who volunteered for two weeks to a month, to members of new agricultural contingents and city residents working urban gardens.[33]

Cuba also mobilized the entire population in an effort much like the victory gardens of World War II. The Agricultural Ministry, Academy of Sciences, labor movement and other national mass organizations have managed to turn just about every available space into vegetable gardens and animal pens.

Las Tunas Province is the model being followed by the rest of the nation. In 1989, the provincial government surveyed every inch of available land surrounding workplaces, schools, service centers and homes. Plans were drawn up to turn the unused land, from patios and parks to roofs and landfills, into gardens and livestock producers. A special manual in one hand, seeds and minerals in the other, Las Tunas residents set to work. 1990 saw the victory gardens produce 2000 metric tons of vegetables and roots and in 1991, 4000 tons. The province reported that of 99,000 homes with the potential to grow food, 91,000 were doing so, as were all municipalities, work centers, schools, etc.[34]

Cuba's Committees in Defense of the Revolution reported at the end of 1991 that there were 796,232 victory gardens across the country; 614,000 gardens were attached to homes and the remainder work centers, schools, etc.[35] Havana lagged behind the nation. City officials estimated that there were 15,000 large parcels of land, amounting to over 7,100 acres, that could go to seed. Forty-one percent was already in production. Seeds and small garden tools were being distributed en masse, with over 100,000 patios already boasting edible greens.[36] Across the island people were given the go-ahead to consume, barter or sell whatever they produced at home. The popular movement not only supplemented family meals and workers' lunch rooms; it helped free up the state system to insure the elderly, the sick in hospitals, and children in school received an adequate diet, free of charge.

BIOTECHNOLOGY

Cuba is already considered the Third World leader in genetic engineering: Cuban scientists have produced over 200 interferons and over 170 other products using the advanced scientific technique. Unique Cuban medications and treatments include the world's first vaccine against meningitis-B; a sugar-based anti-cholesterol drug called PPG that is considered the best in the world; streptokinase, a medication with no side effects for heart attack victims; the epidermal growth factor, one of the most effective burn medications and skin regenerators ever discovered; and the world's first effective treatments for vertiligo and retinitis pigmentosa.

Cuban pharmaceuticals and advanced medical treatment go first to Cubans free of charge. The country's children were the first and only children in the world to be immunized against meningitis-B. At the same time Cuban treatments and medications promise to become big export earners. By 1992, Cuba had also acquired several foreign partners for manufacture and sale in the field, a move aimed at helping the new products break into an otherwise monopoly-dominated world pharmaceutical market.

TOURISM

Tourism represents the third pillar of Cuba's plan to pull out of the crisis. The mafia-run tourism of pre-revolutionary Cuba left such bitter memories that tourism virtually ceased through the 1970s. The early 1980s witnessed an important debate within the Cuban Communist Party over whether to re-introduce tourism on the island, and even gambling on some of its beautiful keys. Tourism was given the green light; but proposals to include gambling were resoundingly defeated.

Today, tourism development is off and running. The largest areas of expansion are at Cuba's world-famous Veradero beach; on a number of its truly exquisite virgin keys; in Havana and Santiago; and to a lesser degree, in the mountains and wildlife preserves.

When I first arrived in Cuba in 1984, international tourism earned the island $80 million. By 1991, that figure had climbed to $400 million, with Cubans reaching for the billion-dollar mark by 1995. With its relatively short turn-around on investment, the idea is for tourism to help pay for fuel, medicines and other urgently-needed essentials. The industry is expected to create some 250,000 relatively high quality jobs for Cuban young people, encourage local production and earn the island new friends as tourists come in contact with the Cubans' undisputed hospitality.[37]

As 1991 came to a close, it appeared Cuba's strategy for survival was working. To be sure, the country still faced the rigors of 1992, when the full impact of the collapse of the Soviet Union would be felt and the United States would step up its efforts to block economic development. However, the country remained at peace; there were no serious social disturbances; and Cuba's kids—and as a matter of fact the entire population—remained better fed, clothed, educated and cared for than any other in Latin America. The country was on all but a war footing, the entire population mobilized to meet the challenges ahead. The government announced projects valued at 1.7 billion pesos had been completed in 1991. They included 27 reservoirs and canals, with a 800 million cubic meter capacity; 4,000 new tourist quarters and the basic projects to service them; a major biotechnology and pharmaceutical plant; and dozens of lesser economic projects. Work was proceeding on a new nickel refinery in Holguin's Moa district, the expansion of Havana Province's Antillana steelworks and the new Las Tunas metal works; development and production of a Cuban engine and the search for oil deposits off Cuba's coast. Foreign investors were being attracted, with over 60 deals signed and many more were in the works. Despite the crisis, Cubans entered 1992 with 400 more family doctor home-offices, 14 new childcare centers, one new special school, 1500 more housing units and with seven of their hospitals expanded and remodeled. More defense fortifications were built than during any year since the revolution. Cuba's infant mortality rate and life expectancy remained stable, and light years ahead of the rest of the Third World.[38]

Chapter Nine:

THE UNITED STATES AND CUBA— CRUEL AND UNUSUAL PUNISHMENT

Bad Dreams

I'm sitting on my balcony 13 flights up, looking out over Havana Bay towards Florida, just 90 miles away. I'm hammering away on my laptop, racing the deadline for a story on the latest crisis in U.S.–Cuban relations. Suddenly, without warning, waves of U.S. fighter planes appear on the horizon and in seconds are overhead. The familiar air raid sirens are already blaring as the first cruise missiles whiz by and nail their targets. Explosions, fire and smoke erupt all around me. A missile slams into the 28th floor of my building, which also houses a radar station. I dive for cover and become nauseous thinking of my daughter and the other 220 children caught in her childcare center now seven long blocks away. My wife is somewhere on the street. I'm pinned down as the roar of war continues all around me. A few hours later, I peer out over the bay to see hundreds of landing craft and helicopters coming my way. The GI's are landing to mop up Havana. Machine gun fire erupts in my building. My door bursts open to reveal three fear-crazed soldiers. "Don't shoot!" I shout. The invasion of Cuba has begun. What took Cubans 30 long hard years to build is being turned into a terrifying mangle of fire, steel and screams. Cuba's independence—and with it, Latin America's—hangs in the balance.

By the time I left Cuba in April of 1991, I was having fantasies like this one—fantasies most Cubans have long since learned to live with.

Spend some time in Cuba and you begin to think you are living in a World War II movie. There are regular air raid drills, mock attacks complete with MIGs, helicopters, ships, tanks and smoke bombs. People can be seen building bomb shelters. Mothers and their children, the elderly, teachers and students, regularly practice scrambling for those shelters and the Red Cross and community volunteers bind up imaginary wounds.

I arrived in Cuba just months after the Grenada invasion. The Cubans believed they might be next in line for a dose of U.S. "democracy and human rights," a la invasion and occupation. Talk inside the Communist Party and on the street swirled around a recent speech by Fidel Castro to the Central Committee, detailing a defense strategy that would relinquish the capital in order to hold the rest of the country—and eventually win.

There is no stranger feeling than to live among people threatened by your own government, preparing to die defending their families and independence from your own country's troops. That is especially the case when you become convinced there is no justifiable reason for such a hostile policy, except to insure that no other small nation dares to buck the powers-that-be in Washington and on Wall Street. I would watch defense preparations from my balcony or walk the streets amidst all the noise and commotion, and wonder if anyone back in the United States understood what our government was doing to these fine people, forcing an entire nation to constantly prepare to defend itself from every possible kind of attack—terrorizing a population of over ten million people while trying to starve them into submission. I learned quickly that the Cubans were still very much under siege. Their civil defense preparations in Havana were just the tip of an iceberg. Hundreds of thousands of people in the countryside were preparing safe zones for children and the elderly, as the army mapped out theaters of operation.

As the months passed, I noticed Cuba took extraordinary security precautions at its agricultural and other scientific centers, on its state farms, at power plants and other important "economic targets." I was told time and again about the biological warfare Washington had waged against Cuban agriculture. I learned about African Swine Fever, which appeared in Cuba—and for the first time in the Western Hemisphere—in May of 1971. The U.S. press reported in 1977 that an intelligence source had confessed he transferred swine fever germs from Fort Gulich in Panama to Miami-based Cuban contras just before the epidemic broke out. There was also tobacco's blue mold and a host of other plagues that struck the island's key crops and livestock in the 1970s and early 1980s.[1]

Most disturbing to me was the story of my friend Marta, a 40-year-old Cuban journalist who confided to me that she would need specialized medical care for the rest of her life. Marta was one of 344,230 Cubans hit by the hemorrhagic dengue epidemic in 1981. She lived, but like many others, suffered permanent liver damage. Dengue, carried by mosquitos, appeared on the same day at both ends of the island. The United States openly blocked Cuba's first efforts to purchase fumigators and chemicals to control dengue's spread. At the end of the epidemic, 158 people—including 101 children—were dead.

Cuban authorities, including top scientists and public health officials, insist the CIA was responsible for the dengue epidemic. They point to extensive CIA research into dengue, revealed during congressional hearings in the 1970s, the fact that it appeared at two different points on the island the same day, and that it was the first outbreak of the disease in Cuban history. The Cubans also trace five separate outbreaks of hemorrhagic conjunctivitis (in the late 1970s and early 1980s) to the CIA. "Omega 7" leader Eduardo Arocena, on trial for drug trafficking in 1984, confirmed the Cubans' suspicions. He testified that he personally transferred dengue germs to Cuba in 1980 . . .[2]

I'll never forget my 1990 interview with Academy of Sciences Vice President, Dr. Ismael Clark, in charge of environmental protection and public health. For some four hours, Clark described pollution control efforts on the island. "What outside environmental dangers do you face?" I asked, thinking about our world's deteriorating ozone layer and ocean dumping of hazardous wastes. But Clark, becoming visibly agitated, responded that the biggest outside environmental threat came from the United States' biological warfare against the country. He described various outbreaks of disease ranging from swine flu to dengue. Clark called in his secretary and within minutes had spread a complicated chart on his desk. He traced the various plagues and epidemics that hit Cuba in the '70s and '80s and insisted Cuba had proof that the CIA was behind many of them. Clark expressed his frustration that the international community did not take such charges seriously enough.

The linchpin of U.S. efforts to destroy Cuban socialism and independence is the economic embargo, the longest such U.S. effort against another country in history. Far from the simple ban on doing U.S. business with the island, the embargo is actually a global economic war unleashed against Cuba by Washington. There is a virtual army of U.S. agents at work day and night around the world with the single objective of disrupting free trade with Cuba and destroying the island's economy.

The U.S. Treasury's Office of Foreign Assets Control has the job, with the help of the State Department, the CIA and other U.S. intelligence agencies, of policing the embargo against Cuba, and in 1991, Congress gave the office more money than ever. Its job: to make sure there isn't a gram of Cuban nickel in Japanese steel imported by U.S. companies; to stop a Swedish firm from selling Cuba a piece of medical equipment destined for a children's heart center, on the grounds that it contained a filter patented in the USA; to stop U.S. citizens from traveling to Cuba; to veto the export to Cuba from Mexico of a pesticide vital in halting the dengue epidemic.[3]

Back in 1987, a high-ranking Cuban intelligence officer, Major Florentino Aspillaga, defected to the United States. That forced Cuba to surface 32 of its double agents who had infiltrated the CIA. Ship captains, truck drivers, doctors, scientists, government officials, air traffic controllers—all had contacted the Cuban government as soon as the CIA contacted them. For decades most of the CIA's operatives inside Cuba actually worked for Cuban intelligence.

The Cuban double agents told their story in a 13-part series on Cuban television. The nation, spellbound, stopped to watch each episode. The agents' testimony was alternated with hidden-camera video footage that over the years had caught 89 U.S. diplomats "red-handed" as they carried out covert operations in Cuba. They were hiding transmitters and cash, mapping out Fidel Castro's routes to work, posing as foreign scientists to visit research centers, obtaining Cuban tobacco leaves resistant to blue mold. I heard taped conversations with CIA officials asking for the details of hemorrhagic conjunctivitis's impact on the country before, during and after one epidemic. Cuban double agents were ordered to obtain the specifics of Fidel Castro's flights, and other inside information on the Cuban economy. The series documented repeated CIA efforts to sabotage Cuban trade and develop "dissident" and "human rights" organizations on the island.

The programs (available from Cuban television), left no doubt in my mind that a massive U.S. covert war was being waged by the United States against Cuba, even before the fall of socialist Europe. The never-ending assault included biological warfare, economic sabotage, new plans to assassinate Cuba's leaders, a desperate search for anyone willing to work for the United States in exchange for the chance to live a comfortable life in Miami. Incredibly, what should have been the CIA scandal of the decade, and one of the most important of the century, was completely blacked out by the U.S. media.[4]

LOW INTENSITY CONFLICT (1990—1991)

"The political fortune tellers inside the Washington Beltway and on Miami's Calle Ocho have declared that Fidel Castro and the Cuban revolution are about to hit the wastebasket of history," wrote Saul Landau, an American scholar on Cuban affairs, in the June 25, 1990, edition of *The Nation*. "John McLaughlin confidently signs off on one of his Sunday TV shows in May with the assertion that 'Castro is out by Christmas.' Vice President Dan Quayle confidently announces that 'Cuba is the last real problem in our hemisphere' (poverty, debt, drugs are not real?) Margaret Tutwiler, speaking for the State Department after the Nicaraguan elections, and with the invasion of Panama still fresh in the memory, declares that 'it's two down and one to go.' Cuba is regularly referred to as 'the last domino.'"

Miami exiles are currently calculating their increased worth, expecting shortly to reclaim their expropriated property, while Florida Governor Bob Martínez, combining machismo with chutzpa, has set up a commission to study the impact of Cuba's collapse on Florida. Some of the paunchy veterans of the 1961 Bay of Pigs invasion have picked up their rusty rifles to train for another assault; as in the past, U.S. police agencies are turning a blind eye to their activities.[5]

Months earlier, the 1989 tripartite agreement ending South African attacks on Angola, making way for Namibian independence and establishing a timetable for a Cuban withdrawal from Angola, seemed to signal that better Cuban-U.S. relations were on the horizon. Cuban officials I talked with at the Foreign Ministry and the Cuban Party's Central Committee were moderately optimistic that President Bush, like Nixon with China, would neutralize reactionary forces in the Cuban American community and improve relations. José A. Arbesú, who played a key role in the tripartite negotiations, was named head of the Cuban Interests Section in Washington, joining another top Cuban negotiator in the United States, Deputy Foreign Minister Ricardo Alarcón, who returned to the UN ambassadorship as Cuba assumed a two-year stretch on the Security Council. Cuba seemed ready to talk. But by April 1992, Abesú was back in Havana heading up American Affairs at the Central Committee. Alarcón, named Cuba's new Foreign Minister, returned to Havana in June. A golden opportunity for improved relations had passed.

Cuban Vice President and Party Political Bureau member, Carlos Rafael Rodríguez, summed up what happened.

We are at a difficult moment in the Revolution. A moment in which part of those mentally colonized Cubans who live in the United States think the Cuban revolution is going to collapse. The United States has come to believe that. I can tell you that when the meetings about Africa were held, attended by both a Cuban and U.S. delegation, the attitude of the Cuban delegation during the discussions demonstrated to the U.S. representatives that, first of all, we were not an instrument of the Soviet Union, that we have our own policies. Secondly, that we were capable of holding talks based on a rational policy. They began to talk about some of the problems in relations between the United States and Cuba. This was just before the collapse of socialism in Europe. Then all those people began to change their points of view, and began to think that the collapse of socialism in Europe would also bring about the collapse of socialism in Cuba.[6]

Indeed, by 1990—and despite Mikhail Gorbachev's call for world peace, understanding, tolerance of differences and non-intervention in others' internal affairs—it became clear that Washington had no intention of ending its 30-year war against Cuba. Quite the contrary! The United States, with Cuba more vulnerable than ever, began what it believed would be its final assault on the fiercely independent island.

SETTING THE STAGE

In the 1960s the United States rationalized its efforts to retake Cuba by charging the island posed a subversive threat to Latin America and the Caribbean. In the 1970s and 1980s Washington told the world and the U.S. public that Cuba, a mere appendage of the Soviet Union, posed a direct threat to the United States. Today, Cuba enjoys normal relations with just about every Latin American and Caribbean government, and the Soviet Union no longer exists. Clearly a new U.S. rationale is in order. That rationale is the fight for democracy, human rights and to save the Cuban people from economic hardship.

Perhaps the most dastardly aspect of low intensity conflict is that it is fought under the banner of "democracy and human rights" even while creating conditions that force the target government to limit both. No country, under siege from as powerful a country as the United States, could afford the liberties Washington is demanding today of Cuba. And much of the economic hardship Cubans are enduring today is the result of the tightening noose of the U.S. blockade. Nevertheless, Washington, combining rhetoric, bribes and intimidation, is intent on gaining international backing for its final offensive against the island.

The United States zeroed in on Cuba at the 1990 United Nations Human Rights Commission's yearly meeting in Geneva. For five years, the U.S. had tried to divert the Commission's attention away from gross human rights abuses in apartheid South Africa, death squad El Salvador, U.S.-backed contra terror in Nicaragua, ongoing extra-legal slaughters in Haiti, Colombia and Guatamala, Israel's brutal suppression of the Palestinians and Pinochet's Chile—and instead rivet them on Cuba, with an infinitely better human rights record than these U.S. allies, albeit not a perfect one. Washington had only succeeded in irritating the UN body. Then, as one source observed, new-found U.S.

allies—Hungary, Bulgaria, Poland and Czechoslovakia—"sold their integrity for 30 pieces of silver" when they tipped the scales to push through a U.S.-written anti-Cuba resolution on March 6, 1990. The resolution called for a special investigation of Cuba.

The Cuban media always gave significant coverage to the annual Geneva human rights hearings, and 1990 was no exception. The Cuban public followed events in Geneva as they unfolded, then listened to their President's assessment during a nationally televised speech March 8, 1990, at the 5th Congress of the Cuban Women's Federation.

Castro urged his people to focus on the message the vote sent: the first clear and open political break in Eastern Europe's 30-year alliance with the Third World's struggle for independence and social justice.

"You know that we've been waging battles in Geneva year after year to oppose U.S. attempts at securing some type of resolution against us," Castro began. "Those battles were waged in spite of the huge economic and political pressures exerted by the United States, backed unanimously by the NATO countries and the few Third World countries whose strings are pulled like puppets."

Castro explained that whenever the UN voted by secret ballot, Cuba came out on top. He cited Cuba's 1989 election to the UN Security Council by the largest number of votes ever on record (145 out of a possible 159) and Cuba's 1988 election to the UN Human Rights Commission itself. But, he noted, all Commission votes are public.

Open balloting is very difficult for us, because other countries must openly confront the United States and they depend on the U.S. for World Bank credits, Inter-American bank loans, International Monetary Fund credits— institutions dominated by the United States. So, a large number of countries abstain, and some are forced to vote against us . . .

Naturally this year's U.S. motion was co-sponsored by several NATO countries . . . But it was also co-sponsored, comrades, by Poland and Czechoslovakia, which until a few months ago belonged to the socialist camp; they co-sponsored with a government that had just invaded Panama and with the U.S.-installed Panamanian government . . .

Castro exclaimed:

This is the negation of everything that has been progressive in the world, the negation of all justice in the world. For countries which until yesterday were allegedly socialist to do this now along with the U.S. imperialists . . .

The revolutionary movement always distinguished itself for its principled, brave, firm position against all colonialism, neocolonialism and imperialism. What decency remains in those countries? What is left of socialism? What is left of the socialist community? What can be left with this repugnant behavior?[7]

PSYCHOLOGICAL WARFARE

Meanwhile, the United States was accelerating its preparations to put TV Martí on the air, and Cuba its preparations to knock it off. To the Cubans, the TV station was part of that sophisticated U.S. weapon known as psychological warfare, in turn part of Washington's arsenal for "low intensity conflict."

"The signal will first be relayed from TV studios in Washington to a ground transmitter, which will then shoot the signal up to a satellite," explained engineer Carlos Martínez, in 1990 Cuba's Communications Minister. "The satellite will beam the signal back down to another ground transmitter on Cudjoe Key, off the Florida coast. It will relay the signal to a powerful 10,000-watt TV transmitter located in the gondola of an aerostatic blimp 3,000 meters over the U.S. military base there. The signal will then be beamed to Cuba."

Martínez, well before TV Martí went on the air, was explaining to a Cuban prime-time TV audience the technicalities of the Spanish-language station the Bush administration and the CIA hoped would allow them to enter every Cuban's home, "to occupy one or more of our channels," as Martínez put it.[8]

TV Martí, or "No Se TeVe" (The TV you don't see) as Cubans came to call it, made its debut on Tuesday, March 27, 1990, at 1:45 in the morning. Its signal, aimed at Havana and other western provinces, was strong for 10 minutes before Cuban jamming dissolved "Good Morning Havana" into a series of scratchy lines and sounds. A Cuban government statement issued a few hours later termed TV Martí "a grave violation of Cuban sovereignty and unprecedented abuse of radio and TV signals." It noted that the broadcast was transmitted on channels duly assigned to Cuba for domestic television, violating international telecommunications regulations.

"Cuba has warned that these transmissions could form part of a larger maneuver," read the statement, "and that the United States could be looking for a pretext to launch a military aggression (against Cuba)." Havana stressed that the problem with TV Martí was not its content, but that it was an act of open intervention into the country's internal affairs.[9]

Cuba let it be known it might respond with an AM radio broadcast to the United States; Washington threatened to retaliate by bombing Cuba's transmitters. Washington chose to air its show from 3:45 to

6:45 a.m., while Havana spent $900 a day jamming the signal and knocked the broadcasts of its five-year-old sibling, Radio Martí off the AM band for good measure. (It still can be heard on the short wave radios owned by almost every Cuban household.)[10]

The United Nations-affiliated International Telecommunications Union (ITU), which regulates the international use of radio and Television, ruled twice that the height and range of TV Martí's antenna was "much greater than normal" and "not compatible with the standard land practices on VHF and UHF bands." The ITU stated TV Martí "is operating in violation of article 158 of the ITU Convention" and other rules as well. It's call to Washington to shut down TV Martí was ignored by both the Bush administration and Congress.[11]

The TV Martí project sparked serious disputes among Cubans living in the United States. Radio Martí's director, Ernesto Betancourt, resigned in March, 1990, charging that the ultra-right Cuban American National Foundation and its leader, Jorge Mas Canosa, were taking over. Betancourt revealed that the Foundation planned to use Radio and TV Martí to promote Mas Canosa as Cuba's next president.

In September, 1990, Havana hosted a visit by 42 members of the more moderate Cuban American Committee, which opposes increased confrontation with the island and advocates normalizing relations. Coalition President José Cruz took Mas Canosa and his Foundation to task for being a "bunch of millionaires" out of touch with Cubans living in the United States. Cruz noted that three out of four Cuban Americans surveyed supported normalized relations. During their visit to Cuba, Cruz said no one in his group found a single person who watched TV Martí, and called on Congress to kill the project.

Mas Canosa thought otherwise. The Miami businessman is an important Republican and sometimes Democratic fund-raiser, and friend of U.S. President Bush's son, Jed Bush. He advocated strengthening TV Martí's signal and some of his friends called on Washington to use force to insure TV Martí got through.

PROVOCATION

U.S. troops, during the first two weeks of the 1989 Panama invasion, held 19 Cuban children, 27 women and over 50 men hostage at the Cuban ambassador's residence in Panama City. The Cubans lived for ten days with the barrel of a U.S. tank gun pointed at the front door, helicopter gunships hovering overhead, snipers' rifles trained on the windows and a contingent of marines who evacuated surrounding buildings and more than once donned gas masks as they threatened to storm the diplomatic property.

The U.S. soldiers barred any Cuban from leaving, including diplomats in search of food and medicine for the 100 hostages. Cuban diplomats who tried to reason with the occupation forces were threatened and arrested. Diplomats from other countries who tried to enter the residence with food and medicine were stopped and turned away.[12]

Angolan UNITA contras attacked Cuban troops north of the 13th parallel in January, 1990. The Cubans were in a designated safe zone under the tripartite agreement that guaranteed the Cuban troops security as they withdrew. Despite the peace accord, Washington gave UNITA $50 million in overt aid and weapons for 1990, more in covert funding, and closely advised their every move. The January attack left four Cubans dead and five wounded. A second raid in March killed one Cuban and wounded five others. A third in November killed one Cuban and left four in critical condition.[13]

On January 29, 1990, the U.S. Coast Guard ship, *Chiconteagua*, attacked a small unarmed Cuban freighter in international waters. Shortly after dawn, a barrage of shots slammed into the *Herman*, narrowly missing members of the 17-man crew. The attack continued until the merchant vessel entered Mexican territorial waters at approximately 7:25 a.m. The *Herman*, carrying chrome, had set sail for Tampico, Mexico, from Cuba's eastern port of Moa. No sooner had the ship entered international waters than U.S. planes were on its trail. The captain maintained radio contact with Cuba during the night; he reported the ship was under continuous harassment from the *Chiconteagua*, which appeared out of nowhere. The United States claimed the *Herman* was carrying drugs, but turned down a Cuban government proposal to have the ship searched in Mexico. When the *Herman* finally docked, Mexican authorities, at Cuba's request, did search the ship, verifying that no drugs were aboard.[14]

Amidst the TV Martí confrontation, the Social Democratic Presidents of Venezuela and Spain warned Cuba that Washington was considering military action against the island, a warning the Cubans took seriously. Cuba's Defense Ministry reported on April 30, 1990, that the Pentagon's annual "Ocean Venture," "Global Shield" and "DEFEX" military exercises were about to be held simultaneously—for the first time ever. "Ocean Venture" is the name given for the Pentagon's yearly Caribbean war games, "Global Shield" for its simulation of global nuclear war, and "DEFEX" for evacuation of the U.S. Naval Base in Guantánamo and war with Cuba.

The Defense Ministry communique stated that together with unusual activity at Guantánamo Naval Base and "secret" military activity around Cuba, the three-in-one exercises had "created a dangerous situation that can only be understood in the context of Washington's escalating aggression."[15]

During the first week of May, Cuba's military was put on maximum alert, the reserves mobilized and the entire country put on a war footing. The May 4th edition of *Granma* newspaper said Cuba had evidence that the war games "could be a smoke screen for a surprise attack," citing in addition, the unusual secrecy and lack of press coverage inside the U.S. of the war games, and the involvement of large combat-ready forces with experience in Grenada and Panama. *Granma* charged that the United States "is mobilizing against Cuba," warning that the Bush administration, gloating over developments in Eastern Europe, Panama and Nicaragua, "might have drawn the erroneous conclusion that now is the long-awaited moment to settle accounts with our country . . . Better to prepare 100 times than to be caught off-guard once," stated *Granma*. "It's impossible to tell if this time the threat will be carried out or if it is just another attempt to intimidate, pressure and destabilize Cuba."[16]

After sending hundreds of bombers and fighters to within just a few miles of Cuban territory, the Pentagon maneuvers wound down, as did Cuba's mobilization. But the threat was real enough for then UN Secretary General, Javier Pérez de Cuellar, to comment to the Hungarian press that TV Martí was "a violation of Cuba's sovereignty," and the war games "an act of intimidation that endangers peace." The world's top diplomat declared: "I condemn any possible U.S. aggression against Cuba."[17] His statement followed similar ones by the 108-country Nonaligned Movement, the Soviet Union, China, Canada, Spain, Mexico, Brazil, Venezuela, Argentina, Peru, Colombia, Uruguay and dozens of other governments. World Peace Council President Romesh Chandra warned, "Washington may try to take advantage of events in Eastern Europe and Central America to directly attack Cuba." Chandra called the maneuvers a "rehearsal for aggression," and called on "all peace-loving forces in the world to express our solidarity with Cuba and demand the U.S. end the Cold War in the Caribbean." Solidarity organizations sprang up, or in some cases simply took on new life, throughout Latin America, the Caribbean, the United States, Canada, Europe, Africa and Asia.[18]

SUBVERSION

The United States also stepped up its longstanding efforts to subvert and disrupt Cuba from within. In May, 1500 Cubans seeking to emigrate to the United States formed the "Committee of Cuban Political Prisoners Denied by the United States." On May 22, the group's three top leaders went on a hunger strike, charging Washington was deliberately denying them visas in order to organize terrorist activity in Cuba.

Under the 1984 Cuban-U.S. immigration accord, Havana agreed to take back thousands of people who left on the 1980 "Mariel Boatlift" and were being held in U.S. prisons. Washington, in turn, agreed to allow up to 23,000 Cubans through its borders each year for political, family and economic reasons. The deal was suspended in 1985 when Radio Martí went on the air, but then renewed in 1987. However, in early 1990, rumors began to circulate in Havana that while Cuba was granting exit visas at a considerable clip, Washington was sitting on the entry visas and thus actual immigration had slowed to a trickle.

"Washington is denying us visas," Committee President Orestes Izquierdo told the press May 22, "to create an internal resistance, a fifth column, in hopes of organizing an uprising against the Fidel Castro government." Izquierdo charged that the U.S. Immigration and Naturalization Service had told members of his group "men like us are needed in Cuba to overthrow Castro." Izquierdo, who spent four years behind bars for acting "against the integrity and stability of the state," said that for two years he had been trying to obtain an entry visa to the States. "We were urged on by the United States in the struggle against Castro, and now they have abandoned us," he said.

The group's Vice President, Ecevelio Ruíz González, who had spent 16 years in prison, told IPS news agency that "Cuba has granted us visas to leave and meanwhile we can't find work, nor are we integrated into society . . . But the U.S. Interests Section has not only denied us entry visas, but is sabotaging our efforts to gain visas from other Western embassies." The group's Secretary, Guillermo Fontané Escobar, charged "the North Americans are urging us to violently oppose the regime."[19]

The Committee's revelations sparked a major split between Cuban "dissidents" on the island and in Miami. The former wanted out and the latter, working with Washington, insisted they remain in Cuba. The United States Interests Section, in an official statement issued May 25, denied the Committee's charges: "It is not the policy of the U.S. government to encourage individuals or groups within Cuba to overthrow the government by violent or other means." The Interests Section questioned the claim by Committee leaders and members to political refugee status.

Thus, men whom Cuba had always charged were common criminals or U.S. agents were now admitting they had worked with the United States, bitterly accusing Washington of denying them their due: the "good life" in the States. At the same time Washington, which had always termed these former inmates "dissidents," "victims of human rights abuses" and "political prisoners," now insisted Cuba had been right all along in characterizing them as common criminals or people simply in search of what money can buy and willing to do anything to get it.

On July 9, 1990, just before the Western powers were to meet in Houston to discuss aid to the USSR (a proposal eventually blocked by the Bush Administration due to the Soviet's aid to Cuba), five self-proclaimed Cuban intellectuals and human rights activists entered the Czechoslovakian Embassy in Havana, demanding visas to tour Europe and speak on human rights violations. Within the hour, Radio Martí was broadcasting the news and all but listing Western embassies that others might approach, if they wished to use breaking-and-entering into diplomatic property as a means to leave the country (one of many "terrorist" acts U.S. special police SWAT teams are trained to violently put down). To anyone monitoring Radio Martí, it was obvious the United States hoped to ignite a mass rush on Havana's embassy row. By July 12th, nine more Cubans had entered the Czech Embassy and five the home of a Czech diplomat. Within days, a row had broken out among the Cubans in the Czech embassy, and on July 16, all of them left.

Three of the original five Cubans who entered the embassy, Lázaro Cabrera Puente, Jorge Luis Mari Becerra and Carlos Eladio Novoa Ponce charged they had been set up. The three, all with long histories of contra activity, met with the Cuban press on July 20th, stating they first had tried to get visas to move to the United States, but had been denied. The three men said they were then directed to the Czechoslovakian Embassy in search of permanent entry visas to that country. Once they had entered the embassy, they had been urged to stay, promised protection and a European tour. They stated conditions had been set up ahead of time for their stay and that the Czech diplomats were in immediate communication with various Western embassies.[20]

The real news, however, was that Tania Díaz Castro and Roberto Puppo Sánchez, two of Cuba's most well-known dissidents and at the time under investigation for violating state security laws, appeared with the three. Díaz and Puppo Sánchez stated they had been approached by German and American diplomats with a similar plan to enter the Canadian Embassy during the annual UN Human Rights hearings in Geneva. Díaz, who along with Elizardo Sánchez, was viewed at the time as Cuba's most important political prisoner, even earning special mention from the U.S. Congress, bitterly denounced

Washington for using Cuba's opposition "for propaganda purposes and to foment violence."[21]

That summer, some 50 Cubans entered various Western Embassies seeking entry into Spain, Italy, Belgium and other countries. Cuba adopted the position that anyone could leave the country after obtaining exit and entry visas, in other words through legal channels, but that no one would be leaving illegally or by force. The government promised amnesty for those who left the embassies by their own free will, and all did by September. Cuba denounced the United States for first refusing to grant entry visas then turning around and calling those who broke into the embassies "heroes" and "human rights activists." What came to be known as the "embassy crisis" eventually was defused, but not without getting its heyday in the Western press and causing serious strains between Havana and important trading partners, especially Spain.[22]

ECONOMIC WARFARE

"Preparing for a post-Castro Cuba" is the name of a Heritage Foundation "backgrounder" issued May 14, 1990. Written by Cuban American National Foundation staff director, Thomas Cox, the title reflected the dominant thinking in Washington and Miami. The collapse of East European socialism and the grave crisis ripping apart the Soviet Union signalled the time had come to strike a final fatal blow to Cuban socialism and independence.

The Heritage "backgrounder" is of special interest because of the think-tank's influence within the Republican and Democratic Parties and as an articulate expression of the thinking and policy proposals that became law in 1992.

"Castro is nearing his last days," crowed Cox. He might even fall, he suggested, with U.S. help, before President Bush ended his first term. Cox then urged a seven-point program "to hasten Castro's demise":

1) INCREASE U.S. ECONOMIC PRESSURE AGAINST CUBA

Cox calls for the revocation of a 1975 amendment to the U.S. embargo that allowed U.S. subsidiaries in foreign countries to obtain a license to trade with Cuba. He states "1,236 licenses have been granted since 1982 . . . only 43 applications have been denied . . . Last year Cuba received ($)300 million in goods, more than a fourth of Western exports to Cuba, from U.S. companies in Argentina, Britain, Switzerland . . ."

2) ESTABLISH CLEAR INCENTIVES FOR MOSCOW TO CUT AID TO CUBA

"Washington," argues Cox, "should deny Soviet access to U.S. technology, security markets and trade credit programs unless Moscow cuts its military and economic aid to Havana in a verifiable way." He urges the U.S. government to "oppose U.S. export-import bank credits to the USSR . . . Oppose the USSR's membership in the oversees private investment corporation . . . Prevent Moscow from raising money by issuing bonds in U.S. securities markets . . . Link U.S. membership in the European Bank for Reconstruction and Development (aimed at pooling loans and aid to the USSR) to Moscow's cutting off support for Cuba . . ."

3) FOSTER WESTERN COOPERATION IN ISOLATING CUBA ECONOMICALLY:

"As Cuba enters a more competitive trade relationship with former communist regimes in Eastern Europe," states Cox, "Havana's economic and political security will depend increasingly on Western trade. Nations like Canada, Japan and West Germany have increased their Cuban imports by some 500 million since 1986 . . . Washington should encourage Canada, Colombia, Japan, Mexico, Peru, and other Western consumers of Cuban sugar and seafood to shift their imports of these goods from Cuba to Barbados, the Dominican Republic, Jamaica, Costa Rica, and other democracies in Central America and the Caribbean. This could be done by having these countries join the U.S. in an economic security agreement limiting trade with Castro."

Cox then advocates some arm twisting of "America's friends" to insure they tow the line. "Washington should also demonstrate that Western allies will pay a price if they undermine U.S. efforts to isolate Castro by trading with Havana. The U.S. trade representative has allocated quotas for 1990–91 that set the amount of sugar that nations can export to the U.S. Several recipients of U.S. sugar quotas, such as Canada, Mexico and Peru, also buy sugar from Cuba that may be resold to the U.S. U.S. trade officials should inform these nations that their quotas will be reduced by the amount of their annual sugar imports from Havana."

Cox's fourth point comes under the heading, "ENCOURAGE WESTERN NATIONS TO PRESS FOR POLITICAL REFORM IN CUBA"; his fifth, "CHALLENGE CASTRO'S POLITICAL INFLUENCE IN LATIN AMERICA"; the sixth, "SET SPECIFIC CONDITIONS FOR NORMALIZATION OF U.S.- CUBAN RELATIONS," calling for no less than a restoration of capitalism and end to Cuba's support for independence struggles."

Point number seven calls on Washington to "OFFER A CLEAR ECONOMIC AND POLITICAL ALTERNATIVE TO CASTRO'S 'SOCIALIST PARADISE'." Cox recommends: "The Bush administration should use the

Radio Martí and TV Martí stations operated by the U.S. Information Agency which broadcast news and entertainment programs to Cuba—to inform the Cuban people about the potential benefits of U.S. economic aid and cooperation with a democratic, market-oriented Cuba . . . This message should stress not only that Castro's revolution is reversible, but that Washington is eager to restore traditional ties of economic and diplomatic cooperation with a free Cuba. Promises of U.S. aid to a post-Castro Cuba should include assurances of Havana's access to such vital raw materials as oil and such emergency assistance as food and medical supplies. The Cuban people should be told that Washington will respect a free Cuba's right to forge its own foreign policy and alliances."[23]

That the Bush administration was listening to Cox and his ilk became clear in June and July, 1990. Secretary of State James Baker, testifying June 12th before the U.S. Congress on the recently concluded Bush-Gorbachev Summit, stated he expected the Soviets to reduce aid to Cuba, in particular military aid. "I hope and expect we will end up seeing a reduction in aid as we already saw in the case of Nicaragua," said Baker. "Whenever we meet with the Soviets, especially when we begin to talk about economic affairs, we bring up the Cuba question." Baker said the United States would not accept fully aiding the Soviets or cooperating with them as long as they continued sending "billions of dollars to Cuba, especially in the form of military aid."[24]

The next day, President Bush, answering a reporter's question on the Soviet hope that Washington would soften its anti-Cuba policies, stated: "I don't accept the idea that the time has come for us to change our policy with respect to Fidel Castro. I have a better idea—the Soviets should stop spending five billion dollars a year in Cuba . . . ."[25]

At the July Western Powers Summit held in Houston, Texas, the United States was adamant in its opposition to a joint $15-billion aid program for the Soviet Union, citing as the main reason Soviet aid to Cuba. The U.S. opposition torpedoed the French plan, and provoked protests from Moscow which stated no country had the right to impose foreign policy on another.[26]

The United States Congress also got into the act. The U.S. Senate, in late 1989, approved a resolution drawn up by Senator Connie Mack (R-Fla) to tighten the 30-year economic blockade. The proposal, which restricted U.S. corporate subsidiaries in third countries from doing business with Cuba, died in the House, only to be revived in 1990 and passed by the entire U.S. Congress in late October as part of the 1991 Foreign Exports Act.

Congressional passage of the Mack amendment provoked strong protests from Canada, Latin America and the European Community. Canada's Foreign Minister, Joe Clark, and Attorney General Kim Campbell, stated their country would overrule the law and forbid U.S. subsidiaries in Canada from paying attention to it. Campbell announced he had notified the companies involved that they had to report to his office "any instructions or directives related to this matter." Clark stated the Mack amendment was "completely unacceptable," since it interfered with Canada's sovereign right to establish and maintain trade relations with Cuba.[27]

Brazil's Foreign Minister, Francisco Rezek, also blasted the Mack amendment. Speaking to the press on November 16, he stated "we will never be in agreement with the use of economic mechanisms that can cause unjust damage to other nations."[28]

President Bush, under fierce pressure from allies, on November 18, 1991, pocket vetoed the 1991 Foreign Exports Act, and with it the Mack amendment. Senator Connie Mack lamented Bush's action and promised to reintroduce the measure in 1991, which he did, only to see it again passed by Congress and vetoed by the President. Other anti-Cuba measures introduced in Congress in 1990, and which died without passage, included bills that would have banned ships that stopped in Cuba from docking in the United States for 180 days, cut aid to countries that traded with Cuba and preferential trade agreements for the same "crime."

The United States, perhaps because its attention was diverted to the Gulf War and final collapse of the Soviet Union, or because it believed its own propaganda that Cuba would fall of its own accord, appeared to step back a bit from its escalating confrontation with the island during the first eight months of 1991. TV Martí remained on the air, but the strength and time of its broadcasts did not change. Over 20 U.S. radio stations continued to broadcast some 500 hours of propaganda at the island, but no new stations came on board. There were no open military provocations nor large scale Caribbean war games. However, new pieces of a strategy aimed at wearing Cuba down, creating an internal opposition and perhaps a pretext for future intervention were put in place.

Washington increased its efforts to isolate Cuba by painting it as the world's worst human rights violator, approved expanded funding to enforce the U.S. economic embargo, stepped up efforts to sabotage Cuba's trade and economic cooperation with other countries and moved to form a united political opposition out of the two dozen tiny

Cuban "human rights" groups and their less than 500 members. Mas Canosa and company collected credit and investment pledges to buy the island lock, stock and barrel after Castro's fall.

Then came the failed August coup in the Soviet Union. Just days after it was over, Mikhail Gorbachev, with Secretary of State James Baker at his side, announced the then Soviet Union would pull a small contingent of troops out of Cuba and examine in general military aid to the country. He also let it be known that all favorable trade terms with Cuba were cancelled. The troops, in place since the Cuban Missile Crisis, had no real military value, but were symbolic of the Soviet's commitment to defend Cuba if attacked. The announcement brought a stinging rebuke from the Cuban government, which pointed out it had often resisted U.S. offers to improve relations and provide aid if Cuba would only turn on the USSR. Havana was particularly angry about the deal because it was struck behind its back. Cuba insisted no Soviet troops should leave without a similar U.S. withdrawal from Guantánamo Naval Base.[29]

Gorbachev's surprise announcement signalled the Bush administration would take full advantage of the rapidly deteriorating situation in Moscow to force Cuba's once-trusted ally into the opposite camp. Further, that a disintegrating USSR and then shaky Russian-led Commonwealth was in no position to buck U.S. demands to cut Cuba off and even join in the U.S.-led campaign against the island. As 1991 drew to a close, most Soviet technicians and their families had left the island, and many Cubans had come home from the disappeared USSR.

The next major confrontation between the United States and Cuba came at the United Nations. Cuba succeeded at placing U.S. efforts to internationalize its embargo on the General Assembly's 1991 agenda. All indications pointed to a UN vote branding the embargo a blockade and violation of international law. Washington, shedding its claim as a champion of free speech, threatened economic and political retaliation against any country that even spoke to the issue, let alone considered voting for the resolution.

A document used by the U.S. to muzzle Latin American governments stated:

> We understand your interest in regional solidarity and your hope that by cooperating with Cuba you can help steer them towards democracy. If Cuba is sincere, however, about improving relations with its neighbors, it would not put its friends in the awkward position of squaring off against the U.S. in an international forum . . . We urge you to instruct your ambassador in Havana to approach the Cubans in an effort to have the resolution

withdrawn. The Cubans should understand that their insistence that you support them threatens your good relationship with the U.S. and could damage bilateral relations with your government . . .[30]

Members of Cuba's UN Mission told me they believed they had the votes to win in the General Assembly. But "the offer they couldn't refuse" convinced many governments that hushing up was the healthiest policy. Cuba's UN Ambassador Ricardo Alarcón, speaking before the international body on November 13, 1991, detailed Washington's dogged worldwide campaign to scuttle the Cuban economy. Alarcón then announced that Cuba, at the urging of its friends, had decided to table the debate until 1992. He also asked those assembled in New York to ponder a "New World Order" in which one nation could quiet the governments of the world.[31]

THE CUBANS RALLY

The Cuban people responded to the Christmas Panama invasion by staging nationwide protest rallies that ran well into the new year. In Havana, young people led a week of round-the-clock demonstrations in front of the U.S. Interests Section. These were by far the largest and most militant rallies I had seen in my seven years in Cuba. The protests marked the start of a Union of Young Communists (UJC) offensive on Havana's streets that continues as of this writing. The UJC, skillfully led by Roberto Robaina, combined music, dancing and other forms of street entertainment with marches and rallies, capturing the imagination and spirit of Cuba's youth. Demonstration followed demonstration, each larger than the one before, each affirming support for Cuban socialism and denouncing U.S. imperialism. At each one, Roberto Robaina gave the keynote speech, nationally broadcast.

Havana's young people followed up the Panama protests with a massive candlelight march on January 28, 1990, the 137th anniversary of José Martí's birth. Fidel Castro joined them, walking arm-in-arm from the steps of the University along San Lázaro street. They turned out again in the hundreds of thousands February 1st, to welcome home the crew of the *Herman*. On April 3rd, they staged an all-night party and midnight rally to protest TV Martí. Robaina, taking the microphone before Fidel, asked: "When will they learn that Cuba is for Cubans? That we can't be pressured and that we can't be bought?" On April 16th, Havana's young people were prominent in a huge rally to mark the 29th anniversary of Playa Girón—the Bay of Pigs—and the declaration of socialism in Cuba. The city of Havana was named the site for July 26 festivities—in recognition of the province's work. Havana Party First Secretary, Jorge Lezcano, speaking to the mainly youthful crowd stated to cheers, "Havana will never be a Budapest, Versovia or Prague because here the young people are protesting in support of socialism, the revolution and its leaders." Lezcano asked the youthful crowd if they wanted to establish a market economy and it roared "NO." He asked if the people wanted a Western-style political system and they answered "NO" again. He asked if they wanted to reestablish private property and the response again was "NO." On May 1st, 1990, and again in 1991 and 1992, Havana's youth made up the majority of the 800,000 who marched in the capital marking International Workers Day. Amidst the May, 1990, Cuban Shield alert, Havana's students marched through the city streets and Cuban youth made up the bulk of mobilized combatants.[32]

And so it went right through the years 1991 and into 1992. Just a week before I left Cuba for home, 500,000 Havana young people rallied in Revolution Square for the call to the Sixth Congress of the UJC. They roared their approval when both Robaina and Castro told the crowd life had presented them with a challenge equal to that of their grandparents and parents, with an opportunity to write new pages in their country's historic struggle for independence, development and social justice.

LOW INTENSITY CONFLICT (1992)

1992 began traumatically for Cubans. Three heavily armed Cuban Americans were captured December 29th, just minutes after they landed along the northern coast. Eduardo Díaz Betancourt, a dropout with a long criminal record, had left Cuba nine months earlier. Daniel Santovenia Fernández, who had served time in the United States for assault and battery, had left Cuba in 1969. Pedro de la Caridad Alvarez Pedroso, a drug addict at 19, had never set foot on the island before. At their trial, the three said their plan was to use the weapons, explosives and grenades found in their possession against economic and civilian targets—including theaters, nightclubs and markets, to panic the population. They explained their weapons and explosives came from the former European socialist countries, to create the false impression that Cubans living on the island were seizing arms and violently opposed the government.

The three stated they belonged to an organization called "Commandos L," one of many armed anti-Cuban groups operating freely in the United States. They insisted their activities were carried out with the knowledge and tacit approval of the United States government. The three men said the names, addresses and phone numbers of leading Cuban "dissidents" and "human rights" activists found on their persons were provided to them in case of an emergency. Finally, they gave the Cuban government the names and addresses of Cubans living in Miami who were part of their terrorist operation. The information was turned over to the U.S. government, which did nothing. Commandos L's self-proclaimed leader, Miami resident Antonio de la Cuesta Valle, told the Mexican TV network ECO that he had thousands of men trained for future missions and that his organization operated with a nod from the U.S. government.[33]

On January 7, 1992, the very day the news broke about the terrorists' capture, seven Cubans living on the island set out for Tarará, a children's camp some 30 miles west of Havana. They were led by Luis Miguel Almeida Pérez, a former Tarará employee and a fugitive on several rape charges—one against a minor at the camp itself—the others with two more members of the group, Rene Salmerón Mendoza and Blas Pérez Boucourt. The three men were accompanied by Almeida Pérez's wife, 20-year old Miderglis Ponce Casanova, her four year old daughter and Pedro and Enríque de la Rosa Guerra, two brothers recruited to captain a boat moored at Taharà. The plan was to steal the boat and head for Miami.

At around midnight on January 8th, the seven Cubans arrived at Tarará, overpowered, beat and bound a night watchman and a coastguardsman, Rafael Guevara Borges and Orosman Dueñas Valero; stole their weapons and headed for the boat. But they had trouble starting the motor, enough time for two patrolling policemen, Yuri Gómez Reynoso and Rolando Pérez Quintosa, to appear on the scene. Almeida Pérez and Salmerón Mendoza opened fire, killing Yuri and gravely wounding Rolando. Almeida Pérez, fearing he could be identified, then pounded all four defenseless men with semi-automatic fire at point-blank range. He then called on the others to run for it, believing all witnesses were dead. However, one of the policemen, 22-year-old Pérez Quintosa, was alive and able to utter the word "rapist" in the ambulance that rushed him to the hospital. With help from the public, the band was in custody within 24 hours. Photos of the young security men, tied up, their bodies riddled with bullets, shocked the nation—where violent crime is not an everyday affair.[34]

The three terrorists' capture, followed by the grizzly events at Tarará, created general alarm and indignation. Anger spilled over into the streets with demonstrations demanding the maximum penalty. Meanwhile, the entire Cuban population followed day-by-day, for over a month, the battle by 50 Cuban specialists to save Pérez Quintosa's life. He finally died Saturday, February 15th, and was declared a national hero. The country went into mourning, more determined than ever to stop future violence before it happened.

The leader of the three terrorists, Eduardo Díaz Betancourt, received the death penalty after losing successive appeals to the Supreme Court and Council of State, while Daniel Santovenia Fernández and Pedro de la Caridad Alvarez Pedroso received 30-year prison terms. Luis Miguel Almeida Pérez and René Salmerón Mendoza were also tried, found guilty and sentenced to death; while the remaining defendants in the Terará massacre received prison terms ranging from 2 to 30 years.

Back in Washington, the head of the House Foreign Affairs Committee's Western Hemisphere Subcommittee, New Jersey Democrat Robert Torricelli, was preparing legislation to plug the loopholes in the embargo and transform it into an official international blockade. The bill, called "The Cuban Democracy Act of 1992," was introduced in Congress on February 5, and was a near carbon copy of the Heritage Foundation Backgrounder, cited earlier in this chapter.

Torricelli claimed the legislation aimed at a "peaceful transition to democracy" in Cuba, and he blasted what he called a lack of free speech and press in the country. The Congressman's district included parts of Northern New Jersey with concentrations of Cuban Americans. I talked with a number of Cuban Americans who opposed his bill, but who had been intimidated into silence for fear of retaliation from the rightwing Cuban American National Foundation and others. The *Miami Herald* got a taste of how real those fears were when its editorial against the bill led to violent denunciations by leading Cuban American "ultras," plus bomb and death threats. No less than *America's Watch* takes aim at these same "Cuban Democracy Act" supporters for their reign of terror against Cubans living in the United States.

The "Cuban Democracy Act" internationalizes the economic embargo against Cuba by forcing the governments and businesses of other countries into line. "It shall be U.S. policy to seek the cooperation of other democratic countries" in U.S. efforts to topple the Cuban Government and "to make clear to other countries that, in determining its relations with them, the United States will take into account their willingness to cooperate in such a policy," it states.

Section 4 of the legislation orders the President to negotiate "with appropriate countries in order to secure the agreement of such countries to restrict trade and credit relations with Cuba in a manner consistent with U.S. policy" and it mandates stiff economic sanctions against countries assisting Cuba or providing preferential trade terms to the island. The legislation incorporates part of the Mack Amendment, making it more difficult for U.S. companies' subsidiaries in other countries to trade with Cuba, authorizes the seizure of any vessel that enters U.S. waters within 180 days of docking at a Cuban port, and while wrapping itself in democratic and human rights rhetoric, tightens restrictions and stiffens penalties against U.S. citizens who travel to Cuba and the travel agencies that help them.

The "Cuban Democracy Act" also legitimizes ongoing U.S. covert action against Cuba. It advocates direct U.S. interference in Cuba's internal affairs and financial backing for domestic destabilization. The bill authorizes the President to put "dissidents" on the U.S. payroll, print their literature and smuggle it into Cuba, provide printing and other communications equipment to "dissident" organizations, etc.

Torricelli tried to cover his proposal to cut off the trade lifeline to 10.8 million Cubans by exempting medical and food *donations* to the island—while restricting the Cuban government's ability to produce and purchase the same. The legislation also holds out the promise of massive U.S. aid and better times to come *(a la Nicaragua?)*, only if the Cuban people do things Washington's way.

Perhaps the only constructive aspect of the legislation is that it calls for improving telephone and mail service between the United States and Cuba, long-standing demands of both the Cuban and Cuban American community, and for greater cultural exchanges and the permanent stationing of Cuban journalists in the United States. In late September, 1992, the "Cuban Democracy Act" was passed through Congress as part of the Defense Authorization Bill, and signed into law on October 23, 1992 by President Bush.[35]

But even before signing the "Cuban Democracy Act" into law, President Bush, with an eye on a second term and the cash contributions of the Cuban American National Foundation, had announced stepped-up efforts to topple the Cuban Government. In a February 27, *Miami Herald* piece, Bush claimed U.S. government radio and TV broadcasts to Cuba were "impartial and unbiased," and wrote: "We will continue to aggressively pursue every opportunity to bring the Cuban people the Martí message . . . We intend to keep squeezing Castro hard on the economic front," he continued, "by asking our friends and democratic allies not to replace past Soviet aid to Cuba by providing economic assistance or preferential trade agreements." The U.S. President denied reports he was working with Cuba to curb terrorist activity aimed at the island, and concluded his article with a barely veiled endorsement of the same: "Our desire is for freedom for Cuba," he wrote, "and we want the process to be peaceful, orderly and without the spilling of blood. At the same time, faithful to our tradition of supporting the fight for freedom throughout the world, we intend to do everything we can within the confines of existing U.S. law to support all those who are striving to achieve Cuba's liberation."

President Bush proved true to his word. On April 1st, TV Martí went daytime for the first time, airing a "documentary" on the demise of European socialism. But this, like all TV Martí broadcasts before and since, was successfully jammed. Fidel Castro, speaking on April 4th, announced Cuba would respond with AM radio broadcasts into the States. Castro, quoting Bush's expressed desire to keep Cubans well-informed, stated his government had the same right to inform the U.S. public. Cuba began broadcasting a four-hour AM radio show that could be heard from Florida to Iowa on April 14th. The next day, the U.S. stopped its daytime TV Martí broadcasts and Cuba followed suit.[36]

But President Bush, getting wind that rival Bill Clinton was about to upstage him by supporting the Torricelli Bill, decided to go another route against Cuba. On April 18th, he announced a series of executive orders to cut further into Cuba's trade. The most important decree ordered U.S. Customs to seize any ship that entered U.S. waters if it had docked in Cuba or was en route to Cuba, carried Cuban goods, goods made with Cuban materials or goods from a company that a Cuban national or company had an interest in. The order, just one step short of a naval blockade, aimed at cutting off growing foreign investment, Cuban trade with other countries and tens of millions of dollars worth of oil, food, medicine and other goods coming into Cuba from solidarity efforts around the world.[37]

Cuba's Foreign Ministry denounced the move as nothing short of piracy, a violation of international laws governing maritime trade and navigation, and an attempt to wreck Cuba's efforts to feed, educate and care for its people. The Cuban statement charged that Bush's orders revealed Washington's growing frustration over international sentiment against the blockade. The Foreign Ministry pointed out that just days before, on April 8th, State Department official Robert Gelbard, testifying on the Torricelli legislation, had admitted that "though some governments agree Cuba should not receive aid, very few want to impose an embargo on the island."[38]

On May first, even as Los Angeles, California, and other U.S. cities exploded over the Rodney King verdict, leaving sixty people dead, three thousand injured, many more behind bars and hundreds of millions in damage—one million Cubans marched through Havana to express their support for socialism, the Communist Party and their government. Four million more Cubans marched and rallied across the island in traditional International Workers Day events. As for the Pentagon, it chose May first to launch its Ocean Venture Caribbean war games and Defex mock evacuation of Guantánamo Naval Base. The war games involved over 30,000 troops, two dozen warships and countless aircraft.[39]

Cuba's May Day celebrations and the Los Angeles riots stood in sharp contrast to the shrill warnings from the CIA and Pentagon that Cuba was about to explode and that the U.S. should be ready to intervene for humanitarian reasons.

The head of U.S. military intelligence, James Claper, testifying January 22nd before the Senate Armed Services Committee, stated "the internal situation in Cuba has reached the point where it could become a security problem for the United States . . . The rapid economic deterioration and rising needs could provoke another refugee exodus and such an event could provoke generalized violence that threaten U.S. forces at the Guantánamo Naval Base."

"The Cuban regime's repression against growing opposition presages a violent social explosion," warned a somber CIA director, Robert Gates, testifying at the same hearing that day.

On March 4, Admiral Ednesy, Commander of the Atlantic Fleet, told the Senate Committee: "Cuba is the biggest security problem we face in the Atlantic. We must have our forces ready to confront any contingency . . . The deteriorating situation in Cuba creates a serious security problem that could arise from a probable massive exodus of Cubans." (Mad Hatter logic indeed, since the United States was unabashedly doing everything possible to further "deteriorate the situation," . . . threatening its own security?)

The Armed Services Committee, on March 10th, heard from general Hanford Johnson, head of Transporation at the Defense Department. "Cuba is a real danger to the security of U.S. military and civilian transportation," the General assured the Senators.

General Carl W. Stecher, head of U.S. Special Operations, told the House Armed Services Committee on March 19th that as the Cuban situation deteriorated "the Armed Forces must be prepared for any contingency, especially a repetition of Mariel."[40]

By May 5th, yet another U.S. military move proved to be the straw that broke the tropical camel's back. A full page *Granma* editorial charged that under the guise of the Haitian refugee crisis, Washington was building up its forces at Guantánamo. The paper pointed out that U.S. forces sent to Guantánamo—ostensibly to deal with the refugees—included the 10th Division of the Light Mountain Infantry and heavy artillery units. There were also a growing number of warships at the base, including a submarine, helicopter carrier and at one point, five missile frigates. *Granma* revealed that Cuba was being subjected to constant provocations at the base, which included repeated violations of its air space and the firing of artillery rounds into Cuban territory. For the first time since the Cuban Missile Crisis, the Chairman of the U.S. joint chiefs of Staff, Colin Powell, had visited Guantánamo, not once, but twice, and Admiral Ednesy no less than five times. The U.S. Joint Chiefs also created a special office to monitor Cuba's domestic situation and report directly to Powell. Cuba, charged *Granma*, was being subjected to an unusually high number of daily air, sea and radar probes and increased CIA activity. Between 1989 and 1992, stated *Granma*, there had been 523 spy flights directed at the island, and U.S. tactical aircraft had flown no less than 83,000 mock sorties. *Granma* warned that the shrill testimony on Capitol Hill, the military maneuvers, provocations, increased intelligence-gathering and the Guantánamo buildup pointed to a possible U.S. plan to organize or provoke incidents near the base and then use them as an excuse for military intervention.[41]

CONCLUSION: THE FOURTH PARTY CONGRESS AND FUTURE OF CUBAN SOCIALISM

The Dance of Millions

Cuba's critics often complain from afar that it is just about impossible to understand what is going on in the country, let alone predict the future. They blame government secrecy, censorship and control. My impression as someone who lived in Cuba for seven years is that secrecy, censorship and control are remarkably limited for a country facing a far more powerful next-door neighbor bent on taking it over and reducing its 10.8 million inhabitants to the subservience, humiliation, violence and poverty that are the lot of other Third World peoples unfortunate enough to have their country's politics and economics dictated to them by Washington and other developed capitalist countries.

Cuba's leaders, from the very start of the revolution, realized majority participation and support were strategic necessities both to defend the country from the United States and to develop. To date, they have garnered both and thus the need for repression has been restricted to legal harassment of isolated opponents whose actions dovetail or are directly tied to U.S. efforts to retake the island. There is no evidence that socialist Cuba has ever resorted to the massive and often U.S.-sponsored death squad-torture repression that has been commonplace in many Third World countries—a repression that has left hundreds of thousands dead or maimed and just as many families scarred for life. As of this writing, socialist Cuba had never even had to use tear gas against a demonstration or riot, nor had it ever violently broken a strike.

The longer I lived in Cuba, the more impressed I became at the level of grassroots participation in policy formation and implementation. What I came to refer to as "The Dance of Millions" would have been impossible if Cubans were not well informed about the world, their country and the foreign and domestic options open to them. I am not arguing that Cuba is some sort of democratic or human rights utopia:

it's not, nor does such a country exist in today's world. However, its record is better than most and there is a constant and conscious effort by both the leaders and the public to communicate, find common political and economic ground, work together towards constructive change and hold in check the gross political and economic opportunism so prevalent in power games worldwide.[1]

I never had a problem understanding the general contours of Cuba's foreign or domestic policies, nor predicting where the country was headed. I found that Cubans do what they say they will—and that perhaps many observers' confusion and inability to understand Cuba, let alone accurately predict where the country is headed, comes from their unconscious and perfectly natural tendency to superimpose their own reality, beliefs and desires onto the country.

For example, the 1986 documents and debates from the Cuban Communist Party's Third Congress elaborate the general foreign and domestic policy guidelines pursued by Cuba through 1990. Similarly, I have no doubt that the debate leading up to the 1991 Fourth Party Congress, as well as the decisions taken at the Congress, provide an excellent guide as to what to expect from Cuba in the coming years, barring a U.S. invasion and the destruction of the island.

RECTIFICATION MOVES TO THE SUPERSTRUCTURE

Plans to hold the Fourth Party Congress were announced on February 16, 1990, after an extraordinary session of the Party's Central Committee. The rectification movement had brought positive results, stated the Central Committee, especially in the areas of social and economic development. However, "conditions have now matured to tackle in a practical and concrete way the rectification of the country's political and institutional system . . ."

The Central Committee stated that taking aim at Cuba's superstructure was a logical continuation and deepening of the country's ongoing effort to identify its mistakes and correct them, an effort it insisted was "a continuous and permanent process of the revolution based on the Cuban situation and free from external pressures." At the same time, the Central Committee stated the Party couldn't "ignore what is happening in the world and in particular, the situation of socialism at a world level." The Cuban Party had been able to avoid certain errors committed by other Communist Parties, but "we must prepare ourselves so as not to commit others, for which there are some basis in our society, determined by the transfer and copying of experiences foreign to Cuba's traditions, history and peculiarities."

The Central Committee resolved to hold the Fourth Congress in February 1991 (later postponed until October) and to set up an organizing commission. Preparations for the Congress would take place under the banner "Cuba, an eternal Baraguá," a clear challenge to the "New World Order" and the United States. A Congress call to center nationwide debate would be issued March 15, 1990, the 112th anniversary of Antonio Maceo's Baraguá protest.[2]

On February 20th, just four days after the special Central Committee meeting, Cuba's parliament, the National Assembly of People's Power, met in special session. The Assembly accepted the retirement of 78-year-old Severo Aquirre as acting President. Aguirre had taken over the job in 1988 when another long-time revolutionary, Flavio Bravo, died. Juan Escalona Regueira was elected the new Assembly President and Zoila Benítez de Mendoza Vice President. Escalona, one of Cuba's most sharp-witted and dynamic leaders, had fought in the revolution, held various military and non-military posts, and as Minister of Justice prosecuted the famous Ochoa corruption and drug trafficking case. Benítez, a former teacher, was director of Havana's education system before her election to the new job. The election of Escalona and Benítez—after nominations from the floor and by secret ballot—signaled a decision to breath some life into the Assembly and strengthen its role.[3]

The special sessions of the Central Committee and National Assembly took place amidst an unprecedented U.S.-orchestrated campaign demanding that Cuba adopt a multi-party system and market economy, similar to those being adopted in a then crumbling socialist Europe. The two meetings sparked extensive international coverage and speculation that "Perestroika" had arrived in Cuba.

Fidel Castro, speaking at the close of the National Assembly session, put such speculation to rest. Castro said the country would continue with its own rectification process, listening to the beat of its own domestic drum. Castro pointed out that it was José Martí, well before Lenin, who called on Cubans to form a single party to unite the nation in defense of its independence. Castro said one of the most important achievements of the revolution was its bringing together of various political currents into a single organization to coalesce national unity.

The Cuban President defended the country's one-party system, pointing out that Cuba had to maintain its independence and develop "just a few miles from the most powerful reactionary empire on earth and amidst its constant pressure, hostility and aggression." He warned that if Cuba became divided into two or more parties, the far more powerful United States, with its wealth and technology, would quickly intervene on one side or the other and once more divide and conquer Cuba.

Castro's explanation reminded me of the story of the Dutchman who plugged a hole in a dike with his thumb. Most Cubans see their one-party system as a dike, holding back a far more powerful United States, ever ready to rush through and drown their independence and the basic social peace and security they have achieved. The Cubans still remember the years of U.S. control over their political life before the revolution: the violence, corruption, gross inequality and opportunism of a U.S.-manipulated multi-party system that alternated with outright dictatorship. They believe that allowing more than one political party would in effect be boring a hole in the dike they have built to prevent just such a U.S.-dominated anti-democratic system from re-emerging. Washington, they reason, would rush through the hole, support the most corrupt and opportunist among them, broaden the breach until the entire dike crumbled, washing everything they have worked and fought for into the sea. Castro put it this way:

> Look, our NATO is unity; our Warsaw pact, what defends us, is unity; and with that weapon and strength we, who don't belong to any pact (and we don't want to belong to any military pact) have been defending ourselves for a long time on our own. We made the necessary estimates to undertake such a decisions long ago. We have a NATO and Warsaw pact to defend us and it is our unity, and we will never accept anything that in any way undermines that fundamental force of our people. . . .

Castro, for the first time in public, then admitted that Cuba's one-party system, while a historic necessity as long as Cuba was under siege, had its problems. "Now, amidst the advantages there are also drawbacks, and that's what we must learn to confront in our process of rectification," he said. "Our Party must improve its leadership methods, its work, its structures, and as we said recently, not just the Party but also the state institutions and mass organizations are over-staffed, and there are certain problems, sometimes dualities of functions and leadership, which is never advisable . . . We must correct all those things and overcome them."[4]

DEMOCRATIZING THE TRADE UNIONS

The battle to rectify Cuba's superstructure had begun in earnest a year earlier. Roberto Veiga, longtime leader of the Central Organization of Cuban Trade Unions (CTC) and a Political Bureau member, was effectively replaced in March 1989 by Pedro Ross, who was named President of the Organizing Committee for the 16th CTC Congress. The Congress, held in February of the following year, elected Ross CTC General Secretary.

Veiga reportedly suffered from alcoholism and had proved unable to keep pace with rectification. Pedro Ross told me "the problem was that there was a time, even after rectification began, when the unions either had a hand in the problems or kept quiet about them." He said there were some union leaders "who were not corrupt but made systematic errors and, even after being criticized, did not change. So, they became isolated from the rectification process and the rank-and-file."

Ross would go on to lead a spectacular nine-month debate among Cuban workers that brought the labor movement into the forefront of the rectification process in each shop, company, industry, ministry, and in the mass media. The CTC Congress, said Ross, was to be just one moment in an ongoing struggle to transform the labor movement and its role in the Cuban workplace and society. The grassroots meetings that led up to the main event would be the real Congress, he noted, and the big fight would be against formalism and phoney unity. The Organizing Commission insisted that participants at shop level meetings be prepared, speak their minds, focus on concrete problems and how to solve them. Every criticism and proposal was carefully recorded and forwarded to the Organizing Committee. Meetings were often cancelled, sometimes more than once, if criticism and debate did not flourish.

"We decided that preparations for the Congress would take the form of a massive consultation with the workers, an open dialogue between the base and their leaders," Pedro Ross told me on the eve of the Congress, in January, 1990. "We held 53,700 local meetings where at least 85 percent of the members attended. The meetings often lasted four or five hours, and in the end some 3,000 changes were made in proposals to be raised at the Congress. We also insisted that the pre-Congress discussion analyze problems in every workplace, come up with concrete solutions and then follow-up to see they were put into effect."

I attended many local union meetings and two provincial ones during preparations for the Congress. What struck me most at the Antillana Steel Works, the Ariguanabo Textile Plant, the main shipping center and truck depot for Havana's ports, the construction site for the 1991 Pan American Games, the Guanabacoa Plumbing Fixtures factory and other Cuban workplaces was just how self-confident and articulate

Cuba's working class is. I saw and heard dozens of people take the floor to talk about Cuba's economy, the vast changes taking place as part of the rectification process and how those changes had affected them. The exchanges were many, often heated, and sometimes with top national political, government and trade union leaders. No one seemed the least bit intimidated about speaking their mind or arguing their point of view.

The 16th CTC Congress endorsed ongoing efforts to rectify Cuba's economy and social services. The Congress then voted to reorganize the CTC's national leadership bodies. The number of National Council members was increased from 187 to 500 and the number of National Commission members from 42 to 170. The new seats were taken by municipal and shop-level union leaders, greatly increasing grass roots participation in the CTC's national leadership. At the same time the Congress decided to cut by half the CTC's national and provincial staffs, placing some of the slots at the disposal of the municipal and local organizations. The CTC Congress called on its 19 national union affiliates to follow suit. Ross told me the CTC and individual trade unions had become "inverted pyramids" that had to be put right-side-up.

The CTC Congress' most important decision was to move towards direct elections at all levels of the labor movement. Cuban workers have always directly elected their immediate leadership through secret ballot. However, in big plants, union committees and their officers were elected indirectly by those already elected at the department level. Now all union positions, no matter how big the workplace, are filled through directly contested elections and a secret ballot vote. The winners not only represent their members before management but sit on each workplace's board of directors.

The 16th CTC Congress also did away with the practice of presenting pre-determined slates for what amounted to rubber-stamp approval of municipal and provincial-level labor leaders. Today, all nominations for municipal and provincial-level union posts come from the shop floor, contested campaigns follow, and then the membership decides by secret ballot.[5]

DEBATING CUBA'S FUTURE

On May 26, 1990, the Organizing Commission for the Fourth Party Congress was formed. It's 72 members included all regular and alternate members of the Political Bureau, 14 of 225 Central Committee members and alternates, and 30 people who were not in the national leadership. This last group included two top scientists, the directors of a number of Cuban workplaces that were rectification success stories, two national UJC leaders, the Presidents of the University Students Federation, Union of Artists and Writers and the Journalists Union, a number of shop-level trade union leaders, the presidents of two farm cooperatives and half a dozen municipal and shop-level Party leaders.

The Commission announced they would proceed much as the CTC had a year earlier. The Fourth Party Congress was to be one moment in an ongoing process; and Party organizations at all levels should not wait until the Congress to take action on local issues where an obvious consensus was reached. That consensus would be hammered out at grassroots meetings open to Party and non-Party members alike, which would debate the Call (Llamamiento) to the Fourth Congress, issued March 15th. The Call stated the Congress was expected to "mark a new stage in the improvement of Cuban society and its democratic institutions and in broadening the process of rectification. This will be its most important content . . ."[6]

Cuba's streets and workplaces were soon a-buzz with tales about the "llamamiento" debates—hot events, even in Cuba where grass roots debate is in fact a constant. Urged on by Fidel Castro and other leaders, the people expressed and defended their views about the Party, government, national mass organizations, the economy and day-to-day life—amid a growing economic crisis and a barrage of U.S. threats.

One of the meetings I attended was with the staff of Cuba's international radio station, Radio Havana Cuba. It was a standing-room-only crowed that gathered at the Radio Havana Cuba cafeteria. As I waited in the late afternoon of October 12th, 1990, for the meeting to begin, I looked around me at the 250 mainly young journalists, technicians and workers jesting, gesturing, smoking a last cigarette before they got down to business. I knew some of them personally, and we had talked of the danger presented to Cuba by international events and by the revolution's own mistakes and weaknesses, too. Anxious about the future, I knew many were just as anxious to speak up about how they felt. The first person to take the floor set the tone that predominated for the next five hours: fierce insistence on defending Cuba's socialism by taking it to task where it wasn't measuring up, and figuring out how to make it work.

"I remember when Che Guevara was a minister," said 52-year-old Marcia, a popular Communist Party militant at the station. "He didn't live in a house outside the city. He didn't have two cars. He wasn't removed from ordinary people. He'd spend half his time finding out from people what was going on and what they thought. But today! When was the last time anyone here talked with a minister? Six months ago a new President was named to Cuba's Institute of Radio and Television and we have yet to meet him. People at the top are distancing themselves from the base."

I flashed back to one sweltering August night when I had met two young communists in a Havana bar. One was a sugar worker and the other, of all things, was in charge of quality control at a shoe factory. I asked them: "The 1986 Third Party Congress was all about rectification, as is the upcoming Fourth Congress—five years later. Does that mean rectification hasn't worked, that its failed?" Both quickly answered, "Not at all!" If the Third Congress was about rectification, the Fourth, they assured me, would be about those who hadn't rectified!

Back to Radio Havana's cafeteria: before the session closed, at least 50 speakers had given their opinions—some talking from a whole list of concerns they had jotted down beforehand. As in most places, they supported the model of social justice the revolution had come to stand for—so all the more was their fury against privilege, bureaucracy, disorganization, what the Cubans call "formalism" or doing things by rote, white-collar and street crime, petty abuse of power, laziness, shoddy work and services. Notes on the issues raised would find their way to a computerized center that tabulated hundreds of thousands of statements, criticisms and proposals pouring in from the 3.5 million Cubans who actively participated in the pre-congress debate—attending 80,000 meetings island wide from June through December, 1990.[7]

A summary of 1,500 Havana meetings recorded over 20,000 criticisms and suggestions. The summary, I believe, accurately reflected a growing consensus among Cubans. Put together for the island's top leaders, it began by stating that an overwhelming majority of participants expressed their support for socialism, the Communist Party and Fidel Castro. At the same time, there was sharp criticism of many of those around Castro and a general lack of confidence in Cuba's 50-odd ministries and national agencies. People were clearly fed up with bureaucracy, inefficiency, disorganization and corruption. They believed over-centralization paralyzed work at the provincial and municipal levels. The summary then broke down the participant's views into various subject areas. A look at each, and then at the policy statements and changes announced before, during and after the Fourth Party Congress, reveals a remarkable responsiveness to popular demands as well as what we can expect from Cuba as it charts a course through an ever more turbulent world towards the year 2,000.[8]

SHAKING-UP THE PARTY

The vast majority of those who attended the "llamamiento" meetings endorsed Cuba's one-party system, given the external threats the country faced. At the same time, they sharply criticized the Party as topheavy and bureaucratized. Many people charged the Party was in danger of losing its ties to the grassroots. They reasoned the Party's role as political leader, guide and trouble-shooter was being undermined by its deep involvement in day-to-day administration of the country. Some people pointed out the Party's structure tended to copy that of the government, state and national mass organizations, and that there was a constant overlapping of responsibility and action. Party members insisted that inside the organization there was too much "formalism," and that often a false unanimity smothered critical thought and debate, healthy pluralism and effective action.

Speakers called on the Party to move away from hands-on administration of the country, do away with bureaucracy, and pay more attention to its role as a guiding ideological and political force. Many people said the Party should hold open meetings from the shop-level on up, following the example of some provinces, where provincial Party meetings were broadcast live. There was near-unanimous agreement that the Party should stop selecting its own members, and return to the practice of the 1960s, when members were nominated by their fellow workers. Just about everyone also agreed the Party should do away with the near-automatic entry of UJC members into its ranks. A person's Party membership should be periodically reviewed by his or her fellow workers, insisted numerous participants. They also said Party candidates and members should be judged not just by their conduct at work but also in their community and at home. After sharp debate, general agreement was reached that religious believers should have the same right as atheists to join the Cuban Communist Party.

The Congress Organizing Commission, as promised, did not wait to respond. On October 5, 1990, a full year before the event, it announced a sweeping reorganization of the Party from top to bottom. The Cuban Party was led by a Political Bureau made up of 14 members and 10 non-voting alternates and a Central Committee with 146 members and

79 alternates. An 11-person secretariat coordinated its day-to-day activity. The Commission abolished the secretariat and category of alternate, the slots now being filled by voting members. The Political Bureau now runs day-to-day Party affairs, and all its members, as well as those of the Central Committee, have full voting rights.[9]

The Central Committee apparatus was drastically reduced from 19 to 9 departments and an astounding 60 percent of its staff re-assigned to other jobs.[10] Cuba's Provincial and Municipal Party organizations also went through a profound shakeup. They were led by Committees headed by a Bureau, in turn led by a First and Second Secretary. Each body had regular and alternate members. The Commission eliminated the Second Secretary post and all alternate member slots. Provincial and Municipal Party organizations were instructed to break with the practice of structuring themselves along identical lines, their re-organization to be dictated by the concrete conditions and needs of each respective territory.

The number of Bureau members leading committees at the provincial and municipal levels was reduced by combining some tasks and eliminating others. The number of provincial departments was drastically cut and the job of department head abolished, the post now being filled, in all but exceptional cases, by Bureau members. Forty-five percent of provincial staff and 10 percent of municipal staff were reassigned. Task forces, made up of provincial and municipal committee members and Party members outside these bodies, were formed to tackle particular tasks and respond to the critiques and proposals coming from area "llamamiento" meetings.[11]

The aim of the reorganization, stated the Organizing Commission, was to "move towards new more integral styles and work methods in the Party leadership bodies and to eliminate dualism, the narrow defense of a single sector, excess personnel and other flaws . . . To set the example in not using a single cadre more than is strictly necessary at each level of the organization. This is indispensable . . . to do away with the sluggishness of leadership bodies of the state, government and the political and national mass organizations."[12]

Several proposals relating to the Party's internal life were also implemented by the Organizing Commission. Some changes were made in the local Party branches when rectification began. Each branch was lead by a First Secretary then Organization and Ideological Secretaries. The latter two posts were abolished in 1987 and the party declared it expected all members to do organizational and ideological work. The second and third elected posts became trouble-shooter positions with those holding them responsible for tackling what ever major problems confronted a workplace.

Branch elections often amounted to a show of hands for single candidates or current office holders. The party was insisting by 1987 that there be more candidates than seats and that elections be by secret ballot. However, Committee, Executive Bureau and Secretary elections in large shops, municipalities and the provinces remained formal affairs, with the next higher level proposing a fixed slate that was confirmed by a show of hands from below. The Organizing Commission declared this practice null and void and announced that candidate lists at each level had to be based on nominations from the rank-and-file, include a minimum of 20 to 25 percent more names than positions, and that all elections were to be by secret ballot.[13]

Delegates to the Fourth Party Congress, meeting in Santiago from October 10 through the 14, 1991, endorsed the Commission's moves, then made some changes of their own. The most important were admission of religious believers into the Party, a return to the practice of workers themselves nominating candidates for Party membership, and the decision to develop Party branches not just in the workplace but also in the community.[14]

The Congress voted to establish a special committee to revamp Party by-laws with the aim of making them more "flexible . . . to insure respect for diverse points of view . . . the promotion of creative, non-dogmatic thought . . . to move towards basing the Party not just in the workplace but the community . . . to insure the full autonomy of Cuba's government, state administration and national mass organizations . . . to lead by example not administrative methods . . ."[15]

Another committee was established to update and no doubt radically change the Communist Party Program hammered out in 1986. The Congress instructed the committee to maintain the Party's commitment to equality and social justice; its opposition to an unjust international economic order; its insistence on the democratization of the United Nations and international political pluralism; and its special interest in Latin American integration.

The program, resolved Congress delegates, should also endorse the rectification process—in particular, the enhanced role of political work and public participation in developing socialist society and the critique of over-reliance on economic mechanisms and the bureaucracy borrowed to a large extent from the European socialist model.

On a more somber note, Congress delegates stated it was impossible to map out a five-year development plan and that even the social and economic goals outlined in the 1986 Program had to be scaled down. The Program should, they said, detail plans for export diversification, import substitution and the generalization of new forms of socialist production embodied in the contingents and Armed Forces initiative. The delegates, after lengthy and often heated debate, agreed that despite U.S. pressures, efforts to open up the media and improve its access to officials and information must continue, along with support for a national cultural movement open to outside influences but not dominated by them.

Finally, the delegates instructed the committee to reinforce that part of the Program dedicated to Cuba's national defense, in particular the "War of the Entire People," and to make clear that Washington's efforts to promote terrorism from Miami and create a fifth column inside Cuba would be met head-on by the people themselves and never be tolerated.[16]

The delegates in Santiago accelerated the renovation of the Party leadership begun in 1986—incorporating new generations of revolutionaries. Fifty-six percent of the 225-member Central Committee was replaced. The new Central Committee was a mix of politicians, administrators, doctors, scientists, soldiers, teachers, artists, blue and white collar workers. The average age of Central Committee members remained at 47 years; but only 29 percent were Party founders, as compared to 46 percent back in 1986.[17]

A new, rectification-oriented Political Bureau was also elected at the Congress. From the older generation, Fidel and Raúl Castro remained at the Party helm, but 14 of the Bureau's members were replaced. Continuing a process begun in 1986, five historic figures—the best known being Culture Minister Armando Hart and heroine Vilma Espín—were not re-elected. Others, such as Carlos Rafael Rodríguez and Juan Almeida, who were with Fidel Castro since the very beginning of the revolution in 1953, held their posts. So, too, such pivotal figures as Osmany Cienfuegos, medical doctor José Ramón Machado Ventura (a key mover in rectification of the superstructure) and Julián Rizo Alvarez.

Cuba's top military men—Julio Casas Regueiro (second only to Raúl Castro), Leopoldo Cintras Frías (head of the Western Army) and Ulises Rosales del Toro (Chief of Staff)—were elected to the Political Bureau, as was Minister of the Interior Abelardo Colomé Ibarra.

The most important newcomers to the Political Bureau were Carlos Aldana Escalante, in charge of ideological work and international relations until he was thrown out of office in September 1992 for egoism and poor judgement; Roberto Robaina González, credited with leading a revolution within the revolution by Cuba's youth, and after Castro, Cuba's best orator and most charismatic figure; and Carlos Lage Dávila, a doctor and former youth leader, now specializing in the economy.

There is a regular rotation of provincial Party leaders on the Political Bureau. However, this time around provincial First Secretaries appeared to be chosen on the basis of their territories' importance, covering both the island's major urban and industrial centers. Estaban Lazo Hernández, from Santiago, was the only provincial Party leader re-elected to the PB. He was joined by Alfredo Hondal González from Ciego de Avila; Alfredo Jordán Morales from Las Tunas; Havana's Jorge Lezcano Pérez and Nelson Torres Pérez from Cienfuegos.

Pedro Ross Leal, leader of Cuba's trade union movement, and Cándido Palmero Hernández from the Blas Roca Contingent, joined the Political Bureau. Science chief, Rosa Elena Simeón, was dropped for health reasons, while another top scientist, Concepción Campa Huergo, became a member. Campa led the team that developed the vaccine against meningitis-B and earned a reputation as a top notch administrator directing the Carlos J. Finlay Research Institute. Two other women were also elected to the Political Bureau: educator turned women's leader and Santiago Party leader, María de los Angeles García Alvarez; and Yadira García Vera, long-time student and youth leader, and a member of Fidel Castro's inner team.

Last, but far from least in significance, poet Abel Prieto Jiménez, President of the Union of Writers and Artists, was elected to Cuba's top political body. Prieto earned his stripes by replacing bureaucrats with well known and active cultural figures. He also proved able to walk that fine line between a fairly conservative older generation and younger artists and writers keen on breaking new cultural ground.[18]

TOWARDS DIRECT NATIONAL ELECTIONS

Ninety-eight percent of Cuba's eligible voters went to the polls in 1976 for a referendum on a new draft constitution. Ninety-six percent of those who voted cast a ballot in favor. The heart of the new constitution was the establishment of Cuba's People's Power form of government. It rests on a foundation of grassroots participation at the precinct or "voting district" level. District delegates are elected by secret ballot for 30 month terms, and there must be at least two (and as many as eight) candidates for each post. Run-off elections are held if no candidate receives more than half the vote. An elected delegate must hold regular public meetings with his or her constituents who can by a simple majority recall their delegate at any time. The Party and all other organizations are banned, by law, from running candidates.

The last local election I witnessed in Cuba took place on April 30, 1989, and was followed by run-off elections May 7th. 29,597 candidates were nominated for 14,300 delegate positions. The "campaign" consisted of posting each candidate's biography or qualifications, and word-of-mouth endorsement. 98.3 percent of Cuba's 7,117,807 registered voters turned out to cast their votes; 47 percent of the 13,815 delegates elected in the first round were incumbents, while 53 percent were new. Run-off elections were then held in 431 voting districts.[19]

The delegates make up the Municipal Assembly (one for each of the island's 169 municipalities), or local governing body. The assembly elects a president and Municipal Council. The Municipal Assemblies, until 1992, also elected representatives to Provincial Assemblies and the National Assembly of People's Power, or parliament. The National Assembly meets two or three times a year, each session lasting less than a week. The Provincial Assemblies meet more frequently as do those at the municipal level.

Cuba's government and electoral process, along with its democratic centralist form, has two important characteristics that came under heavy fire during the "llamamiento" meetings. First, district delegates were volunteers, carrying out their political jobs along with their regular jobs. The same held true for almost all municipal and provincial Assembly members and even many National Assembly deputies. Second, some 40 percent of National Assembly members were elected by the municipal assemblies without ever coming up before the voters at large. For example, Fidel Castro (who could easily beat anyone in any district in Cuba) was not directly elected to the national legislature— the municipal assemblies elected him. Thus 100 percent of municipal assembly members were directly elected, while the figure dropped to 60 percent of the National Assembly members.

Participants at the 1500 Havana meetings insisted that the government be strengthened at all levels. They called for a clear separation between the government and state with the former exercising real authority over the latter. Many people expressed concern that government executive bodies, while theoretically subordinate to the broader municipal, provincial and National assemblies, in fact dominated the political process. They attributed the problem, in part, to the fact that many executive office-holders worked full time on government matters, while delegates to the various assemblies held regular jobs and had to conduct their political work in their spare time.

Some people ridiculed the fact that the National Assembly, theoretically Cuba's highest decision making body, met only two or three times a year for a total of no more than 15 days. They called for greatly increasing the time spent by the National Assembly on the country's affairs. There was a sharp critique of indirect elections, people exclaiming that they often did not know who their national deputies were. There was a general consensus that the National Assembly should continue to elect the national executive, as is done in most European countries, but strengthen its check-and-balance role vis-a-vis the same.

During the debate leading up to the Congress, both the Party and National Assembly set up special commissions to study constitutional reform. The Party commission presented a series of resolutions to the Fourth Party Congress. The resolutions, in the form of recommendations to the National Assembly, sparked the most important debate during the Congress because of their far-reaching implications.

The Congress called for direct elections to the Provincial and National assemblies, a move to strengthen both bodies' authority and independence. In its July, 1992, session, the National Assembly adopted direct elections among a host of other constitutional reforms, paving the way for a new electoral law and general elections in 1993. But Cuba has just one party and says it is determined to avoid the commercialization of politics so prevalent in our world—and in Cuba before 1959. The obvious question: how then will candidates be chosen and compete for the vote? As of this writing, the new electoral law is still being debated—nevertheless, it looks like the elected municipal assemblies, with the advice of Cuba's various popular organizations, may do the nominating of provincial and national candidates. One thing is already expressly clear: the Communist Party will not be asked or allowed to do any nominating.[20]

The Fourth Party Congress also asked that longer district delegate terms be looked into, a request turned down by the National Assembly; that committee structures be strengthened within all elected bodies; for the allocation of more resources to elected government; and that there be a clearer delineation of and increase in the powers and responsibilities of the municipal, provincial and national governments.[21]

POPULAR COUNCILS

The Congress also endorsed the development of a new level of government—"Popular Councils"—and called for their formation across the country.[22] On October 10, 1990, the Organizing Commission had announced ninety-three Popular Councils were being constituted in Havana on an experimental basis.[23]

Havana residents for a number of years, and with increasing insistence during the "llamamiento" meetings, pointed out their city is not just another province. It is home to 20 percent of Cuba's people and has a population density far higher than that of the nation. The public insisted district level delegates were swamped and often didn't have time or real authority to act. Delegates had become mere go-betweens for their constituents with the big city bureaucracy. At the same time municipal executives also had too much to handle, were often removed from day-to-day district life, and appeared unresponsive to local needs. During the Havana meetings complaints focused on consumers suffering at the hands of poor services, neighborhood deterioration, and the impotence of district delegates in the face of the people's day-to-day woes.

The Popular Councils are designed to fill the gap between district and municipality and rekindle active community involvement in local problem solving. The Councils, formed largely along historic neighborhood lines, are composed of all elected district delegates in the neighborhood (on average 15), a representative from the area's Committees in Defense of the Revolution, Women's Federation and Trade Unions, the commercial network, any large enterprise and the health and education systems. The Council elects a president, who must also be an elected district delegate, to work full time organizing residents and representing the neighborhood.

The Popular Councils do not replace the municipal assemblies and do not have legislative power. What they have is full authority to enforce the law in their neighborhoods, insure services function well and honestly, mobilize residents to solve local problems, and they possess far more clout than an individual volunteer district delegate. By the close of 1992, Popular Councils had formed across the island.

THE NATIONAL (MASS) ORGANIZATIONS

Cuba's national or mass organizations have traditionally been far more active than those in the former European socialist countries. They have exercised a real influence over policy formation. Cuba's national mass organizations include, by importance: The Central Organization of Cuban Trade Unions, with its 19 affiliated unions to which

96 percent of Cuba's workers belong; The Committees in Defense of the Revolution, Cuba's block associations, with over six million members; The Federation of Cuban Women; the Association of Private Farmers; and a series of youth organizations from the Pioneers, made up of young people through Junior High, to the High School Students Federation and University Students Federation.

"Llamamiento" meeting participants said they wanted Cuba's national organizations to follow the example of the Central Organization of Cuban Trade Unions; rid themselves of bureaucracy, formalism and false unanimity; institute direct versus indirect elections; and re-orient their resources and work to the grassroots. The public expressed its exasperation over being meetinged to death—meetings which, they charged, often had little value. People were critical of the government and various ministries for assigning to the mass organizations jobs that were, in essence, theirs to perform. Cubans demanded that the mass organizations be freed of dual functions, secondary tasks, and paper work, so they could focus on their primary objectives.

For example, at the time of the "llamamiento" meetings, the Committees in Defense of the Revolution were expected to carry out 98 different tasks, from cleaning streets and recycling glass, to filling out various government surveys and organizing blood donations. At the meetings it was pointed out that many of these responsibilities should be carried out by the government, leaving Cuba's block organizations free to help keep Cuba's streets crime-free and the counter-revolution at bay. By the time the Fourth Party Congress convened, a sweeping reorganization of Cuba's national mass organizations was well underway, and along the same lines as that of the Cuban labor movement.

HUMAN RIGHTS

Human rights violations, at least as defined by the United States, were not an issue during the "llamamiento" meetings. Most Cubans are well aware that multi-party systems throughout Latin America and the Caribbean often serve as covers for U.S. and domestic elite control over policy-making, tens of thousands of death squad killings, massive torture and other forms of violent repression. Most Cubans also believe their public ownership of the mass media is preferable to its being in foreign corporate hands or those of wealthy individuals and business advertisers.

The Cubans believe the right to life, an education, health care, a job, home, political and economic independence are fundamental democratic and human rights; and that the United States, through its political, economic and military domination of other countries, its exploitation of their resources and labor, its low intensity and high intensity wars, and the increasing poverty and repression of the U.S. people themselves, in particular people of color, is the world's worst human rights violator.

A majority of Cubans believe their country's human rights record is one of the world's best. They base their position on Cuba's elimination of hunger, illiteracy and many diseases that kill millions of Third World children, the development of Cuba's excellent health and education systems, Cuba's real political independence, the People's Power form of government and other forms of grassroots participation in policy formation and the economy. They also point to Cuba's advances in the struggle for racial and sexual equality and the revolution's elimination of torture, death squads and violent repression in general.

According to the summary of Havana "llamamiento" meetings the question of human rights did surface in three different areas. First, during the debate over whether religious believers should be allowed into the Communist Party. Many speakers favored their inclusion and stated their exclusion from the Party's ranks violated their democratic right to participate fully in Cuba's political life. Second, over Cuba's tight restrictions on travel, especially to the United States and other Western countries. The majority of participants opposed any travel restrictions, stating they violate basic human rights. Third, the issue of human rights came up around the problem of crime. Cuba, in 1989, liberalized its criminal code, reducing sentences for many offenses. The move was opposed by a clear majority of Cubans who felt the government was bending to pressure from the United States and international human rights organizations. Havana residents brought the issue into the "llamamiento" forum. They demanded the government ignore international pressures and crack down harder on white collar and street crime.

In May, 1991, the Cuban government eliminated all travel restrictions for Cubans 18 years of age or older. The one exception: Party members, who first had to request permission. Thus Cubans could legally travel to the United States, but U.S. citizens, with few exceptions, could not legally travel to Cuba.[24]

The decision was welcomed by the Congress, the Cuban people and their relatives abroad, many of whom live in the United States. As many as 50,000 Cubans applied at once for U.S. tourist visas. Washington, which for years had pointed to Cuba's travel restrictions as a human rights violation, did a quick about-face. The Bush administration charged Cuba's move was aimed at ridding the country of undesirables who, after obtaining a tourist visa, were illegally staying in the United States. The U.S. State Department announced in September, 1991, that it had frozen the issuing of tourist visas to Cubans. This would be opened up again months later, in a constant game of now-you-see-it, now-you-don't.[25]

It is true that some Cubans, mainly the elderly visiting relatives in the U.S., opted to remain illegally. However, most Cubans returned home after stays of a few weeks to a few months. There is no doubt that Cuba's lifting of travel restrictions helped ease tensions on the island, especially among young people, and brought in some hard currency earnings. However, anyone living in Cuba during the "llamamiento" meetings knows full well the travel restrictions were lifted due to public demand, and the disastrous results of similar restrictions applied in the European Socialist countries, in particular East Germany.

The summary revealed that people were exceptionally critical of Cuba's Interior Ministry, which combines the island's version of the FBI, state and local police. Participants charged that it was slow in responding to street crime, that corrupt mid-level administrators and Party officials diverted scarce resources and goods to the black market with relative impunity, that in some cases Interior Ministry officials and employees were on the take. Word had it on the street that in many "llamamiento" meetings, people named names, a rumor backed up by the summary itself.

In November 1990, the Interior Ministry launched an assault on official corruption, the black market and street crime. Called "Operation Cascabel" or "Bell the Cat," the dragnet pulled in hundreds of corrupt administrators (many Party members) along with those who sold stolen goods on Cuba's streets. Their trials, and the stiff sentences they received, garnered unusual coverage by the Cuban media. The crackdown continued through 1991 and was fully endorsed by the Congress.[26]

INFORMATION AND CULTURE

Virtually all radios sold in Cuba include international short wave bands, in contrast to the United States, where most radios just carry domestic AM and FM bands, and you have to go out of your way to equip yourself to hear another country's point of view. Cuba's internationally acclaimed literacy efforts and educational system also attest to the island's efforts to keep people informed. Every Cuban can read and write, and every household can tune in to government-run radio from all four corners of the globe, including the Voice of America and its special anti-Cuban broadcasts. Many commercial Florida radio stations and—depending on the weather and your antenna—television stations, are picked up on the island. Cuba has two national TV networks, and dozens of local and national radio stations on the air, ranging from all-music to the all-news station, Radio Reloj, an easy match for any news service in the states.

Up to 1992, when Cuba drastically reduced TV broadcasts because of the energy crisis, the two TV networks imported 30 percent of their programming from abroad. One station ran a morning news and information show and headline news again at 1:00 pm. Both stations ran 8:00 pm prime-time news. Except for weekends, TV was largely an evening affair, with both stations going off the air sometime between midnight and 1:00 am.

I randomly picked the week of Monday April 9th, to Sunday, April 15, 1990, to look at the week's television programming.

Cuba-Visión went on the air at 6:00 pm with cartoons from around the world that included a U.S. production "The Jetsons," broadcast Monday through Thursday. "The Jetsons" also entertained kids Sunday morning for two hours. The station ran a British production of Robin Hood, three evening soap operas (one from Brazil, another from Britain and one Cuban). One of the station's best shows is "Prisma," 90 minutes of documentary and fiction shorts. That particular Wednesday night, Prisma featured one Spanish, two U.S. and three Cuban films. On Thursday evening, viewers watched an Agatha Christie mystery and a music video show, again featuring material from around the world. Friday evening's programming included the regular West German educational program "The Human Body" and the weekly 45-minute "CNN World Report." Two U.S. films ran Saturday night and two more Sunday afternoon. There was also an Italian movie Tuesday evening. The station's late night news wrap-up, "24 Hours," was a news junky's dream.

Tele-Rebelde, the other Cuban station, showed international music videos week nights from 7:30 to 8:00. Monday evening featured the Prague Spring Music Festival; while Cuba's favorite sport, baseball, dominated the screen Tuesday through Thursday evenings, Saturday evening and Sunday afternoon. Friday night featured a talk show on elections in the USSR, a two-hour meeting between Fidel Castro and

Cuban religious leaders and a U.S. movie. Sunday night there was another U.S. film, in the regular comedy slot.[27]

Saturday, April 14, 1990, *Granma* listed showings at Havana's 77 movie theaters, some of which were shut down in 1992: U.S. films were running at 18; Cuban movies at 15; Japanese at nine; Italian at eight; Spanish at seven; French at five; Mexican at five; Argentinan at three; Brazilian at two; and then one or two theaters ran films from Poland, India, China, Venezuela, Peru, the USSR, Costa Rica, Switzerland and West Germany.[28]

Up to November 1990, Cuba had three national newspapers: *Granma*, the Party daily; *Trabajadores*, the trade union daily; and *Juventud Rebelde* for the country's young people. Hundreds of weeklies, local newspapers and specialized magazines were also published in Cuba.

Movies, music and dancing are national pastimes. Recordings and musicians stream in from all around the world. On stage at my first Havana concert back in 1984 was an Italian "punk rock" band. Many visitors who also spent time in Eastern Europe and the Soviet Union remarked to me over the years about the difference between Cuba's lively night and cultural life and what exists or existed in those countries. Every weekend in Havana you could pick from dozens of concerts, outdoor music, discos, cabarets and dances that are either free or nearly so. Havana's streets were alive with crowds of young people into the early morning hours, Thursday through Sunday. As some night haunts shut down in the Special Period, young people have taken over major thoroughfares in Havana—including the seaside drive—just to party.

Cuba has become an important center of Latin American and Caribbean culture. "Casa de Las Américas" is one of the most prestigious cultural institutions in the region and its yearly literary prizes draw scores of entries from aspiring young writers. Cuba's calendar is also filled with cultural festivals which attract participants from around the Americas. The 1989 calendar included the Latin Jazz Festival in February, the International Humor Festival in the Spring, an International Handicrafts Fair and the Caribbean Cultural Festival in June, an International Fashion Fair, and the Varadero Music Festival also during the month of June. October brought to Cuba an International Opera and Light Opera Festival, a Theater Festival and a Concert Music Festival. November saw the International Fine and Plastic Arts Biennial and in December there was the annual New Latin American Film Festival.[29]

Cuba also excels in sports of all kinds, and since rectification began there is a new emphasis on mass participation in Cuba's remarkable sports program. The island regularly comes in second to the United States at the Pan American Games, beating out such large countries as Brazil, Mexico and Argentina. At the 1991 Pan American Games Cuba, for the first time, was the gold medal winner; and at the 1992 Summer Olympics, Cuba placed an incredible fifth.

The 1986 Third Party Congress took a close look at Cuba's information and cultural policies, as did the year long grassroots discussion that was part of it. On July 17 and 18, 1986, the Party Central Committee met and parts of the proceedings were broadcast on Cuban television.

"It's better to have the dirty laundry come tumbling down on us than to have society come tumbling down," Fidel Castro told the gathering.

Castro strongly opposed the view that the press had to be muted to protect Cuba from imperialism and its international media campaign against the island. That view, manifested as self-censorship on the part of editors and journalists or the crutch by some to cover up their own incompetence, had led to glossing over many problems existing in the country which, in turn, limited public debate. Cuba, argued Castro, was being deprived of a key weapon in its battle to build socialism:

"The most important thing," he stressed, "is that we must use the press in this battle of the revolution to exert greater pressure on cadres, officials and ministers . . . What is required is that we give the press more information so it can say what's going well and what's not, especially for subjective reasons. If there are material reasons these should be explained . . .

"I believe there should be criticism, counter-criticism and criticism of the critics. The press has helped develop patriotic feelings. Now we must say: help us in this battle; look into this report or that, the problems which exist; analyze, study and formulate an opinion on what is happening."[30]

And along these lines, a new information policy was ratified at the deferred Third Party Congress session at the end of the year.

The battle to improve Cuba's media is far from over, with Fidel Castro, other Cuban leaders and the Journalist Union pushing hard for change and more openness. Directors and editors have come and gone, journalism schools and curricula have been turned inside out. Evaluation procedures and journalist pay scales have been upgraded, while access to officials and information improved. There is a marked change in the content and style of TV and radio news and information and some papers. For example, *Trabajadores* and *Juventud Rebelde* have been so shaken up that they are unrecognizable when compared to the pre-rectification period.

"Llamamiento" meeting participants strongly endorsed efforts to improve and open up Cuba's media and cultural scene. They were critical of the press for dragging its feet on important domestic issues and events and sometimes missing them entirely. People directly involved in the media and culture, while overwhelmingly supporting the revolution, often charged their work was still stymied by bureaucracy and government stonewalling.

The debate spilled over into the Fourth Party Congress, often becoming heated between those who insisted on continued openness and those who argued that the Special Period and new U.S. threats should lead to greater control over the media and culture. The debate is still not over—in fact the media was one of a handful of key issues remanded to the new Central Committee for a deeper look.[31]

THE STATE ADMINISTRATION, ECONOMY AND SERVICES

The "llamamiento" meetings unfolded just as Cuba's Special Period began. Few, if any, direct challenges were made to leadership proposals to radically restructure trade, the economy and the labor force; nor to the belt-tightening and search for alternatives to traditional imports. Rectification, as far as it had gone, also received high marks, though many people said they were frustrated at its slow pace, especially at the top. That frustration was expressed in an avalanche of criticism of Cuba's 50-odd ministries and national agencies which run the entire economy and all social services.

People island-wide charged overcentralization, bureaucracy and corruption were still crippling the system and undermining their efforts. They demanded that the government be restructured and streamlined, bureaucrats sent packing, paper work and forms cut to the bone, more local control over the economy and services, and more room for local initiatives.

Government-run economic services were ridiculed time and time again as worse than worthless. People asked why individuals, working in their spare time, couldn't legally, for example, repair others cars, make clothes or fix someone's plumbing. They charged poor government services and legal restrictions on individuals providing such services simply lead to black market activity and, in effect, were forcing even the most stalwart Party members into subterfuge.

By the time the Congress convened, the full impact of the collapse of European socialism was upon Cuba. Its no wonder then that the economy took up the bulk of the delegates time. They heard detailed reports on the contingents, Armed Forces economic initiative and other efforts at economic reform. They reviewed Special Period plans, spent long hours discussing tourism, science and efforts to attract foreign investment. There was little debate on the need to diversify exports, further cut imports, save resources and attract foreign capital, nor on the need to extend implementation of more efficient forms of socialist production. The delegates' attention focused on how most effectively and quickly to accomplish all this, and in particular, on foreign investment formulas centered on Cuba's development interests.[32]

Cuba's Joint Venture law, passed in 1982, does not allow foreign ownership of land; nor foreign majority control of joint ventures. Labor is supplied by a Cuban company insuring workers basic rights are respected. The Congress gave its blessings not just to more foreign investments, but to all sorts of possible arrangements from joint marketing to cooperatives and allowing foreign firms to manage some tourist enterprises and services. They also decided to open up new sectors of the Cuban economy, for example mining, textiles and food processing, to foreign investments, in effect stating that where ever a lack of capital, raw materials or a market had shut down production, foreign partners, able to solve one or more of these problems, were welcome.[33]

The Congress backed exceptions to the rule that government must own over half the shares in a joint venture—exceptions to be applied exclusively with Latin American and Caribbean partners. And the Congress endorsed direct trade with foreign customers and suppliers by selected government enterprises, which would not be bound to do their business through the Foreign Trade Ministry.[34]

The need to trim and reorganize the central ministries was taken as a given by Congress delegates, and they called on the government to begin the process as soon as possible. The shape that reorganization will take was not spelled out, but it promises to be dramatic with a number of ministries merging, a few disappearing, perhaps one or two new ones taking shape and all down-sizing.[35]

The Congress resoundingly endorsed centralized planning of investments and most resources, while giving high marks to continuous planning within these parameters, to make the process more flexible. Delegates rejected any generalized return to private ownership of the means of production or services and anything resembling the capitalist marketplace. Private sector business and market economics, said the Congress, is tantamount to capitalism—and for Third World countries this means prolonging their neocolonial status on the road to economic disaster. However, popular demands for the right to provide certain services were met, the Congress endorsing the idea that individuals should be able to sell their talents and services under the rubric of "self-employed."[36]

CHAPTER TWO, pp. 41–56.

1. Program of the Cuban Communist Party, (Havana: Editora Política, 1986). Rodríguez, José Luis; "Cuban Social and Economic Development: The Results of 30 Years of Revolution," (Havana: Cuba Socialista #39, May-June 1989). Gutierrez, Alberto Salazár and Galdós, Victor Pérez; "Vision de Cuba," (Havana: Editora Política, 1987).

2. Latin American and Caribbean Economists Association, "The Foreign Debt, Unequal Exchange and the New International Economic Order," (Havana: February, 1990).

3. For economic growth in the seventies, see the main reports to the First and Second Communist Party Congresses, (Havana: 1975 and 1981). For economic growth in the eighties, see the main report to the Third Party Congress, (Havana: 1986). Thereafter, see the year-end JUCEPLAN economic reports to the National Assembly of People's Power. The 1989 report on Cuba from the UN Economic Commission for Latin America and the Caribbean (ECLA), sets average annual growth between 1980 and 1988 at just under 4 percent.

4. All of Latin America's major labor federations charge real wages have fallen by more than 50 percent. Government and international reports give varying figures. The International Labor Organization (ILO) reports the average real wage dropped 7 to 16 percent depending on the country. The Regional Program on Latin American and Caribbean Employment states the real earnings of the informal sector, which amounts to 40 percent of the population or more, dropped 40 percent during the 1980s. Logic seems to go with the labor federations, as virtually every country in the region, with the exception of Cuba, experienced hyper-inflation and growing unemployment during the decade. In addition, International Monetary Fund and creditor-imposed economic policies applied throughout the region are designed to limit internal demand and imports by cutting available income, thus freeing up resources for increased export and hard currency earnings needed to meet debt service and interest.

5. *Granma Weekly Review,* October 18, 1987.

6. *Granma Weekly Review,* October 15, 1989.

7. *Granma Weekly Review,* June 10, 1990.

8. At least six new Blas Roca brigades were organized in October and November 1990 to work in agriculture, in particular banana production. *Granma,* October 3, 1990.

9. The figure of 61 contingents was mentioned numerous times by Fidel Castro and the Cuban press in June and July 1989. *Juventud Rebelde,* July 13, 1989.

10. *Granma,* August 13, 1990.

11. 1989 interview with the head of the Blas Roca contingent, Candido Palmero. *See* also Fidel Castro, "Speech on the Second Anniversary of the Founding of the Blas Roca contingent," *Granma Weekly Review,* October 15, 1989. And; Fidel Castro, "Speech Opening Varadero's International Airport," *Granma,* January 7, 1990.

12. JUCEPLAN, "Year end report to the National Assembly of People's Power," *Granma,* December 29, 1989.

13. Ibid.

14. *Granma Weekly Review,* December 29, 1991.

15. JUCEPLAN, "Year end report to the National Assembly of People's Power," *Granma,* December 29, 1989.

16. Ibid.

17. *Granma Weekly Review,* December 29, 1991.

18. *Granma Weekly Review,* November 19, 1989.

19. *Granma*, November 8, 1990.
20. *Bohemia*, September 28, 1990. For more on the contingents in agriculture see; *Trabajadores*, January 31, February 7, March 26, May 9, 1990. *Granma*, March 20, October 30 & November 21, 1990. *Juventud Rebelde*, April 13 & 14, 1990.
21. *Granma*, November 16, 1990.
22. I was not able to interview any of the major figures involved in the Armed Forces Initiative. Therefore, the following is taken from: Betancourt, Armando Pérez and Sánchez, Berto González; "Perfeccionamiento empresarial en el MINFAR," *Cuba Socialista*, #36, November-December, 1988. And by the same authors, "El perfeccionamiento de los sistemas de costo en el MINFAR," *Cuba Socialista*, #40, July–August, 1989. *See* also Interview series with Lt. Colonel Armando Pérez Betencourt, head of the military commission, *Trabajadores*, Oct 12, 13, 16–20, 1989. For the process in the state sector, *see Trabajadores*, June 18, July 6, August 22 & November 16, 1988. *Trabajadores*, May 10, 1989. *Granma*, April 5, 1989.

CHAPTER THREE, pp. 57–78.

1. The Cuban trade union daily *Trabajadores'* coverage of changes taking place in the Cuban economy provide a good example of the new journalism haltingly emerging in Cuba with rectification. For this reason, I quote extensively from *Trabajadores* in this chapter.
2. *Trabajadores*, November 20, 1990.
3. *Trabajadores*, June 1, 1990.
4. *Trabajadores*, April 14, 1989.
5. November 1990 interview with Roberto Blanco, First Vice Minister, Cuban State Finance Committee.
6. *Granma Weekly Review*, October 2, 1988.
7. *Trabajadores*, February 7, 1989.
8. *Trabajadores*, October 12, 1989.

9. *Trabajadores*, July 23, 1988.
10. *Trabajadores*, December 15, 1988.
11. *Trabajadores*, July 23, 1988
12. Ibid.
13. National Cadre Commission, "1987 Year End Report," January, 1988.
14. *Trabajadores*, January 4, 1989.
15. Ibid.
16. Ibid.
17. *Trabajadores*, October 14, 1989.
18. *Trabajadores*, March 23, 1988.
19. *Trabajadores*, February 23, 1989.
20. *Trabajadores*, August 27, 1988.
21. *Trabajadores*, January 13, 1989.
22. *Trabajadores*, January 4, 1990.
23. *Juventude Rebelde*, October 12, 1988.
24. *Trabajadores*, March 14, 1989.
25. *Trabajadores*, July 3, 1989.
26. Fidel Castro, "Speech Closing Annual Basic Industry Meeting," *Granma Weekly Review*, February 21, 1988.
27. *Trabajadores*, June 30, 1989.
28. *Trabajadores*, July 4, 1989.
29. *Granma*, October 30, 1990.
30. *Trabajadores*, February 15, 1990.
31. *Trabajadores*, February 24 & 25, 1988.
32. Ibid.
33. *Trabajadores*, February 15, 1990.
34. *Trabajadores*, May 9, 1989.
35. *Trabajadores*, July 28, 1989.
36. *Trabajadores*, August 9 & 23, September 17 & 18, 1990. *Granma*, March 13, April 24, August 1, September 26, 1990.
37. *Granma*, November 17, 1990.
38. "Este es el Congreso más democrático," (Havana: Editora Política, 1991).

CHAPTER FOUR, pp. 79–98.

1. State Statistics Committee, "Cuba En Cifras 1989," (Havana: Editora Estatistica, 1990).
2. Ibid.
3. *Trabajadores*, December 15, 17 & 25, 1989.
4. Report delivered by Havana microbrigade movement leader, Máximo An-

dión, on the third anniversary of the revitalization of the microbrigade movement, September 30, 1989.

5. Report delivered to the provincial meeting of the Havana Central Organization of Trade Unions (CTC) in preparation for the 16th CTC Congress, December 1989.

6. For an example, see; *Granma*, March 18, 1989.

7. Report delivered by Havana microbrigade movement leader, Máximo Andión, on the third anniversary of the revitalization of the microbrigade movement, September 30, 1989.

8. JUCEPLAN, "Year End Report to the National Assembly of People's Power," *Granma*, December 29, 1989.

9. The author visited the community's social microbrigades half a dozen times in 1989 and 1990, then returned in June 1992.

10. Provided to the author by the Havana Department of Education.

11. *Granma*, June 18, 1992. According to UNESCO developed countries had one teacher per 50 to 80 students and Third World countries one teacher per 100 to 200 students.

12. Provided to the author by the Havana Department of Education.

13. Ibid.

14. Ibid.

15. Ibid.

16. Provided to the author by the Havana Public Health Department.

17. Children's Defense Fund, "Annual Reports," (Washington, D.C.: 1987–1989).

18. The Washington figure comes from the Children's Defense Fund and the Havana figures from the Havana Public Health Department.

19. *Trabajadores*, April 12, 1990.

20. Cuban Attorney General's Office, "Report to the National Assembly of People's Power," July, 1990.

21. United Nations Economic and Social Council, "Report of the Committee on Crime Prevention and the Fight Against Criminality," (Vienna, February 5–16, 1990).

22. Cuban Attorney General's Office, "Report to the National Assembly of People's Power," July, 1990.

CHAPTER FIVE, pp. 99–120.

1. *Granma*, May 15, 1989.

2. *Juventude Rebelde*, June 7, 1989.

3. *Granma*, May 15, 1989.

4. Benjamin, Collins & Scott, "No Free Lunch: Food and Revolution in Cuba Today," (New York: Grove Press, 1986).

5. Ibid.

6. Adolfo Díaz, Vice President of the Executive Committee of the Council of Ministers, "Report to the National Assembly of People's Power on the Status of the National Food Program," *Granma*, December 27, 1990.

7. Ibid.

8. The figures are estimates based on a number of sources, including: *National Assembly of People's Power, special session on the National Food Program*, December 26–28, 1990. Education Ministry, "1990 Year End Report." And from the interviews cited in this chapter.

9. Adolfo Díaz, Vice President of the Executive Committee of the Council of Ministers, "Report to the National Assembly of People's Power on the status of the National Food Program," *Granma*, December 27, 1990.

10. Proceedings, Third Congress of the Cuban Communist Party and Seventh Congress of the National Association of Small Farmers, January and May, 1986.

11. National Assembly of People's Power, "Report on the Food Program," December 26, 1990. The author received a copy of the report used for debate during the Cuban parliament's special session on the National Food Program. Unfortunately, this excellent 138 page report has not been pub-

lished, though copies may be available from the Cuban government.
12. Ibid.
13. Ibid.
14. Ibid.
15. Ibid.
16. Ibid.
17. The information in this section comes from two primary sources. Agriculture Ministry, "Report to the National Assembly of People's Power," (Havana: José Martí Publishers, 1987). And; National Assembly of People's Power, "Report on the Food Program," December 26, 1990.
18. *Bohemia*, March 30, 1990.
19. 1990-1991 sugar harvest from, *Granma Weekly Review*, December 29, 1991. 1991-1992 sugar harvest from, *Granma Weekly Review*, September 13, 1992.

CHAPTER SIX, pp. 119–126.

1. Gutierrez, Alberto Salazár and Galdós, Victor Pérez; "Vision de Cuba," (Havana: Editora Política, 1987).
2. *Granma*, May 20, 1990.
3. National Assembly of People's Power, *Report on the Food Program*, December 26, 1990.
4. Agriculture Ministry, "Report to the National Assembly of People's Power," (Havana: José Martí publishers, 1987).
5. For a general overview of infrastructure development see: *Granma*, March 14, 1990. *See* also National Assembly of People's Power, "Report on the Food Program," December 26, 1990. For electricity see; *Granma*, May 20, 1990. For highway construction *see Granma*, Jan 4, 1989 & February 24, 1990.
6. *Granma*, May 20, 1990.
7. National Assembly of People's Power, "Report on the Food Program," December 26, 1990.
8. Ibid.

9. Ibid.
10. Data provided by Israel Rodríguez Castro, National Director of the Coffee and Cacao program.
11. *Granma*, February 24, 1990. *See* also National Assembly of People's Power, "Report on the Food Program," December 26, 1990.
12. *Juventude Rebelde*, April 5, 1990. *See* also National Assembly of People's Power, "Report on the Food Program," December 26, 1990.
13. Agriculture Ministry, "Report to the National Assembly of People's Power," (Havana: José Martí publishers, 1987).
14. Ibid.
15. *Juventude Rebelde*, June 4, 1990.
16. National Assembly of People's Power, "Report on the Food Program," Havana, December 26, 1990.

CHAPTER SEVEN, pp. 131–136.

1. *Granma Weekly Review*, December 17, 1989.
2. Cannon, Terrence; "Revolutionary Cuba," (Havana: José Martí publishers, 1983).
3. *Granma Weekly Review*, December 17, 1989.

CHAPTER EIGHT, pp. 137–158.

1. *Granma*, January 22, 1990.
2. Cuban National Bank, "Second trimester Report," 1990.
3. As cited by Eduardo Díaz, "The Transnationals," *Latin American Economic Panorama*, April 15 and 30, 1990. (Havana: Prensa Latina News Agency).
4. Ibid.
5. Association of Latin American and Caribbean Economists: "The Foreign Debt, Unequal Exchange and the New International Economic Order," (Havana: 1990).
6. UN Economic Commission for Latin

America and the Caribbean: "Preliminary Report on the region's economic activity in 1989," *Latin American Economic Panorama*, March 15 and 30, 1990. (Havana: Prensa Latina News Agency).

7. Permanent Commission of Latin American Political Parties, "Report on the Foreign Debt," as cited in *Granma*, December 4, 1990.

8. Dr. José Luis Rodríguez, "The Economic Relations Between Cuba and the European Members of the CMEA. Actual Current Situation and Perspectives," *Latin American Economic Panorama*, December 15, 1990. (Havana: Prensa Latina News Agency). The article is the best I've seen on Cuban-Soviet economic relations from a Cuban perspective.

9. Cuban National Bank, "Second Trimester Report," 1990.

10. Author's estimates based on various reports and conversations with Cuban officials.

11. *International Press Service*, August 29, 1990.

12. For example, see Bertrand Rosenthal, *Agence France Press*, June 13, 1990.

13. Csaba Nagy, "Hard Currency With Cuba Also," *Nepszabadsag News Agency*, August 16, 1990.

14. *Granma Weekly Review*, April 29, 1990.

15. Fidel Castro, "Speech at the 30th Anniversary of the CDRs," *Granma Weekly Review*, October 14, 1990. This is a key speech where Castro details growing problems with the former Socialist Camp. He also presents the first detailed outline of plans to cope with the crisis. For a detailed review of deteriorating trade relations with the former USSR see, Fidel Castro, "Speech opening the Fourth Congress of the Cuban Communist Party," *Granma Weekly Review*, November 3, 1991.

16. Fidel Castro, "Speech opening the Fourth Congress of the Cuban Communist Party, *Granma Weekly Review*, November 3, 1991.

17. Ibid.

18. *Granma Weekly Review*, October 18, 1987.

19. Fidel Castro, "Speech delivered on the 36th Anniversary of the Attack on the Moncada Garrison," *Granma Weekly Review*, August 6, 1989.

20. Fidel Castro, "Speech closing the Fifth Congress of the Federation of Cuban Women," *Granma Weekly Review*, March 18, 1990.

21. *Granma Weekly Review*, September 9, 1990.

22. *Granma Weekly Review, See* just about all issues from September, 1990 through the end of the year.

23. *Granma Weekly Review*, September 30, 1990.

24. Ibid.

25. *Granma*, November 24, 1990.

26. *Bohemia*, November 16, 1990, interview with Francisco Linares Calvo, head of the State Labor and Social Security Committee.

27. *Granma Weekly Review*, December 29, 1991.

28. Kaplowitz, Donna Rich and Michael; "New Opportunities for U.S.-Cuban Trade," Cuban Studies Program, The Paul H. Nitze School of Advanced International Studies, John Hopkins University (April, 1992). The study is by far the best I've seen on the Cuban economy and trade and is available from the University.

29. National Assembly of People's Power, "Report On the Food Program," Havana, December 26, 1990. Also see; Fidel Castro, "Speech at the 30th Anniversary of the CDRs," *Granma Weekly Review*, October 14, 1990. *See* also *Granma*, September 25 and November 19, 1990.

30. *Granma*, February 23, 1991.

31. *Granma*, November 9, December 8, 1990 and May 16, October 5, 1991.

32. Through 1991, see "Todas las preguntas tienen respuestas," *Latin Ameri-*

can Economic Panorama, May 1991. (Havana: Prensa Latina News Agency). For 1991–1992, see *Trabajadores*, April 20, 1992. *See* also Fidel Castro, "Speech closing the Eighth Congress of the National Association of Small Farmers," *Granma*, May 19, 1992.

33. *Trabajadores*, January 25, 1992.
34. *Trabajadores*, December 16, 1991.
35. *Granma*, December 26, 1991.
36. *Granma*, December 4 and 21, 1991.
37. "Turismo," "1990 Report of Cuba's Tourist Agencies to the National Assembly of People's Power," (Havana: Ediciones Turisticas, 1990). For 1991, see Gail Reed, "Cuba's Tourism Revival: No Country is an Island," *Cuba Update*, April 1992. (New York: Center for Cuban Studies). Gail Reed also has an excellent piece in the same issue on the social ramifications of Cuban Tourism, "Mirror Images."
38. *Granma Weekly Review*, December 29, 1991.

CHAPTER NINE, pp. 159–184.

1. Franklin, Jane; "The Cuban Revolution and the United States—A Chronological History," (Melbourne, Australia: Ocean Press 1992). pp.40, 50, 54, 62, 71, 89, 90, 150, 159, 192.
2. Franklin, Jane; "The Cuban Revolution and the United States," pp. 159, 162, 192, 225.
3. Murray, Mary; "Cruel and Unusual Punishment," (Melbourne, Australia: Ocean Press, 1993).
4. Morera, José Luis and Calcines, Rafael; "The CIA's War Against Cuba," (Havana: National Information Service, 1988).
5. Landau, Saul; "Fidel Will Be Around Awhile," *The Nation*, June 25, 1990.
6. *Granma Weekly Review*, November 25, 1990.
7. *Granma Weekly Review*, March 18, 1990.
8. *Granma*, Sept 4, 1989.

9. *Granma Weekly Review*, April 8, 1990.
10. *Granma Weekly Review*, April 29, May 6, June 24, 1990.
11. *Granma*, April 4, June 26 and August 30, 1990. *See* also *Cuba Update*, Summer and Fall issues, 1990. (New York: Center for Cuban Studies).
12. *Granma Weekly Review*, December 31, 1989 and January 7, 1990.
13. *Granma Weekly Review*, February 4, April 1, December 9, 1990.
14. *Granma Weekly Review*, February 4 & 11, 1990.
15. *Granma Weekly Review*, May 6, 1990.
16. *Granma Weekly Review*, May 13, 1990.
17. *Granma*, May 12, 1990.
18. From May 2nd to the 19th, 1990, the Cuban press featured solidarity statements and news of Cuban support organizations forming around the world. The May, 1990, issues of *Granma Weekly Review* also carried some of the reports and statements.
19. The formation of the organization and its denunciations were carried by the major news agencies with offices in Cuba. *See International Press Service*, May 22 & 24, 1990. *Agence France Press*, May 24, 1990. *Reuters*, May 25, 1990.
20. *Granma Weekly Review*, August 5, 1990.
21. Ibid.
22. The Embassy Crisis was covered both in the *Granma* and *Granma Weekly Review* through its conclusion on September 4, 1990. A good source for the Cuban position can be found in Fidel Castro's July 26th speech, *Granma Weekly Review*, August 5, 1990.
23. Cox, Thomas; *Heritage Foundation Backgrounder*, "Preparing for a Post Castro Cuba," (Washington, D.C.: May 14, 1990).
24. As reported by the *Spanish News Agency*, June 12, 1990.
25. As reported by *Agence France Press*, June 13, 1990.
26. The U.S. position at the Summit as well as the Soviet response was cov-

ered by the U.S. press and major international news agencies.

27. *Granma Weekly Review*, November 18, 1990.
28. *Prensa Latina News Agency*, November 16, 1990.
29. *Granma Weekly Review*, September 22, 1991.
30. Cited by Joseph Rubin, "UN Vote on Embargo Deferred," *Cuba Update*, April, 1992, (New York: Center for Cuban Studies).
31. Murray, Mary; "Cruel and Unusual Punishment," (Melbourne, Australia: Ocean Press, 1993).
32. The author attended all the rallies. For rally coverage and photos one can look at the issue of *Granma Weekly Review* following each event.
33. *Granma*, January 8,9 and 16, 1992. *Granma Weekly Review*, January 19 and 26, February 9 and 16, 1992. For day of mourning see *Granma*, February 18, 1992.
34. *Granma*, January 9, 10, 11, February 6, 1992. *Juventude Rebelde*, Jan 12, 1992. *Granma Weekly Review*, January 19 and 26, February 9 and 16, 1992.
35. From a copy of the legislation issued by the office of Representative Robert Torricelli, Congressional Office Building, Washington, D.C..
36. *Miami Herald*, "U.S. Halts T.V. Martí Daytime Transmissions to Cuba," April 15, 1992, p. 13a.
37. Federal Register #15216, April 24, 1992.
38. *Granma Weekly Review*, May 3, 1992.
39. *Granma Weekly Review*, May 10, 1992.
40. Cited by Lázaro Barredo Medina, "Los Políticos Dicen: No Agresión. Los Militares: El Hacha de la Guerra" (Havana: unpublished, 1992). Also see; *The Congressional Record*.
41. *Granma Weekly Review*, May 17, 1992.

CONCLUSION, pp. 185–209.

1. Amnesty International, "1990 Annual Report."
2. *Granma Weekly Review*, February 25, 1990.
3. *Granma Weekly Review*, February 25 and March 4, 1990.
4. *Granma Weekly Review*, March 4, 1990.
5. The Congress proceedings and its conclusions are available from the Central Organization of Cuban Trade Unions.
6. *Granma*, May 26, 1990. For the Call see; *Granma Weekly Review*, March 25, 1990.
7. The figures on Congress preparations were released during the Fourth Party Congress and are cited by Gail Reed, "Island in the Storm," (Melbourne, Australia: Ocean Press, 1992). P.17.
8. The Summary, which was never released, was passed to me by a protected source to read, take notes on, and return.
9. *Granma*, October 5, 1990.
10. Reed, Gail; "Island in the Storm," p. 80.
11. Reed, pp. 80–81.
12. Reed, P.9.
13. Reed, P.9.
14. Reed, pp. 92–94.
15. Reed, pp. 80–94.
16. Reed, pp. 95–110, and 142–153.
17. Reed, pp. 154–160, and 161–187.
18. Reed, pp. 161–176.
19. *Granma*, May 2, 1990.
20. Reed, pp. 111–126.
21. Reed, pp. 111–126.
22. Reed, pp. 11–126.
23. *Granma*, October 10, 1990.
24. Gail Reed, "Cuba Update," Summer and November issues, 1991. (New York: Center for Cuban Studies).
25. Murray, Mary; "Cruel and Unusual Punishment," (Melbourne, Australia: Ocean Press, 1993).
26. Reed, pp. 96–97.
27. *Granma*, April 9–14, 1990.
28. *Granma*, April 14, 1990.
29. Author's notes. *See* also *Granma Weekly Review*, 1989.
30. *Granma Weekly Review*, August 3, 1986.

31. Reed, pp. 95–100.
32. Reed, pp. 127–141.
33. Reed, pp. 127–141. Also see Cuban Council of Ministers, "Possibilities of Joint Ventures in Cuba," (Havana: March 1991).

34. Reed, pp. 127–141.
35. Reed, pp. 123–141.
36. Reed, pp. 127–141.

INDEX